Challenged and Changed

Challenged and Changed

Living and Learning in Central America

LINDY SCOTT

KIM HERNÁNDEZ

Foreword by Esther Louie

RESOURCE *Publications* · Eugene, Oregon

Resource Publications
An Imprint of Wipf and Stock Publishers
199 W. 8th Ave., Suite 3
Eugene, OR 97401

www.wipfandstock.com

PAPERBACK ISBN: 978-1-5326-6040-5
HARDCOVER ISBN: 978-1-5326-6041-2
EBOOK ISBN: 978-1-5326-6042-9

Manufactured in the U.S.A.   AUGUST 28, 2019

Dedicated to Ron and Marianne Frase, and to all the CASPians, who have had the courage to walk with Jesus throughout the highways and byways of Central America. May the truths you have learned and the Central American friends you have cherished in your hearts be with you the rest of your lives.

Contents

Foreword

THIS CENTRAL AMERICA STUDY program over the years developed its own mythical legends on our campus as previous students returned and shared snippets about their experiences. The students knew they would face new and different experiences, and even challenges, by participating in this study travel program. But if you were to ask them how and what changes they expected, I'm sure they would not have been able to tell you exactly.

The faculty knew that applying learning concepts and theories into individualized student and team engagements with their daily experiences across the expanse of social, political, economic, historical, and personal dimensions while encountering new communities and countries would be a fulfilling and challenging teaching task. And thus I joined this program with hopes and wishes for supporting the students' learning and intercultural experiences, and for expanding my own learning about Central America. Little did I know that the magic of traveling, studying, and living with each study group and with our Central America communities would open such an invigorating world perspective and provide me the most outstanding experience of my lifetime. And along with our students, we were all transformed by this longest and shortest semester of our lives.

—Esther Louie

Former Whitworth Assistant Dean of Student Life-Intercultural Student Center, and CASP Faculty Leader (2002-2005)

Statement from the Whitworth University Historian

FROM THE VERY BEGINNING in 1975, the Central America Study and Service Program has been one of the most distinctive and important programs in Whitworth's history. The impact on students and faculty has been profound; the impact on the university has been undeniable. When Ron and Marianne Frase designed and led the program in its initial years, they clearly had little idea that 43 years after its beginning, students would continue to be challenged, moved, and exhilarated by their experiences in a variety of Central American countries. Ron and Marianne could not possibly have imagined how students would want to return repeatedly for reunions to reminisce about their times together.

Whitworth at its best has been a place where both on and off campus students have been provided the opportunity to read and reflect deeply about difficult issues. Whitworth at its best has been an institution that believes that students should explore their faith and wrestle with its possible connections to the world around them. Whitworth at its best is a place where faculty and students develop mutual trust and lasting relationships where difficult issues can be explored together. The Central America Study Program reflects all of these elements and more that have formed such an important part of the Whitworth experience.

Over the years, I have visited with many students, as well as faculty, about their experience in Central America. They have consistently remarked about how much they grew and matured as individuals. They comment on how their homestays exposed them to people who were dealing on a daily basis with poverty and yet for the most part retained a posture of gratitude, humility, and joy which directly challenged the student's middle-class American assumptions about wealth and happiness. Students comment consistently on their struggles with the role the United States has played and continues to play in both the politics and the economies of Central American countries. Students consistently comment on the way that their faith has often been challenged on the one hand and strengthened on the other as they grappled with the ways in which God seemed present and sometimes absent in the lack of justice for many people. This compilation of stories and reflections by students and faculty reinforce those general observations and will provide a lasting testimony and legacy to the experiences of Whitworth students.

From its beginnings with Ron and Marianne Frase to its current leaders Kim Hernández and Lindy Scott, the Central America Study and Service Program has been an integral part of the Whitworth experience. Whether students have gone on the program or not, I truly believe Whitworth has benefitted from the program in so many ways. As indicated above, the program reflects the very best of Whitworth in its willingness to be courageous in the many ways it has challenged and nurtured students. It has truly been an expression of what it means to have an education of the heart and mind.

Dale E. Soden, PhD
Professor of History
Whitworth University Historian

Preface

WHITWORTH UNIVERSITY STUDENTS AND faculty have been learning, living, and serving in Central and South America for over forty years. The university's mission to provide an education of mind and heart guides the purpose and principles of the study abroad program that Ron and Marianne Frase began in 1975. While students learn about the language, culture, and sociopolitical issues of the region through traditional coursework, they get the chance to live these topics in daily life, in community with the people of Central America. It seems that people grow best in their commitment to addressing problems like cross-cultural difference, poverty, injustice, and environmental degradation — and working toward a biblical understanding of Shalom — when they have witnessed the broad consequences of a broken world. We are just two among many Whitworth faculty who have accompanied students in this quest to learn, grow, and witness new ideas in Central America.

This program is unique; it invests in communities and individuals; it changes lives. It is one of the best, most transformative experiences for the Whitworthians who participate during their time as a student or faculty member at Whitworth.

The legacy established by the Frases created a four-decade story that needed to be told. This book seeks to capture the stories, the adventures, the growth, and the lasting impact of all the groups who have been part of this remarkable program. It is our hope that the chapters and other features in this book will be a reminiscent journey for the participants and an insightful exploration for other readers.

There are many people we wish to thank for their important contributions to the book:

- Ron Frase and Jim Hunt who gave us access to their files, pictures, and correspondence.

- All of the CAST/CASP alumni who contributed to this volume with vignettes, anecdotes, pictures, and revision of chapters.

- Dale Hammond from the Whitworth Office of Alumni and Parent Relations who encouraged us in the writing of the book.

- Erik Blank (CASP 2018) who helped with the acquisition and placement of the pictures in the book and other important aspects of the final editing process.

- Hannah McCollum (CASP 2016) who helped out in the early stages of the book.

- Students from Whitworth Professor Thomas Caraway's book editing class, Madison Douglas, Devin Manlove, and Madeleine Danusiar, who provided excellent suggestions regarding the style and format of the book.

- Our colleagues at Wipf & Stock for their invaluable assistance in bringing this book to publication.

Although we tried to obtain accurate information, in a book of this length, there will be some historical inaccuracies. We are responsible for these errors.

It is our hope and prayer that upon reading the stories of Whitworthians in Central America, readers will be stimulated to walk more faithfully with our God and to serve more deeply our neighbors near and far with the love of Jesus.

Paz de Cristo,
Kim and Lindy

Abbreviations

CAST   Central America Study Tour
CASP   Central America Study Program or Central America Study & Service
              Program (as of 2014)
TA   Teaching Assistant
PC(USA)   Presbyterian Church, USA (denomination)
CIA   Central Intelligence Agency (of the US government)
YAV   Young Adult Volunteers (a service program of the Presbyterian Church)
FSLN   Frente Sandinista de Liberación Nacional
CEDEN   Comité Evangélico de Emergencia Nacional (Evangelical Committee for
              National Emergencies in Honduras)
CNT   Centro Nacional de Trabajadores (National Center of Workers in
              Guatemala)
ESA   Ejército Secreto Anticomunista (Secret Anticommunist Army in
              Guatemala)
CEPAD   Consejo de Iglesias Evangélicas Pro-Alianza Denominacional (Council
              of Protestant Churches in Nicaragua)
PLO   Palestine Liberation Organization
MIGs   a Russian military aircraft

SECTION I

Testimonies from Each Trip

1960s and Early 1970s: Ron and Marianne Frase

The Vision is Born

THE CENTRAL AMERICA STUDY and Service Program has been Whitworth University's most prominent overseas program for over forty years. Although the program has changed along the way, Whitworth students and faculty have been experiencing Central America, and parts of South America, since 1975. Over the years many people have asked the founders, Ron and Marianne Frase, how the Central America Study Program came about. Here is the beginning of the program in Ron's own words:

Frase Family in Brazil

My wife Marianne and I, together with our two young daughters, went to Brazil in January of 1961 on a life appointment by the Presbyterian Church USA. It was a profound experience which was destined to shape our future in ways we could not have anticipated at the time.

In the summers of 1963 and 1964 we had university students from the United States come down to spend a couple of months with us. They worked with Brazilian students in a variety of work projects, visited points of interest, shared meals together and spent hours in discussions in an attempt to understand each other's culture. The North American students were surprised to discover that the Brazilian students knew a great deal more about the US than they knew about Brazil. The visit in 1964 occurred during the Goldwater–Johnson presidential campaign and the Brazilians were shocked to learn that some of the American students were staunch Goldwater supporters.

It was during these visits that the concept of "experiential learning" began to form in my mind. While learning does occur through lectures and the reading of books, learning via experience is far more penetrating and not easily forgotten. You don't forget your experience. Little did I realize at the time that this concept would later play an important role in my life.

In August of 1965 we returned to the States after five years in Brazil for the customary furlough. We went to Princeton Theological Seminary and I entered a program titled "Church and Society". This was essentially a program in the field of Sociology with all but two of my seminars taken at Princeton University. After finishing my residency, we moved to Atlanta, Georgia where I was hired by Westminster Schools to teach while I also continued to work on my doctoral dissertation. While there, the Brazilian Presbyterian Church severed relations with our North American Presbyterian denomination in 1973 which terminated our life appointment.

This unexpected termination meant that we were not going to return to Salvador, Brazil, where we had left our household belongings in 1965. It also meant that I would need to explore possibilities for future employment as we had no desire to remain in the South. Marianne was raised in California, and I had lived there for thirteen years prior to our going to Brazil. We knew that we wanted to return to the West Coast.

I wrote a letter to Dr. David Winter, Dean of the Faculty at Whitworth College (now Whitworth University) in 1973 asking him if he knew of any colleges looking for a college chaplain on the West Coast. Twenty-three years earlier, when I was a student at Fuller Theological Seminary in Pasadena, California, he helped me start a Young Life club at South Pasadena/San Marino High School where he was a high school senior. Dave replied to my letter by asking if I would be interested in teaching Sociology at Whitworth. He later visited us in Atlanta. This was followed by an invitation to visit Whitworth in the spring of 1973 as a candidate for a faculty position.

Marianne and I were still reeling from the disappointment of not being able to return to Brazil where we had invested so much energy. It was difficult to let go of the dreams we had for the projects we had started in Salvador, Brazil, and to realize that we would never see them fulfilled. We were struggling to understand why, after spending five years in Brazil and an additional five years in graduate school in preparation to return to Brazil, only to learn belatedly that we were not going to be able to return there. I shared this with the Dean and said that our next move had to have some continuity with the past ten years. He offered to help me establish a Latin American program if I came to Whitworth. That was the decisive reason for our coming, and it opened a door into the future that I had never dreamed of.

My family and I arrived at Whitworth in August of 1973. I was hired as a professor in the Sociology Department and immediately began strategizing about launching our first trip to Latin America for the summer of 1975 in consultation with Dr. David Winter.

The foundational components of Whitworth's Latin American program were sown in those early years. Over the life of the program, key ingredients for experiential learning have been the following:

- Language Study—Although significant communication can take place via a translator, there is nothing comparable to communicating with Latin Americans in their own language. Therefore, the Central America program has required that students know some Spanish before their departure from Spokane. They then build on this knowledge by intense Spanish language and culture study for the first month, which has usually taken place in Guatemala.

- Homestays—"*Mi casa es tu casa*" (My home is your home) is a famous saying among Latin Americans. You cannot understand a different culture well until you have seen it from the inside. That is why every Central America study trip has always included a homestay experience; sometimes two or three.

- Adequate preparation—An emphasis on experiential learning does not mean that books and lectures are unimportant. The program has always included preparation courses in which students would read books and listen to lectures about Central American history, culture, economics and politics. They would also be led into exploring how personal change takes place, what is the role of "unlearning" as well as learning, and the need for intercultural humility.

- Journaling—The value of keeping notes in a diary or journal was stressed from early on. Over time, this practice developed into the famous field journal where students learned the importance of observing very carefully before making too hasty a moral judgment of a different or unusual event or practice. Although the discipline of journaling did not come easily to some of the students, in the end, most recognized the value of such a practice. Some alumni continue this discipline to this very day.

- A profound quest for the truth—Followers of Jesus recognize that He is the truth. In addition, they should seek to know the truth about God's creation, and especially, human society within that creation. The program has continuously urged participants to follow the truth wherever it might lead, even if it might differ from perspectives commonly found in the United States. Healthy discussion between people with different interpretations of what is really "true" can lead to great personal growth and the betterment of society.

- Community—Although truth can be learned individually, much true knowledge comes to us in community. To compensate for the excessive individualism of the United States, the Central America program has given a special place to community. "As iron sharpens iron, so one person sharpens another," Proverbs 27:17 (NIV). Not only during the trip itself, but throughout the years, alumni frequently celebrate reunions to continue the sharpening process. One student wrote, "Marianne and Ron together form one of the very most influential couples in our lives. Their continued contact with all of us through the years sets such an example. They truly created and sustained a sense of community with our group that is quite unusual."

- A Pedagogy of Transformation—Not all pedagogical methods are helpful. Brazilian educational specialist Paulo Freire developed a pedagogical approach that encourages education as the practice of freedom. It intentionally utilizes the tensions of opposing points of view to bring about transformation at both the personal and group level. Over the years, the Central America Study Program has not shied away from exposing students to the many complicated sides of an issue.

- Justice—Spanish Bibles use the word "*justicia*" in New Testament passages where the English versions use "righteousness." Most New Testament scholars agree that the Greek word "*dikaiosune*" has this interpersonal, societal aspect of justice as in, "Seek first the Kingdom of God and his *justice*," Matthew 6:33 (NIV; author's emphasis). From the very beginning, Ron and Marianne emphasized in the Central America program that followers of Jesus need to seek, promote, and implement justice for all, but especially for the most vulnerable.

- The immense value of every human being—Every person is important because we all bear the image of God. Although society relegates the poor, women, the foreigner, children, and the sick to the fringes or margins, these are the very people that Jesus lifted up. They have always had a special place in the Central America program because they nobly bear God's image and truly are ambassadors of the Lord Most High.

1975: The First Trip

Whitworth Explores Mexico and South America

1975 COHORT:[1] VICTORIA (ABBEY) Del Greco, Wayne (Akana) Akana-Wung, Ann Berney, Betsy (Elizabeth) Brownlee Gano, Cindy Bryggman, Amy (Dinnison) Mc-Donald, Mary Dowse, Lynn (Griesbaum) Onley, Robert Kroeger, H. Scott Matheney, Carolyn (Mooney) Bigbee, Cindy Smith, Lee Smith, Marilyn Strong, and Stephen Walker. Faculty Leader—Ron Frase.

Whitworth's first Latin American study program took place in the summer of 1975. Five countries were chosen—Mexico, Peru, Chile, Argentina, Brazil, and then back to Mexico for a time of reflection and debriefing. Professor Ron Frase, together with his wife Marianne, led the program. Ron used his personal contacts to provide amazing opportunities for students to meet Latin Americans.

The 1975 cohort at a Mexican seminary

1. For identification purposes, throughout the book we strive to provide names as currently used. Names used in college (frequently before marriage) are indicated in parentheses, if known or unless requested otherwise by the participants.

During the academic year of 1974–75 there was a Latin American theme house just off campus. Most of the CAST members took special Portuguese classes there taught by Marianne Frase, so that they would have some linguistic preparation for their time in Brazil.

According to Professor Ron Frase, many of the students were "blown out of the water" by what they experienced. Brazilian Christians had been wrestling with the challenges of living under a military dictatorship for over a decade. Chile's situation was also very tense. A CIA supported military *coup d'état* had taken place on September 11, 1973 and replaced the democratically elected president Salvador Allende with General Augusto Pinochet who would carry out two decades of a brutal dictatorship. This was also the high point of "liberation theology" as Christians, especially within the Catholic Church, developed a more holistic understanding of the Christian mission. This meant identifying with the poor and the politically oppressed, together with the persecution that was their daily bread. The impact on the students was so powerful that some of the students decided not to return to classes in the fall of 1975, although all of the cohort later graduated.

The program was physically and emotionally strenuous from the very beginning. The group met up in Mission Viejo, California at the home of student Lynn Griesbaum's parents. After reaching Tijuana, Mexico, they boarded a bus for a grueling 48-hour trip to Mexico City. They stayed for a week in a seminary dormitory and studied Mexican history and culture, from the Aztecs to the present.

Then they flew to Lima, Peru for more tours and lectures on history and culture. A special component was going to the two-mile-high city of Cuzco. Several students got altitude sickness and had to drink coca-leaf tea to acclimate themselves to the high altitude. One student did admit that after drinking the tea, some students had "wild dreams." Most of the group hiked to the fabulous Inca ruins of Machu Picchu. The four altitude-sickies were given a private tour of Cuzco by a fledgling movie star.

Group on top of the Teotihuacan pyramid

Chile was the next stop on the tour, and this beautiful nation proved to be deeply unsettling for the group. The United States Central Intelligence Agency (CIA) had been involved in the *coup d'état* that had taken place in 1973 in which the democratically elected president Salvador Allende was overthrown, and the dictator Pinochet was installed. During his two-decade long reign, Pinochet ordered the death, torture, or disappearance of some 30,000 Chileans.[2] Ron Frase describes one profoundly important, but distressing, interview:

> While staying at the Methodist Center in Concepción, Chile, I was asked by the director if our group would like to visit a married couple who had recently been released from prison and was staying at the Center under house arrest. After saying that we would, we were taken to a small apartment and introduced to Camilo Cortéz and his wife Jeri. At the end of our three months in Latin America, our group unanimously voted this encounter to be the most memorable event of the trip.
>
> Camilo introduced himself as a Methodist lay pastor who was serving two congregations and was also the manager of a factory during the week. In addition to this, he was the leader of the Socialist Party in Concepción.
>
> While eating breakfast the morning of September 11, 1973, military personnel arrived at his home and placed him and his two adult sons under arrest and took them off to prison on a naval base located on an island in the harbor. He was charged with being one of the leaders of a *coup* that was planning to overthrow the government! All of which he denied.[3]
>
> He took off his shirt and showed us a scarred back and explained a series of tortures he had suffered which included the dunking for eight hours in a tank of water during a cold Chilean winter, hanging by his feet and bounced off a wall until he lost consciousness, and electrodes which burned his body.
>
> They took him out of his cell and placed a bullseye on his chest and told him to look at the sun as it would be the last time he would see it. The next morning, they took him outside again and tied him to a post in plain view of the other prisoners. The firing squad cocked their guns and were ordered to fire. Unknown to Camilo, they fired over his head. He thought he was dead but saw no holes nor blood gushing forth. They hurried him away to another part of the prison leaving all of his fellow prisoners with the impression that he had been killed. The colleagues were later questioned, and they confessed

2. At the time, the United States government denied any involvement in the *coup*. Nevertheless, years later the truth came out and the CIA's involvement was clearly exposed. For a thorough account of that involvement see Peter Kornbluh's *Chile and the United States: Declassified Documents Relating to the Military Coup, September 11, 1973* at https://nsarchive2.gwu.edu//NSAEBB/NSAEBB8/nsaebb8i.htm; downloaded February 23, 2018.

3. Note—This accusation was blatantly absurd and illogical. September 11, 1973 will go down in infamy because, in fact, the CIA conspired with some Chilean officers to implement a military *coup* in order to remove the democratically elected Socialist President Salvador Allende and to replace him with General Pinochet who then ruled Chile as a ruthless dictator for the next two decades.

that Camilo was the leader of a plot to overthrow the government. Later he was presented with a huge dossier of incriminating evidence. He 'redeemed the time' by spending his months in prison serving in the informal role of chaplain comforting and encouraging his colleagues. When he was finally released to the Methodist Center, the guards carried his bag to the gate in a show of admiration.

He told us to return to America and let people know that Pinochet was not the ruler of Chile. Christ was! As he spoke, Jeri, his wife, quietly wept in a corner. He spoke with unimaginable courage. As we quietly filed out of the room, it never occurred to any of us that we would ever see them again. The military regime expelled them from Chile to New York City. Much later, Camilo came to Whitworth for a week. He spoke to the student body in the Forum Program. We had the privilege of hosting him in our home and our high school age daughters had the opportunity of listening to his story.

Ron Frase

After Chile, the group travelled eastward to neighboring Argentina. The contrast was striking. In Buenos Aires, there were no curfews nor machine-gun-toting soldiers on every corner as they had experienced in Chile. Some of the group participated in a huge, political rally in downtown Buenos Aires where they heard the *Presidenta* Isabel Perón give a public message.

After spending some weeks in Argentina, the group traveled to Brazil. Professor Ron Frase describes a powerful interview that took place there.

> Our group briefly visited Campinas, Brazil where Marianne and I had lived a year while attending language school in 1961. In addition to sightseeing, we had some seminars. One of the speakers was Jim Wright who was the Director of the Central Brazil Mission of the Presbyterian Church (USA). He was our "boss" while we were in Brazil. We were also friends with his brother, Paulo Wright, who was a state legislator and supported the labor unions. That was a dangerous position to be in under a military dictatorship. Paulo turned up missing and later his death in a Brazilian prison was verified and reported in the *New York Times*. In 2014 the World Council of Churches repatriated to Brazil thousands of documents that were used to write *Brasil: Nunca Mais* (Brazil: Never Again). This book documented state-sponsored repression and torture during the 1964–1985 military dictatorship. The three authors who wrote the book were Roman Catholic Archbishop Paulo Arns, Reverend Charles Harper and Reverend Jim Wright. Both Charles Harper and Jim Wright were Brazilian born sons of Presbyterian parents and both became PC(USA) ministers. Wright became the Director of the Central Brazil Mission as indicated above, and Charles Harper worked at the Human Rights Desk in Geneva, Switzerland.
>
> The repatriation of these documents came at the time of the beginning of the National Truth Commission which was created with the purpose of trying to understand why the Brazilians did not oppose the military dictatorship, including many members of the Presbyterian Church who truly believed that the nation was under threat and that even torture was justified.

From the very beginning, there has been a deep involvement of Whitworth alumni in the successive trips of the program. For example, Albert and Cathy Reasoner graduated from Whitworth back in 1955. They were Presbyterian missionaries serving in Brazil, and they were friends of Ron and Marianne Frase. This first group slept in sleeping bags in the Reasoner home in Brasilia. Four years later, their son Donald went on the 1979 trip throughout Central America. and later served as a Teaching Assistant for the 1981 tour and helped CAST as a consultant in Nicaragua during the 1980s. Don's sister, Carolyn (Reasoner) Ward participated in the Central America Study Tour during the summer of 1985.

After the group's sojourn in Brazil, the tour returned to Mexico City. They stayed at the Wycliffe Bible Translators headquarters where they reflected on the powerful experiences that had become embedded in their hearts. The long bus ride back to Tijuana gave them time to further reflect on both the pain and the hope they had seen.

Back on the Spokane campus in the fall semester, the students gave a presentation to the entire campus at a Forum session.

Students at Teotihuacan

1977: Jan Term Trip to Guatemala

As a follow up to that first program in 1975, Whitworth sponsored a short three-week course in Guatemala during Jan Term 1977[1]. Although it was a forerunner of the future programs in Central America, it was not considered a full-fledged Central America Study Tour.

Student participant Susan Lonborg writes, "I was part of one of Dr. Frase's study tours to Guatemala. It was in December 1976—January 1977, a year after the major earthquake there in 1976. We spent a little bit of time in Guatemala City, a few days at Lake Atitlan, and most of our time in and around Quetzaltenango. Part of that time included staying with local families. We had a little bit of money left over at the end of the trip, so we took a flight to the ruins at Tikal and spent a couple of days there. Others on the trip included one of Ron's high school aged daughters, a woman named Kak Logan who was a high school English teacher, and a young man who was a farmer in Eastern Washington. There were about a dozen of us on the program. It was certainly a life-changing trip."

Guatemalan children

1. A complete roster of the Jan Term 1977 cohort was not available at the time of publication.

1979: The First Central America Study Tour

Can Violence Be Used to Overcome a Dictator?

CAST 1979 COHORT: STEVEN Benz, Michael Bovee, Albert Cahueque, Robert Campbell, Cindy (Chapman) Weber, Gayle (Donnell) Moir, Kim (Higdon) Harry, Robin Houlton, Tim Marshall, Lyman Miller, James Motteler, Corinne (Parkinson) Thompson, Carol Prentice, Don Reasoner, Dixie (Reimer) Marshall, Chany Sak-Humphry, Adriana (Schilperoort) Havnaer, Dana Schilperoort, Susan Schilperoort, Mark Smith, Rebecca Staebler, Sharon Stratton, Kirsten Thompson, Leslie Vogel, Julie (Weinman) Lays, Debora (Youmans) Hanssen, and Linda (Zenger) Zenger-Obrien. Teaching Assistant—Susan (Bittner) Bittner-Bonebakker. Faculty Leader—Ron Frase.

The political context was extremely important for the 1979 Central America Study Tour participants, given that Central America was experiencing civil wars on many fronts. The main rebel force in Nicaragua, the *Frente Sandinista de Liberación Nacional*, had been formed back in 1961, but it had taken the better part of two decades to bring the dictator Anastasio Somoza to the end of his reign. On January 10, 1978, Pedro Joaquín Chamorro, editor of the opposition newspaper *La Prensa* was assassinated (probably under orders from Somoza). Much of the middle and upper classes began to turn against the dictator. United States President Jimmy Carter had made human rights a bedrock of his foreign policy, and therefore, in 1978 he withdrew his support of Somoza. Through urban guerrilla warfare, the Sandinistas gained control over more and more of the Nicaraguan territory. Guatemala and El Salvador also had repressive regimes, and rebellion had emerged in both countries. There were two prevailing interpretations of the civil strife that had gripped Central America. Some saw it as a local playing out of the Cold War. According to this view, the rebels in each country had been persuaded by the Communists, especially from Cuba, to fight against their freedom-loving, capitalistic governments. The other interpretation saw the rebels as justly fighting against authoritarian regimes that oppressed their own people. The Whitworth students would need to navigate between these two general perspectives as they searched for the truth.

January in Guatemala

This program began in the fall of 1978 with a three-credit orientation course on "Contemporary Latin American Problems" and was taught by Professor Ron Frase. Topics covered in the class included foreign aid, trade, debt, race, and Latin American families and cultural values. Some of the important textbooks included Paulo Freire's *Pedagogy of the Oppressed* and Eugene Nida's *Understanding Latin America*. Many years later, Ron Frase commented on the relationship between book knowledge and experiential learning:

> Although students were academically prepared for the trip and exposed to many of the issues, by traveling to Central America students were exposed to a whole new world and learned from profound experiences that touched their heart—not just their mind. This was an experiential learning course that changes your life.

On New Year's Day 1979, the students, together with Professor Ron Frase and Teaching Assistant Sue Bittner, met up in Los Angeles to begin their four-month sojourn. First stop: Costa Rica for 6 ½ weeks. They were immediately immersed in the culture by living with Costa Rican host families. Student Corinne Parkinson described her family:

> To me Costa Rica is a land of music and laughter. My family there includes some of the finest people I have ever met. The house was constantly filled with talking, singing, and guitar playing. *Mami* was fun, loving, understanding, and she and I grew particularly close. *Papi* was one of the kindest, most sensitive men I've ever known. They and the children all adopted me, and I now have a second family. I think of my mother's eyes or the red and yellow flowers, or the tears when I left. I miss it all, and I secretly promise myself that I'll go back someday.

Students spent their afternoons in intensive Spanish language courses at the *Instituto de Lengua Española*. Mornings were spent at the *Seminario Bíblico* where the group heard speakers deal with the tough issues of politics, economics, theology, and poverty. One especially powerful conversation took place when students were able to interview three Nicaraguan exiles together with renowned theologian John (Juan) Stam. Ron Frase recalls:

Ron Frase

John Stam arranged a meeting for us with three Nicaraguan exiles: Doña O-livia, Bosco Centeno, and Felipe Peña. John introduced them as refugees from the island of Solentiname who had fled the island located on Lake Managua to escape Somoza´s soldiers who were destroying their community. These three peasants were members of a church that Ernesto Cardenal had formed in 1966. He was a Nicaraguan who had gone to a Trappist monastery in Gethsemane, Kentucky, where Thomas Merton was his spiritual director. He decided to return to Nicaragua with Merton´s blessing. He went to the primitive island of Solentiname and created a small community called the "*Familia de Dios*".

Felipe Peña told us how people of Solentiname were transformed by Cardenal´s arrival. They felt resentment toward their former priests who had not shared the "true gospel." These priests had talked about the rosary but not about real love for one's neighbor. Instead of hearing a sermon each Sunday on the Gospel, the Solentiname people would have a dialogue/conversation following the Gospel reading. Many of these people were illiterate. The Scripture was read and then commented on, verse by verse, and everyone contributed to the conversation. Over time, they developed a desire to join the struggle with the FSLN (the guerrilla group called the Sandinista National Liberation Front) in the mountains.

Doña Olivia entered the conversation. She spoke with passion and excitement. She spoke of how Ernesto Cardenal had brought the "true Gospel" to Solentiname. She described a new level of human existence. They discovered that they had people who could paint and sell their paintings and improve their standard of living. She told us how Ernesto Cardenal had delivered them from "conformist religion" to "authentic religion" and their obligation to serve the poor. Slowly they came to the realization that they had to fight for the liberation of the people from the exploitation and corruption of the Somoza government. This meant that they had to leave the island and join the struggle with the hope that all Nicaraguans would become free to know a life of love and justice.

Bosco joined in the conversation to say that they did not arrive at this decision impulsively, but only after much prayer and discussion. They came to the conclusion that they couldn't remain comfortably in Solentiname while Somoza's army harassed the people on the mainland and the Sandinistas in the mountains.

John Stam explained to us that Felipe had been taken prisoner after a failed Sandinista attack on the National Palace. Felipe followed up by saying that he now saw oppression and corruption from personal experience. He had been beaten and tortured and had heard the groans of peasants being tortured. To see and feel torture is very different from hearing about it. He told us that he had been handcuffed for 16 days, but that he had never felt discouraged because as a Christian he knew that what he was doing was right. The prisoners prayed for a miracle. Their prayer was answered when the Sandinistas captured the palace on August 22, 1978. The prisoners were freed in a hostage swap for the government officials and cabinet members who had been taken prisoners in the capture of the palace.

On our return from our Central American experience, our flight briefly landed in Managua. Nicaragua was still in the hands of Somoza who bombed his own people and whose National Guard ravaged the countryside. As we sat in the plane (we were not allowed to enter the airport), we remembered the conversation we had in San José with John Stam, Felipe Peña, Bosco Centeno, and Doña Olivia when we had started our journey. We admired them and the people they represented, but it seemed that the struggle against Somoza was in vain. They were no match against Somoza's Air Force and the United States support of the Somoza regime.[1]

---

1. Against heavy odds, the Sandinistas did in fact overthrow the Somoza government later that year on July 19.

The revolution taking place in Nicaragua continued to spark controversy among the students, especially regarding the use of violent versus nonviolent means for effecting social change. This issue arose out of some first-hand encounters with members of the Sandinista guerrillas who were fighting against the Somoza regime in Nicaragua. The following vigorous discussion was presented back at Spokane in the fall at the campus-wide Forum. It illustrated the complexities of the Nicaraguan civil war.

Leslie Vogel: Saturday at Playa El Coco, Susan and I went for a walk down the beach. A Latin man spoke to us in English, admiring the shells we had collected. We quickly learned that he was a Sandinista, recovering from being shot seven times while fighting in the Nicaraguan civil war. He spoke of Somoza's oppression — of the rape, torture, and massacre of innocent people. His words brought questions to our minds of the horror of civil war, of killing fellow countrymen with American guns, and forced us to recognize that our own country has played a strong role in creating and maintaining that situation.

Susan Schilperoort: I could sense Antonio's bitterness against the fact that Somoza and his national Guard had been trained by the United States government, and the fact that our multinational corporations, which feed our blind desires for a higher standard of living, are doing so at the expense of the lives and freedom of Nicaraguans. He said that he doesn't hate Americans personally, but that he hates our system . . . a system which encourages us to be ignorant about the effects that our selfish, materialistic lifestyle has on nations like Nicaragua. How true, and I was faced with the fact that by doing nothing to express my disapproval, I was, and am a part of the system that is exploiting and oppressing his people. He told us that now we have to live with our consciences. We have a responsibility to continue to be informed and to inform others. We know what their situation is, so how can we live with ourselves if we choose to ignore it?

Leslie: Antonio told us we could also help, directly, by sending medical supplies that the Sandinistas need, and he pointed out that by doing so, we would become Sandinistas, his sisters. I was no longer merely an observer. I had a choice to make. The complexity of the world's problems and the complete reality of this situation overwhelmed me. Tears streamed down our faces as we walked on down the beach. I couldn't forget Antonio looking into my eyes and saying, "We're not in a classroom, and I'm not just teaching you a lesson. This is for real!!"

Susan: So, what do you do when you think you've got your non-violent philosophy all wrapped up in a neat little package and then this Nicaraguan who doesn't like war, who'd rather be home writing poetry and playing with his kids, sits in front of the room and says that even Christ would have taken a weapon had he lived in Nicaragua under Somoza; that a Christian must show commitment through action, and in the case of Nicaragua the action is violent. Then he says, "Don't call it violence; call it justice against injustice"

Leslie: I always believed that violence was wrong, but after talking with the Sandinistas, I can see where they find violence to be a necessary response to their situation. Still I'm not at all resolved about whether violence is right or wrong.

Linda Zenger: Doña Olivia broadened our understanding of the issue by her own belief that any violence they participate in is done out of love to counter the oppressive violence of Somoza. They felt themselves required to join the fight out of love for future victims—preventing future oppression by stopping it now.

Leslie: But doesn't violence breed more violence?

Tim Marshall: At the time we talked with them, before Somoza's downfall, we all felt they were overly optimistic about their ability to overthrow him, and we didn't really believe them when they said that when it did happen, the violence would not continue afterward. But look at what has happened, Nicaragua has not become another Cuba or Iran.

Leslie: Still, centuries of historical evidence support the fact that any violence leads to more violence.

Linda: Does that become an excuse not to act? The situation demands a response. The thought of participating in the violence there is not as frightening to me as the thought that I might do nothing. We are struggling with the morality of violence, but might failure to act be just as wrong or worse?

Leslie: It is also possible to believe that violence is wrong, but still see it as the only alternative. In Mexico, I met a Nicaraguan who had been forced to leave his country, and I asked him if he would have fought had he stayed. He said, "Of course, but thank God I haven't had to add that to my list of sins."

Tim: If violence shouldn't be used, how would you bring about social change in a violent situation? Our system allows for significant changes without violence . . . but how do you peacefully or non-violently deal with someone who would bomb the innocent people of his own country?

Linda: We can't know, because we haven't experienced the reality of oppression . . . they have. We enjoy the luxury of being able to intellectualize about the issue of violence and non-violence They have to make a decision.

Tim: Although I don't know if I could ever use a gun, I can't tell them that they shouldn't. In talking with Doña Olivia, Felipe, and Bosco, we began to understand their answers, but found more questions for ourselves.

From Costa Rica, the group flew to Honduras where they spent the next six weeks in service projects. An immediate problem arose when the plane landed in Tegucigalpa. The group had to wait several hours on the tarmac of the airport as Ron, Susan, and the leaders of CODE/CEDEN, our local host organization, tried to negotiate with the Honduran immigration authorities who refused to allow Chany Sak-Humphry to enter the country. She was a Whitworth student, traveling on a UN passport because of her status having fled the Khmer Rouge in Cambodia. In the end, she was put on a plane and sent back to the US.

The students were surprised and troubled by the general conditions of Hondurans. Susan Schilperoort wrote, "We were immediately struck with the great differences between Costa Rica and Honduras. Some of the main things that stood out in our minds were the extreme poverty, the number of armed military men in the streets, and the rustic countryside." Given the similarities in geography and climate, students strove to understand the causes of the economic and political differences. The personal integrity/corruption of political leaders was a small, but significant factor. Structural differences seemed more influential. For example, Costa Rica abolished its military in 1948. Public funds saved from not needing to invest in a military were channeled into health, education, electrification of the countryside, and other infrastructure investments which led to benefits for the general population. A viable democratic tradition in Costa Rica was another significant factor. Nevertheless, the Whitworth students expressed great admiration for the inner strength of the Honduran people.

Dixie Reimer: The Miskito Indian people are strong and friendly. They live simple but hard lives. La *Miskitia*, they claim, was forgotten by God and the government. Recently two hurricanes destroyed their homes and farms. The government sent only two bags of black beans.

Don Reasoner: I really don't know what the Miskito people are doing. They have no place to live, nothing to eat but the fallen fruit which will rot in a few days. They have no materials to build a new house. It hasn't stopped raining long enough for them to get materials or dry firewood. The school went down so the kids were sent home two months early. I am living through a personal crisis, and yet I am warm and have food to eat. It is mind boggling to think that people around me suffer yet because I am from the USA, I don't. I always have something to fall back on, my family, the US, something. And these people have nothing.

Nevertheless, Tim Marshall articulated an observation echoed by many, "There is a basic blessedness here."

Some of the students made the following comments about their Honduran experiences:

Tim Marshall: I live at a truck stop, Honduran style. Truck drivers hauling logs, Honduran style—a swig of water, spit on the floor, and back on the road again.

Albert Cahueque: Maybe I'm being too judgmental, but I sure wish these d . . . nurses were better instructed in setting IVs. Wow! I am here in Choluteca, Honduras, flat on my back, dehydrated from the parasitic infection and burning with fever from malaria: What a strange way of furthering my education. Education or not . . . as soon as Doc says I am well enough to leave, I'm whipping out whatever money it takes and getting the hell out of here!

Julie Weinman: I am mad this morning! I have diarrhea, little bites all over my feet and hands . . . today I want a break! I want a beach; I want to hear English; I want a brownie!!

Albert: I wish I had some sort of exciting news to tell, but I really don't. Major events just don't occur. Each day is like the one before.

Adriana Schilperoort: I've become a Nun! I live with a Franciscan sister and rise to the church bells at 6:00am. I am learning about the Catholic beliefs and enjoying life in La Libertad.

Rebecca Staebler: We're starting to do things for the last time. I don't like the feeling. I want to be on with the trip and soon to be home, but I don't want to leave Buenos Aires (the name of her town in Honduras). I don't want the evenings to never again be full of joking with *Agar*, hearing stories, then writing by the kerosene lamp, listening to the crickets and the people in the road. I don't want to never again see Maribel's red hair and smiling eyes. I don't want to miss *Osmín* and *Walda* saying "Adiós Rebecca." I don't want to never again laugh at *Juancito's* funny ways in the morning, I don't want to leave *Dorotea's* warm hugs. Will they miss us as we will miss them? They say they will. They tell us not to go. Do the children realize there will be no more *Kinder*; no more *gringüitas*? Tomorrow will be hard; perhaps the hardest goodbye I'll ever have to say. These people are so special to me. They have accepted me, opened their homes to a stranger. Life will go on here in Buenos Aires. When I return to the US, I leave behind what is almost another world. A world which will be difficult, if not impossible to return to. It's been an experience which, in actuality, has lasted five weeks, so I must hold it inside of me for a lifetime.

Due to the civil strife taking place in El Salvador and Nicaragua, the group could not visit these countries. The group was scheduled to spend a week in San Salvador. They were going to visit a Whitworth alumnus working with Archbishop Oscar Romero and with the church's displaced peoples program. The itinerary was changed, and the group flew from Honduras directly to Guatemala. Several months later, Archbishop Romero was assassinated while celebrating mass in the chapel. He has been universally recognized as a martyr because he pursued the kingdom and justice of God here on earth through peaceful means. Down through the years, Whitworth students, upon reading or hearing of his testimony, have held Romero in high esteem. His life and martyrdom have encouraged many Whitworthians in their faith.

The group then went to Guatemala for the next two and a half weeks. The students were confronted with a stark contrast—a country of striking beauty and deep pain. One student wrote:

> A land of color, tradition, beauty and tranquility. The unsuspecting tourist would see the resort area of Lake Atitlan and remark at the charm of Indian women carting their wash to be pounded clean on the river rocks. They would be taken by Antigua, the colonial capital of Central America; intrigued by the market-place bartering; and then take home memories in the form of hand-woven cloth and embroidered dresses. But we saw much more; a people serving under the rule of military oppression and political tyranny.
>
> The country of Guatemala is about the size of Tennessee, with a population that is 70 percent Indian. The land and wealth are unequally distributed. A tiny elite control most of the country. Illiteracy is high and growing with the population's growth. Seventy-five percent of the people are thought to be malnourished, and nearly half of the children die before the age of six.
>
> Amnesty International has said that the military government of Guatemala apparently holds no political prisoners. They have all been killed by security forces and free-lance death squads. Ana Colom Argueta, widow of the former Mayor of Guatemala City, said that in the first 3 months of this year (1979) 2,000 people have already been killed. Her husband, leader of the United Revolutionary Front Party, was killed last March by a squad of men in front of his office in Guatemala City.

The students were very impressed by two women lawyers that they met. Instead of choosing lucrative safe careers, they were risking their lives to be advocates for their people. Ron Frase describes what happened to one of those lawyers:

> While in Guatemala City we attended a meeting of the CNT (National Center of Workers) chaired by Yolanda Martínez de Aguilar, a lawyer. In Guatemala at that time there were daily stories in the newspapers of the struggle between the *Ejército Secreto Anticomunista*, or ESA, (Secret Anti Communist Army) and the efforts of labor to organize. The ESA had a long list of names of people

they were going to kill. The list was published in the newspapers and over the radio. Yolanda was on that list. Labor leaders were assassinated with alarming frequency. The struggle was highlighted by the battle between the Coca Cola company and its union members. Two years before we arrived, the union leaders were jailed for 613 days. In 1978, an attempt was made on the life of the Secretary General of the Union, Israel Márquez, and in fact, the union treasurer, Pedro Quevedo, was assassinated. We were very impressed by the bravery of these people in their struggle for justice.

The next day we left for Oaxaca, Mexico—a five-hour bus drive. We spent the day in Oaxaca and continued on the next morning over a very winding road to arrive in Mexico City eight hours later. The students were very impressed with the accommodations at the seminary in which we all stayed.

The next morning, I discovered that a committee from the World Council of Churches was also staying at the seminary studying the issue of development in Latin America. A member of the committee, a Guatemalan lawyer informed me that Yolanda Martínez de Aguilar had been arrested by the police at 5:30pm on April 20 (the day after she spoke with the group) at the airport when she went to see her mother off for Puerto Rico.

On that same April 20, the army broke into the building we had visited. They arrested the union leaders we had spoken with the day before. The students were in Mexico for ten days, part of the time in Oaxaca and the rest of the time in Mexico City. The group worked through the conflicting myriad of events and emotions. They pondered together the tough issues they had encountered on the trip: Communism and Christianity, violence and revolution, ostentatious wealth surrounded by immense poverty. One student wrote about a conversation she had on the flight home:

For me, these issues were brought together in my final moments on Latin American soil. Helping a young woman in the Mexico City airport, I carried her few things onto the plane while she clutched tightly at her newborn son. We sat together for the flight to Los Angeles, and she told her story—a Nicaraguan escaping the war, her husband dead . . . shot by the National Guard. She knows no English and has no money—only a son and the pain and agony of a murdered family, a destroyed homeland. As we came over the endless lights of Los Angeles, she stared out the window, and as we began our descent, she turned to me, tears running down her cheek. "*Es tan grande, y somos tan pequeños*" (It's so big, and we're so small). I realized as we left the plane that she meant much more than just the size of her new home. It was the poor and the rich, Latin America and the United States, humanity and the universe. Entering the airport, she was shuttled behind closed doors by immigration officials, while I turned toward the customs line with my bags of presents and souvenirs. Now after four months of questions and searching—the trip meant something.

Back on campus in the fall, the group shared their experiences at a Forum presentation. After sharing their stories and reflections, the students pointed to the life of Chilean musician, Victor Jara, He had raised his voice against injustice, poverty and foreign imperialism. His life was a worthy example of moral integrity and consistency until the very end. He was brutally tortured and murdered while a prisoner of the Chilean Armed Forces on September 15, 1973.

One student summed up the trip with a personal call:

> Through my experience in Central America, I have learned that I have a great responsibility to use what God has given me. Christ says in the Gospel, "To him whom much has been given, much is required," Luke 12:48 (NIV). I cannot destroy poverty, but I can help a person who lives in poverty. I cannot wipe out oppressive institutions, but I can lend help to an individual who lives under that oppression. Awareness and concern are a start, but Christ has challenged me to do more; to step out against the injustice—here in the US, in Central America, and in so many other parts of this world. If I, if we accept this challenge, great changes will occur.

The Central America program sparked healthy discussion and controversy, not just among the participants, but also back on the Spokane campus. Ron described the response that emerged after the 1979 Tour:

> There was some concern from faculty that I was taking students down to Central America and making "fanatics" out of them. I was able to remind them that they had never themselves been to Latin America, and that a kind of reverse learning happens when students and faculty that have experienced Central America return and share what they have learned. There was a difference of opinion among the faculty. The fact that I had been a missionary in Brazil prior to coming to Whitworth did help with my credibility and not to be judged. There was always some pressure with differing viewpoints, but I tried to get them to see that what students returned with was an understanding of the complexity and nuances of the issues, not the more narrow, black and white opinions of those who had not participated in the trips.

1981: Service Projects in Troubled Honduras[1]

CAST 1981 COHORT: MARCOS Archuleta, Carolyn (Bandy) Petek, Paul Brassard, Elizabeth Calvin, Lorrie Hungate, Coburn Ingram, Dorilyn (Kooy) Kooy Roome, N. "Erik" Lampi, Bradley McGuire, Laurie McQuaig, Sara (Nilson) Bos, Lori Ann (Price) Donner, Elizabeth "Liz" (Raymond) Schatz, Carol Rose, Kevin Sea, Ellen Skillings, Margaret "Meg" (Symons) Gregory, and Tamara (Watson) Anderson. Teaching Assistant—Donald Reasoner (CAST 1979). Faculty Leaders—Ron Frase Ross Cutter, Jim Hunt, and JoAnn Atwell-Scrivner.

The 1981 group had a new set of challenges. The Sandinistas were now governing Nicaragua. Ronald Reagan had just been elected president which signified an important change in US foreign policy. President Carter had made human rights a bedrock of his foreign relationships. This led Carter to stop arms sales to the Nicaraguan ruler Somoza which was a significant factor in the Sandinista triumph over the dictator. President Reagan had a different understanding of what was happening in Central America. Instead of seeing these civil wars as justified rejection of repressive regimes, he believed that the Soviet Union was spreading communism throughout Central America and around the world. Reagan began to support the various repressive, anti-communist regimes in the area, and he began a strategy to overthrow the Sandinista government in Nicaragua. The Whitworth students wrestled with the question of whether the Cold War would wreak havoc on the Central American countries.

During the fall of 1980, Professor Ron Frase taught his Contemporary Latin American Problems class. His Teaching Assistant was Donald Reasoner who had participated in the 1979 tour. Some of the themes of the course included Latin American history and politics, social change, and Latin American culture.

The group began the program in Costa Rica where they spent five weeks in intensive Spanish language study at the *Instituto de Lengua Española*. To immerse themselves more deeply in the Costa Rican culture, each student stayed with a local host family. They were accompanied in this process by Whitworth Physical Education Professor and Tennis Coach, Ross Cutter.[2] Ross became known as *"Señor Cien"* because he would hand out a weekly allowance of one hundred colones. It was his way of

1. For some good insights of the impact of this trip, see the article "Central America" in *Whitworth College Today* 50:1 (September 1981), p. 4.

2. Coach Cutter was much loved by Whitworth students and staff alike. He passed into the presence of the Lord during the Fall of 2017.

checking in personally with every student. Urban legend has it that Ross was ordering breakfast at the *Hotel Nacional* and said, "*Una grape-a-fruito, por favor.*" The students with him laughed until they thought they would die.

The group then traveled to Nicaragua where they spent a week learning about what the new Sandinista government was trying to achieve, including their successes and failures. The group took a bus to Managua and stayed at the Baptist Seminary the first night, then went to a retreat center up the hill towards Masaya, where it was much cooler. The Council of Protestant Churches CEPAD (*Consejo de Iglesias Evangélicas Pro-Alianza Denominacional*) organized the local transportation and a group from their Youth Department showed the Whitworth students around and told stories about what it was like to be young adults in the midst of civil strife.

The students traveled to Honduras by bus. Physical Education Professor and Volleyball Coach JoAnn Atwell-Scrivner accompanied the students on this portion of the tour. They spent the next 6 weeks in service projects with a variety of organizations. For example, Ellen Skillings and Liz Raymond worked with *CEDEN* (*Comité Evangélico de Emergencia Nacional*). They were sent to a small village in the mountains east of Choluteca called *Las Casitas*. They were given the task to set up and run a preschool for the children of the village which they successfully accomplished. Students Lori Ann Price and Lorraine Hungate were asked to help start a similar preschool in the town of Cayanini. They also completed their task.

Liz Raymond and Ellen Skilling getting ready to leave Las Casitas

Teaching Assistant Donald Reasoner explained the need for wisdom and flexibility in the Honduran placements.:

Liz and Ellen's preschool class

Liz Calvin was assigned to work with the refugee program near the border with El Salvador. I traveled with her to the location, but we were stopped by the Honduran military about 2 hours from the camp and sent back to Tegucigalpa. We found out later the army did not want any foreigners in the area who could report about the massacre of refugees crossing the Lempa river between Honduras and El Salvador. We managed to find another assignment for Liz. Over the next month, I then made at least one visit to each of the locations where the students were placed.

The group then visited the Mayan ruins of Copán on their way to Guatemala City. After a few days in the capital, they had a week of reflection and debriefing in Lake Atitlán, Guatemala. The final two weeks of the program were spent in Mexico (Oaxaca, Cuernavaca, and Mexico City). Participants studied Latin American history with Professor Jim Hunt. This was Hunt's first experience with CAST, but he would become a major faculty member in the program for the next three decades.

1982: A Challenging Conversation with Salvadoran Seminarians

CAST 1982 Cohort: Susan (Cerruti) Nery, Cynthia (Chamberlain) Archuleta, Karen (Cornwell) Fortlander (who would leave the group in the first few days in Costa Rica, but would later return with another tour!), Craig Dander, Melissa (Frase) Alfstad, Michelle (Frase) Owen, Mitch Frey, Linda (Gillingham) Sciaroni, Kathryn Haisman Boice, Pamela (Hudspeth) Hudspeth-Johnson, Cynthia (Huggins) Tidd, Elizabeth (Kinsler) LeDesma, Susan (Moore) Barnes, David Ramaley, Sally Scrivner, Shelley (Smith) Boucher, William Sherwood, Craig Stein, Susan (White) Ford, and Reid Ziegler. Teaching Assistant—Susan Schilperoort (1979 inaugural group). Faculty Leaders—Ron Frase.

1982 cohort with Salvadoran seminarians

Excitement and anxiety were in the air on a rainy May morning at SeaTac Airport in Seattle as twenty Whitworth students began to gather in the boarding area for a day long flight to San José Costa Rica. Less than three years earlier, the Sandinista revolution overthrew longtime dictator Anastasio Somoza Debayle of Nicaragua in June 1979. Following the seizure of power, the Sandinistas ruled the country as part of a Junta of National Reconstruction led by nine members, including Daniel Ortega, who would become president for many years. When the Sandinistas began to implement the nationalization of certain industries and formally defaulted on World Bank and International Monetary Fund loans abused by the Somoza regime, the Reagan administration began a series of programs to systematically destabilize the newly formed Sandinista government through economic sanctions and asset seizures. During that summer of 1982 Lt. Colonel Oliver North, from within the White House in Washington, worked to assemble, fund, and arm former Somocistas in southern Honduras that would later be known as the "Iran/Contra Affair."

Just sixty days prior to the group's departure, a military *coup d'état* occurred in Guatemala on March 23 after self-appointed leader General Ríos Montt declared the presidential election fraudulent and assumed the presidency. After his seizure of power, he initiated a brutal campaign of repression and massacred political opponents that often included whole communities of Guatemala's indigenous population.

During the planning of the trip, El Salvador, a hoped-for destination, turned out to be far too dangerous a place for foreigners to travel that summer. Violence against its own citizens was rampant in the spring of 1982 and orchestrated primarily by its military, government officials and para-military organizations all backed and funded by the Reagan administration.

During the spring of 1982, in preparation for the study/service tour, all of the students took language, history, and Latin American studies classes while also attending orientation events over the months leading up to the trip. Susan (Cerruti) Nery recalls:

> Our studies began with a series of orientations designed to prepare us for our trip, including the inevitable "culture shock" we were sure to experience. I vividly remember Ron telling us that catcalling should be expected and that some Latin American women were actually offended if they were not catcalled ... and we needed to be prepared not to feel offended when it happened.

Another student added:

> We also learned about socially acceptable customs, how to conduct ourselves in public, with our families, strange foods and to be aware of our surroundings and that we were walking, talking ambassadors for our country. Ron also told us that because we were gringos, we would be sticking out like sore thumbs. So, we were not to make spectacles of ourselves by gathering in large groups, or by speaking English loudly in public places. He spoke of other important topics, (from eating whatever you are served to busses that might not come

on time), but those two bits of advice have made the most significant impact on me.

Against that backdrop, the students boarded their plane destined for San José Costa Rica. Dr. Ron Frase, his wife, Marianne, and Teaching Assistant, Susan Schilperoort were leading the group. Susan had been on the first ever Central America tour in 1979 as a student. In spite of the fact that the group would not be traveling to highly dangerous countries, many of the places they would visit did produce their own forms of fear, trepidation, and anxiety for the group. Susan's level head, calm demeanor, and positive attitude, in addition to how well organized and prepared she was, made the stress and consternation the group often felt far more tolerable. Without her tremendous language skills and organizational talents, the trip overall would have become an overwhelming emotional, physical, and mental struggle for everyone involved.

San José Costa Rica was home for the participants during the next month. The group attended sessions in the morning at the Seminario Bíblico where guest speakers addressed the group discussing Latin American culture, history, politics, and the role of the church amidst it all. They had intensive Spanish language study every afternoon that one student labeled as "brutal." They would then go back to their host families for a conversationally-laden *cena*. This was during Costa Rica's rainy season, so dinner was usually accompanied by rain showers almost every evening.

One of the most emotionally difficult events took place in Costa Rica. The CAST group would listen to speakers at the *Seminario Bíblico* in San José. There were some Baptist students from El Salvador who were studying at the seminary. The Salvadoran students asked to have a meeting with the Whitworth group. This promised to be an ideal encounter. Although the Whitworth students had read much about El Salvador, they were not going to be able to visit the small country because of the violence taking place there. To meet with Salvadoran seminarians of their same age seemed like an excellent alternative. The Baptists from El Salvador shared painful stories of disappearances, torture, rape, and murder that their friends and families had experienced from the El Salvador military and security forces. Then the seminarians asked a poignant question, "If the United States is truly a Christian country that promotes freedom and democracy around the world, why are they sending money and arms to the El Salvadoran government that so horribly oppresses its people?" The CAST students were taken aback. They felt shame and embarrassment because they couldn't reconcile the violence that the United States was indirectly supporting with the noble ideals of their own country. They also felt impotent because they were unable to change the US foreign policies regarding El Salvador.[1]

Student Craig Dander recalls that awkward setting:

---

1. This dialogue with the Salvadoran students had a deep and long-lasting impact on Ron Frase as well as on the students. See his reflection eleven years later in the 1993 chapter on Archbishop Romero.

We were all well aware of current events there; we'd studied and read a great deal about El Salvador and especially the violence taking place there against its people. These seminarians were our peers in age; so as they began to share painful stories of disappearances, torture, rape, and murder of their friends and family at the hands of Salvadoran military and paramilitary forces, the experience became all too relevant for us. All of what we had learned before this moment had been in academic settings often simply memorizing information in preparation for tests. Here suddenly we were listening to young adults our age who were far more mature, politically-sophisticated, and in-touch with the realities of the world than we could possibly imagine. Theirs was a world we had never experienced. It all culminated when one of the seminarians asked us that poignant and most difficult question. It was a difficult moment, as all of us felt a sense of powerlessness. We had no response and what was worse, we felt completely helpless and incredibly naive. Until that moment, the world we came from did not contain these realities and at best these sorts of discussions and questions had been intellectual exercises and nothing more back on campus at Whitworth.

The time in Costa Rica also had its share of comic relief. Some female students relate a funny experience with catcalling:

The catcalling at a construction site happened every single day without fail. We got used to it. It became comical. As the days passed, we would get a bit bolder. We would walk a little slower and try to sideways glance to see what they looked like, and what was going on. One day, we reached the street right before the block where the construction workers were busy on the opposite side of the street. Just as soon as one spotted us, it fell silent. We noticed a head pop up out of a manhole and as we set foot on the curb, the whistling and cat-calling commenced on cue, and the worker in the manhole followed us, turning his head and keeping his eyes focused on the gringas, either out of curiosity or obligation, saying whatever he was expected to say. As soon as we were setting foot off that block, his head went back down the manhole and the noise of construction began again. We burst out laughing. We were no longer afraid, but amused. And, I think, had they stopped this ritual, we would have been rather disappointed.

From Costa Rica the group traveled by bus to Managua, Nicaragua to the Baptist Seminary. It was one of the few buildings in the old downtown area that had survived the earthquake of 1972. Managua was hot and muggy at night and hotter and muggier during the day. The students heard more speakers each morning, mostly about the Sandinista revolution—the culmination of which was Ernesto Cardenal who was a well-known Catholic priest and a member of the original junta that had taken over power from the Somoza regime in June 1979. Cardenal had served as the Minister of Culture from 1979—1987. He had a very bad cavity in one of his back teeth the morning the group met with him, so his talk was quite short as he was not feeling well.

Later the same day, the group visited the US embassy, and there was a large protest outside the front gates. With the Iranian hostage crisis still a fresh memory, the Marines in the Embassy took unusual precautions. Professor Ron Frase narrates:

> On June 25, we visited the US Embassy and had an interview with newly-arrived Ambassador Anthony Quainton. He spoke with us for about twenty minutes. It was not a very useful conversation. Next Roger Gamble followed him and was more informative and disarming. He acknowledged that the United States had failed in Nicaragua. He also broke the news to us that Alexander Haig had just resigned as Secretary of State. While we were in the Embassy, a massive pro-PLO (Palestine Liberation Organization) rally was forming outside the Embassy protesting the Israeli invasion of Lebanon. The Embassy staff had been released earlier to avoid a confrontation. The demonstration stopped in front of the gates where Uncle Sam was burned in effigy. We were not able to leave because of the crowd at the gates until an hour later. They finally surreptitiously sneaked us out through a back entrance. This was the first and only time we were held captive in a US Embassy.

After a few more days in Managua, the group departed for Honduras. One student recalls the bus trip to Nicaragua's northern neighbor:

> Our "work" home stays were to take place in Honduras. The bus trip to Honduras was awesome simply because we were traveling north and getting higher into the mountains the further north we went. By the time we arrived at the Nicaraguan/Honduran border, the temperatures were quite pleasant, and there was no humidity. Nicaraguan border guards were super friendly to us, and then we walked 200 yards over to the Honduran side of the border crossing where we received a very cool reception. The Honduran guards went through all our personal effects, bags, backpacks, literature, and papers, including diaries we were required to keep. It took hours and was kind of scary.

Susan Cerruti and Pam Hudspeth continued to have creative responses to the machismo they experienced. Susan remembers:

> Pam and I spent lots of time together. While we were used to standing out, we stood out even more in Tegucigalpa. We were that much taller, that much lighter-skinned and more gringa than ever. So, we would always get lots of stares and attention when we walked downtown. It would make us terribly self-conscious, and we tried to figure out ways to fit in better. We even attempted or pretended to have conversations in Spanish only as we walked down the street. We didn't want to speak English and call any more attention to ourselves than we already did. We knew we couldn't make ourselves

shorter, so we thought we could try dressing differently, but all the clothes were tiny, and we didn't have a ton of money. Then we passed by a window that showcased turbans. We looked at each other and said, "Turbans!" What could be more perfect? They were cheap, they covered our light hair, and they would surely make us fit in better! We bought a green and a red one. Pam got the green one. I remember because after we put them on and started walking down the street with our newfound confidence, I turned to look at her, and I realized that we both looked ridiculous! We laughed about that for a long time.

Students had fascinating and life-changing home stays in rural Honduras. The group then traveled to Guatemala and spent a few days of rest in the beautiful city of Antigua. The last days of the trip were spent in Cuernavaca and Mexico City. Students commented that they felt that they had run an emotional marathon, but they had become stronger because of it. The participants flew to Los Angeles and then returned to their homes for a few weeks before classes started up in the fall in Spokane.

Don Chepe y Doña Guadalupe

1984: The Trip that Provoked a Debate Back on the Spokane Campus

CAST 1984 COHORT: SANDRA (Canepa) Canepa-Swan, Karen (Cornwell) Fortlander, Kurtis Dale, Delene (DeForest) DeForest-Dale, Scott Donner, Katharine "Kay" Eekhoff, Bill Sherwood, Rachel Sibley, Joanne (Sleeper) Captein, Jeff Steve, Bradley Taplin, and Bill Turnmire. Teaching Assistant—Leslie Vogel (CAST 1979). Faculty Leaders—Ross Cutter, JoAnn Atwell-Scrivner, and Ron Frase.

1984 cohort in the colonial city of Antigua, Guatemala

The mid 1980s continued to be tumultuous times in Central America. The Contra War was blazing in Nicaragua. In late 1983, President Reagan´s foreign policy advisors urged him to place mines in Nicaragua´s harbors, and he began to do so. Back in the United States, public opinion polls showed that a majority of US citizens were not in favor of backing the Contras. Through the legislation of the Boland Amendment, the US Congress prohibited the federal government from providing military support for the purpose of overthrowing the Government of Nicaragua. Nevertheless, President Reagan would try to do an end around by selling arms to Iran and having the Iranian government fund the Contras (Oliver North´s infamous "Irangate"). Guatemala and El Salvador were also experiencing civil wars against authoritarian regimes. How would the Whitworth CAST students navigate these propagandistic minefields in their search for truth and justice?

In the fall of 1983 an orientation course was taught by Professors JoAnn Atwell-Scrivner and Ron Frase. It treated Latin American history and culture, family life, and politics. An unusual twist was that almost all the participants lived in the "international" Baldwin dormitory in order to enhance group cohesion and to improve their Spanish skills.

The trip began with six weeks in Costa Rica. Physical Education Professor and Tennis Coach Ross Cutter led the group in this period. Professor and Chaplain Ron Frase also came down for a brief visit. The students had several hours of intensive Spanish language study daily in San José. They were immersed in the culture by having the privilege of living in home stays with Costa Rican families. During this period Teaching Assistant Leslie Vogel organized the schedule so that students could hear many guest speakers from a wide range of positions at the *Seminario Bíblico Latinoamericano*. A conflict pedagogical model was intentionally utilized. These alternative versions of reality were not only representative of Central America, they also forced students to improve their abilities of mental and ethical discernment.

Although participants lived in the central valley of Costa Rica, they did have the opportunity to visit the east coast city of Limón. They were impressed with the Afro-Caribbean influence of the area and became inquisitive about the racial history of Costa Rica. They uncovered both similarities and contrasts with the US history of forced slavery of Africans.

This CAST tour was not permitted to go to El Salvador due to the civil war in that country. Nevertheless, students were able to talk to many Salvadorans in the city of Heredia, west of San José. Many Salvadoran women testified that their husbands and sons were killed under orders of the military junta backed by the US government. The Whitworth students struggled to understand the inconsistencies of the US foreign policies. On the one hand, there was purported support of people's freedom and liberty, yet that was contrasted by our indirect support of military dictatorships in Central America and around the world.

TA Leslie Vogel took the dozen students to Panama for an intense period of learning. Participants were amazed to discover that there were fourteen US military bases in the canal zone. Many Panamanians were upset that the US flag was flying over their national territory and some tried to take down the foreign flag. The CAST students were horrified to find out that those Panamanians were shot and killed for their patriotic actions.

TA Leslie Vogel among the bananas

On the way back into Costa Rica, the students were surprised that they were rigorously searched for drugs at the border. This was a rude awakening for them to some aspects of the "War on Drugs."

Whitworth Professor and Volleyball Coach JoAnn Atwell-Scrivner joined the group as they traveled to Nicaragua. The participants learned an extremely important biblical lesson while in Nicaragua. According to the Scriptures, followers of Jesus should not only "believe" the truth, they also need "to walk in the truth," "to speak the truth," and "to obey the truth".[1] They had discovered for themselves truth about Nicaragua. That truth was that most Nicaraguans were striving to build up their country after a popular revolution had overthrown the dictator Somoza. Their truth meant that the US government's military and financial support for the Contras who were attempting to overthrow the Sandinista government was morally wrong and sinful. They had an extensive briefing given by Ambassador Anthony Quainton at the US Embassy and heard the Reagan administration's perspective. It was claimed that the Soviet Union was moving weapons through Cuba to Nicaragua and then on to El

---

1. 1 John 1:4, 3 John 1:4, Ephesians 4:15, Galatians 5:7, 1 Peter 1:22

Salvador to foment civil war. The students felt that the Ambassador himself was not very convinced of his own argument.

Students later decided to join a protest in front of the Embassy to show their disapproval of the support for the Contras. The entire CAST group decided to send a message to the Whitworth community via the student newspaper, the *Whitworthian*. In their letter, they listed the crimes against humanity that the US-backed Contras had committed against the Nicaraguan people. As could be expected, their letter raised a heated debate in the *Whitworthian* back in Spokane. Student Kurt Dale wrote an additional article for the newspaper in which he described the CAST tour in greater detail and how they arrived at their position.[2] A few months later, there was a bit of satisfaction among the participants because the US Congress prohibited further funding of the Contras.

The time in Nicaragua also included service projects. The twelve students were divided up into three groups of 4 students each and sent to the towns of Juigalpa, Nueva Guinea, and Rama. Contra attacks came close to these last two villages, so an abrupt decision was made to bring all the students back to the relative safety of Juigalpa. Sandy Canepa's experiences in Rama and in traveling were so profound, she wrote the following poem for her *compañeros*:

Three Days in Nicaragua
for mis compañeros

    Day One: The Road to Juigalpa
    We travel on a Ticabus.
    I close my eyes to block out the picture
    of the cows with sunken sides,

---

2. For the complete letters and two reactions that appeared in the *Whitworthian*, see the Appendix at the end of this book.

children with bloated stomachs
and the dry, dry dusty roads.
Our bus is accosted,
every time we stop,
by the children tapping
on the windows.
They're selling *platano* chips,
bolsas of sticky Coca Cola,
and pork rinds.
I lean my head against the window—
ignoring the greasy fingerprints.
The bus stops for three people.
They pay with an iguana
that rides in the aisle two seats down from mine.
Halfway to Juigalpa our bus breaks down.
The local people begin to walk
We pace around the bus wondering
what went wrong.
A truck of Sandinista soldiers stops—
asks if we need help.
We accept a ride.
I clutch the side of the truck trying
to keep myself from resting against the soldier
next to me.
I stare at his gun.
I look into his eyes.
He is no more
than nine or ten.
We spend the night in the attic of a bar.
I dream of raven-haired children
chasing me—
their hands outstretched,
dust in my mouth that I can't spit out,
and the sound of gunfire in my chest.
Day Two: The Road to Rama
Banana trees line the cool dusty road to Rama.
Days are spent painting the Catholic Church orange
and discussing *Liberation Theology* with Padre Adolfo.
I am a woman
so I just paint.
Children hang on
to the scaffolding and compete
for my smiles.

I wash my hair with rain water and my clothes on a rock.
In my ignorance, I rub holes in my underwear.
Padre Adolfo offers me a boiled iguana egg.
I suck the middle from the soft shell.
Nights are spent by the riverside.
I watch the shrimp fishermen—
their lanterns sway like fireflies.
I lean against your back
while you read old *National Geographic* out loud.
They come for us without warning.
We barely have time to pack—
there is only time to say good-bye to the school teacher.
We climb into the back of the Toyota.
The smell of slash-and-burning hangs in the distant air.
I hear gunfire but think nothing of it.
Day Three: The Road to Nueva Guinea
Pedro touched your hair and whispered
to you about The Revolution.
He taught you how to hold an AK 47.
You dreamt of the glamour of army fatigues,
eating rice and beans for days on end,
and making love in a hammock.
You traveled in a Jeep and surveyed the pueblos.
You listened to stories that kept you silent
for weeks when you came back—
a wife whose husband disappeared into the hills
with his hands tied behind his back,
a mother who watched her daughter raped,
a child whose father was hanged.
On Tuesday you just missed traveling in a Jeep
that was ambushed by The Contras.
You were whisked away—
back to The Capitol,
back to safety.
I did not understand
your silence
or your rage.
You hear gunfire and think everything of it.

    – Sandy Canepa-Swan, 1984

The program continued as the students travelled with Coach Atwell-Scrivner to Mexico City and Cuernavaca for an extended time of debriefing and reflection, both individually and as a group. In the fall semester, the group shared with the entire Whitworth campus in a Forum presentation.[3]

3. The audio recording of this Forum presentation can be accessed at https://digitalcommons. whitworth.edu/forum/93/.

1985: (Summer) Conflicting Conversations with Refugees in Costa Rica[1]

CAST 1985 COHORT: JEFF Boyd, Cathy Brown, Matthew (Jones) Morgan-Jones, Carrie Susan McLain, Phyllis Hurrah, Carolyn (Reasoner) Ward, Marjorie Richards, Doug Segur, Margaret Strong, and Cathy Verdier. Teaching Assistants—Ken and Chris Arkills. Faculty Leaders—Ron Frase, Bob LaCerte, Ed Miller, and Kris Kropsey.

This study tour was very special in many ways. It took place during the summer and included the country of Panama. It continued to be a volatile time in Central America. The government in Guatemala was brutally oppressing its own people. President Reagan's support of the Contras in trying to overthrow the Sandinista government in Nicaragua was highly controversial. The war in Nicaragua was taking a heavy toll upon the people. The students on the CAST program had a heightened sense of responsibility. They felt it was their duty to visit the Central American countries and then report back to the campus what they had seen and experienced.

Students were selected in the fall of 1984. During spring semester, Professor Bob LaCerte offered an extensive course in Latin American history in order to prepare the students for what they might face in Central America. Although he was an Associate Professor of Library Science at Whitworth, he was a specialist in Latin American studies.[2] The history course was complemented with a course on "Contemporary Latin American Problems" taught by Professor and Chaplain Ron Frase.

On May 22, the students boarded a plane in Seattle accompanied by Bob LaCerte and Spanish Professor Kris Kropsey. One student remembered Kris in glowing terms:

> Her language capability was top notch, and she had the most warm, welcoming, unflappable personality. She spent a year or two at Whitworth teaching Spanish prior to the tour. She was a stable, calming force on the tour when patience ran short in the various challenges we faced in traveling together—delays, lost luggage, unexpected issues at border crossings, personality tensions that come up when traveling, etc.

1. For a brief summary of the tour, see Sue McLain's article "Students use Summer to Study, Serve" in *The Whitworthian*, September 16, 1985, p. 4.

2. Bob was quite the expert on Central America. Earlier that year he delivered a paper on "U.S. Policy Options in Central America" at the annual meeting of the Pacific Northwest Political Science Association in Olympia. After the CAST trip was finished, he presented many more papers at professional venues including "A Policy of Principled Realism toward Nicaragua".

It took the group forty-eight hours to reach San José Costa Rica. They spent the next five weeks studying intensive Spanish at the *Instituto de la Lengua Española*. They also stayed with host families to have a more complete immersion experience. One student describes, "Relationships with our new family members were sometimes frustrating and tiring, but they were also sources for fun times and a lot of information. They were an aspect of the culture in Costa Rica to which we felt we belonged." Costa Rica was perceived as quite different from the other Central American countries, and students were inquisitive to know the factors that contributed to this uniqueness. In San José, people were very well dressed and cared about their appearance. The city was very cosmopolitan, the people there were very proud of the fact that they had no military, and they had the highest literacy rate and the highest life-expectancy in Central America.

Being a participant in CAST did not mean that one was immune from typical illnesses and trials. Marjorie Richards learned about medical practice in Costa Rica from the inside, because she had an appendectomy. The group traveled through Cartago and the jungle to the Jamaican-influenced port city of Limón, on the Atlantic Coast. The train derailed three times. Each time, the crew got out the gear they needed and put the train back on the tracks . . . all in the course of a normal day's work. On the trip east, the group visited the Dole banana plantation near Limón. They learned about the pros and cons of the banana industry in Central America. This was a challenging experience because on other occasions the group heard about the negative impact of this industry, such as low wages and human diseases caused by dangerous pesticides. One student shared his journal entry:

> Saw the Dole banana plantation in Limón. Quite large, workers' houses on the plantation looked a little better than some in town, worse than others. Pretty simple. Workers could cut through a banana tree with one swipe of a machete. All of us tried it and couldn't make it through more than 1/3 or 1/2 of the tree. Struck by how this could be a year-round operation since bananas ripen at all different times. Picked very green. Remember the sorting line—small bananas that still would have been edible once ripened were culled and shredded for compost—not even given to locals as food source. I remember that I was troubled by that.

The students visited a refugee camp which housed dozens of Nicaraguans who had fled the civil war in their home country. One participant shared the following:

> The refugees had fled their homeland on the volatile east coast of Nicaragua, seeking refuge in Costa Rica. We met people who left in order to flee the draft; others who sought food and supplies. Some were women who fled after having lost sons or husbands in the war, caring now for their own lives. Still others carried their criticism of the Sandinistas to the extent of joining the Contra

forces in northern Costa Rica. They were resting in that camp in Limón before returning to fight again.

Once again, the CAST members were faced with a reality that did not lend itself to an easy analysis.

Another memorable experience was the "Plunge." Students were given a name of a town in the country and were told to go there and make discoveries on their own. They had to research and secure their own transportation and find a place to stay once arriving at their destinations. No advance logistical support and no advance reservations. It's what made the Plunge exciting, navigating on one's own in a foreign country. This was an examination that the professors enjoyed, a true test of how well students had learned the language, and how well they could adapt to the unexpected. They made up a list of 15 questions that they would ask the people of Costa Rica. Those questions ranged from what they did with waste disposal, to what they felt about their Nicaraguan neighbors. One group consisting of Marjorie Richards, Margaret Strong, and Doug Segur got to venture to the tiny town of Tilarán, a few hours northwest of San José. In a journal entry, Doug describes their adventure:

> One of the highlights of the plunge weekend for us was to visit a Nicaraguan refugee camp on the outskirts of Tilarán that we knew might be in this area when we came. We ventured out to the camp, again with no contacts or pre-arrangements. We encountered a *guardia civil* at the gate and discussed with him who we were and why we were there. At first, he was reluctant to let us in. After showing our passports and talking with him, he eventually let us visit. We learned from him that the population of the camp was about 3,000 people. We spoke with a small group of three to four men from Bluefields, who told us, "It took us fifteen days on foot with no shoes to reach Costa Rica." They discussed their reasons for leaving—fearful of the Sandinista conscription that they felt for sure would ensnare them. We asked if they had known of anyone directly who had been taken, and they said they didn't, "but we know they take them and we didn't want to be faced with fighting our brother or neighbor, so we left."
>
> We remembered running into this dynamic in Limón earlier that month in another refugee camp. People speaking of accounts of troubling things like conscription but no one with direct connections to a specific friend or family member that they knew were taken. They were all acting on things they had heard were happening. In talking with people on the street in Tilarán, we encountered some who were vehemently opposed to the Sandinistas and what was happening there. It was interesting that they referenced countries like Guatemala, El Salvador and Honduras as being better places to live than Nicaragua because, "They are not oppressive like Nicaragua. Life is better in those countries because they are democracies, unlike communist Nicaragua." It's interesting that when we later visited those countries, what we witnessed

in the spirit of the people in these countries was a spirit of hope and optimism in Nicaragua, while in the other countries the collective spirit seemed much more oppressed and hopeless—not to mention all the accounts of oppression of workers' rights and the accounts from family members of the "*desaparecidos*"—the disappeared who went missing for speaking out against their governments.

In mid-June Spanish Professor Ed Miller joined the group. The group pulled up stakes and took a bus to Panama. One fact that amazed the students was that the United States had 14 military bases in Panama. Questions arose in their minds, "Why such a huge demonstration of US power in such a small country?" The students later confirmed that they felt safer in Nicaragua than they did in Panama. Some had their pockets picked and a few other items stolen in Panama, but nothing like that had happened to them in Nicaragua.

In early July the CAST students traveled to Nicaragua. The day they arrived the headlines of a major newspaper warned of a possible US invasion of Nicaragua. Although students commented that their families in the States were worried for their safety, their experiences were quite positive. At the Forum presentation back on the Spokane campus in the fall, one student shared the following:

> For me it was the high point of the summer. One thing that I am grateful for is the fact that we did not have to rush through Nicaragua. We were there to live for more than a month. In retrospect, I think how lucky we were to be able to experience the area with significant depth. I think we were able to see the positive life of the country; the life we rarely, if ever, get to hear about up here. We didn't just "tour" the country. We lived it.

The students lived in Nicaragua for five weeks and worked in service projects organized by *CEPAD*, the Council of Protestant Churches of Nicaragua.[3] Jeff Boyd and Matthew Jones worked with a farm co-op, Marjorie Richards and Carrie Susan McLain served a mountain community south of Managua, Carolyn Reasoner and Catharine Verdier did research in Carazo, Margaret Strong and Doug Segur worked in schools, and Phyllis Murrah worked alongside Nicaraguans in a reforestation project. The Teaching Assistants Ken and Chris Arkills visited the students at their service projects. The home stays were not always easy. Student Matthew Jones remembered his:

> When I signed up for the Central America Study Tour, my world was small. I grew up in a small rural Alaskan town and was steeped in Presbyterianism. The portion of the trip that had the largest impact was the immersion experience in Nicaragua. I was dropped off in the countryside at a farm cooperative.

3. *CEPAD* is the *Consejo de Iglesias Evangélicas Pro-Alianza Denominacional*. It was founded by Dr. Gustavo Parajón shortly after the earthquake that devastated Managua on December 23, 1972. It was formed to serve the Nicaraguan people in their multiple needs. Although it was a Non-Governmental Organization (NGO), it worked in a cooperative way with the Sandinista administration.

My Spanish was marginal, and I was on my own. My water needs were explained . . . boil, but then the water was too hot, so cool water was added. Water was heated over a wood fire in the 'kitchen' with slits in the wall for the smoke to escape. The kitchen door was closed at night to keep the animals out, and then it was my bedroom. The five members of the family slept in a lean-to on fold out cots. That is the superficial story. The rest of the story was unveiled through the next several weeks. There was a dysfunctional irrigation pump without replacement parts. Nightly prayer services that the community attended. 'Sick' farm workers that were hungover. Men who were anxious to have more kids and more wives. The reliance on oxen to move goods and people and to do the heavy labor in the fields. This is again a superficial story that would become richer over time, but that has taken a lifetime to integrate into my thoughts and actions.

The participants were quite impressed with Luis and Carlos Mejia Godoy, who were brothers and famous Nicaraguan musicians. Their songs, including *Yo Soy de un Pueblo Sencillo*, were thoroughly Nicaraguan in lyrics, melodies, and instruments. Simple music, but oh so powerful!

In some ways the Nicaragua part of the CAST trip had a sequel. Student Doug Segur came back two years later as the Teaching Assistant for the 1987 program. He writes:

While I was in Nicaragua the second time, I was fortunate to be able to return to my host family I had lived with for 3–4 weeks in the *campo* during the CAST trip in the summer of 1985. When I found out I was returning as a TA on the 1987 trip, I let my home church, Carmichael Presbyterian, know of my intent to return. The outpouring of support was amazing. I left for Central America in 1987 with $2,160 in cash and all the basic medical supplies I could carry. While in Nicaragua, the scheduling needs of the trip afforded me a couple of days to try to get out and see my family. I essentially had to find a dirt road off the main highway that I had seen two years previous. I had some help since I knew the community name of *Mesas de Acicaya*. I eventually ended up making connections and getting out to the family. It was great when I saw Narciso (my host father)! It felt like I had been gone only a couple of months. We saw each other and said our hellos with ear-to-ear grins and hugged each other. It was such a great gift to be reunited with him. We headed up the hill to the community. I was so glad to be walking with this man whom I had begun to love two years prior and whose love for me had been made evident while we were together. I was able to reunite with this family of seven or so. I learned the two oldest children, a brother and sister, had moved into Managua to find work. I took $100 of the money I brought down and gave it directly to the family. This converted into 320,000 córdobas. It would help, but not immensely. Just in the time before I left, the exchange rate jumped from C3,200 to C4,500.

I presented the money to Narciso and a few of the community leaders. They wanted to use $800 to build a church for the community and asked that the rest be channeled through CEPAD to use for a well and a school.

Antigua, Guatemala was the last leg of the study tour. There they pondered together their experiences and how they would be affected in the future. In spite of the warnings about the governmental repression of its people, the Guatemalans that the students met were impressive in their generosity and simplicity. A student commented that he saw an immense sign carved and painted (probably) by the government into an outcrop along the highway. "*Trabajemos! No critiquemos!*" ("Let's work and not criticize"). It struck the student to be in stark contrast to the freedom and hopefulness he had found in Nicaragua.

The CAST group gave a Forum presentation back on the Spokane campus in the fall.[4] Students shared their insights about each country they had visited on the tour. In light of the violence in El Salvador, Guatemala and Nicaragua, and the role the US government had in that violence, they then urged their fellow Whitworthians to follow God's exhortations in Isaiah 58.

There is another sequel to the 1985 trip. A few years later, Professor Ron Frase described the story of one of the participants:

> Jeff Boyd, a math and computer major, went on the 1985 Central America trip. When he returned he made an appointment with me in the fall of 1985 to discuss the trip. I did not go on that trip, but I taught the "Contemporary Latin American Problems" course that the students took prior to the trip. Therefore, I had established a relationship with Jeff. He began our conversation by saying that after the four months in Central America, he had decided that he wanted to pursue a career in missions and was wondering how a math and computer major could do this. He was a senior due to graduate in December of 1985. This was a dramatic moment that he had never anticipated.
>
> As I listened during our conversation, I remembered receiving a letter recently from a British missionary in Pakistan, Ken Olds, who was married to an American nurse serving the Presbyterian Church (USA). He wrote asking me if I knew of a computer person who could come and teach young Pakistanis how to use them. The British government had sent him ten computers. Ken also worked with the PC(USA) in Pakistan and was responsible for several trade schools training young Pakistanis for the labor force. He had no experience with computers and needed someone who could teach students how to use them. I explained to Jeff the request I had received from Ken and his eyes lit up. Here was an answer to his prayer! This conversation took place in September and he graduated and found himself in Pakistan by the end of December 1985.

4. The audio version of this presentation is available in the Whitworth archives at: http://digitalcommons.whitworth.edu/forum/105/

Arriving in Pakistan he began teaching computer courses. A couple from Holland was working with the Presbyterian mission in Pakistan at that time and their daughter, Christi, came to visit them. Jeff and Christi struck up a romance which culminated in their marriage. They were sent by the Presbyterian World Mission to Africa where they have remained until this day serving in several African countries. Currently Jeff is the regional liaison person responsible for the Democratic Republic of the Congo, Cameroon, and Equatorial Guinea.[5]

---

5. Authors' theological reflection—God's leading frequently includes "chance" happenings. Jeff Boyd described how he heard about CAST in the first place. "I'm not sure of all the things that contributed to me deciding to join the 1985 CAST. One of the factors may have been a chance encounter that I had with Ron Frase several years before. About half a year before I transferred to Whitworth, I went with my older brother and one of his friends to a faith-based conference on peace and justice in California. I already knew that I would be attending Whitworth, so when I saw that one of the workshops was to be taught by Ron Frase, the chaplain at Whitworth, I decided to join that. I do not recall the particulars of what was presented and the discussions that followed, but my interest in the US policies and practices in Central America grew."

1987: A Tearful Class, a Newborn Baby, and Troubling US "Aid" for the Contras

CAST 1987 Cohort: Michael Barram, Christopher Berg, Robert Clancy, Karen Cordova, Nan Marie (Durst) Kartvedt, Cheryl (Fox) De Genner, Robert Gronhovd, Terri (Jiménez) Jiménez-Sutton, Mikal Kartvedt, Laurena (Kerber) Ketzel-Kerber (Jan Term only), Michael LeRoy, Kurt Liebert, Emily Lower, Juliane (Meagor) Brown, Susan (Odone) Stevenson, Sue (Sherwood) Hastings, and Dodge White. Teaching Assistant—Douglas Segur (CAST 1984). Faculty Leaders—Ed Miller, Ron Frase, and Don Liebert.

Students in the 1987 cohort soon realized that life was very difficult in Central America. The civil war was continuing in Nicaragua. Despite the US Congress' prohibition of military support of the Contras, the Reagan administration had implemented a clandestine policy to arm the Contras via sales to Iran (Irangate). This secret policy had become public knowledge in 1986 and was coming under increasing scrutiny. Civil strife was increasing in each Central American nation in particular ways. The 1987 CAST participants faced a reality not well understood by their North American families and friends back home.

During the fall of 1986 students prepared for their trip while on the Spokane campus. They took the course "Contemporary Latin American Problems" taught by Sociology Professor Ron Frase. Little did they know that the extensive readings would become so helpful in understanding Central America in the following months. Even more important was Ron's teaching style. Student Michael Barram remembers one very special class:

> I have a memory that I was sitting in the back somewhere, probably with a ball cap on, scarcely paying attention. All of a sudden, I got this terrified sense that something had happened, but I didn't know what. It had gotten super quiet, and when I realized that mentally I had been in a completely different world, no one in the room seemed to be breathing. My first thought was that Ron had called on me to answer a question—but, if so, I had no idea what the question might have been. I was completely unprepared for the moment. And then, when I looked up, I realized what was going on. Ron (to my severe teenage-boy discomfort) had tears streaming down his face and was having difficulty composing himself enough to keep speaking. I had never seen such a thing. I

was uncomfortable. I felt like squirming and wished the class session would end. But it didn't. As Ron regained his voice and continued, I realized that he had been talking about something horrible that had happened somewhere in Latin America, something that had happened to someone he had actually known personally. That classroom experience became a personal metaphor for true education—pedagogy that was engaged, passionate, involved . . . invested. I realized then that I had never really seen what education could really do—indeed, what real education could do. Ron Frase showed me something that I had completely missed. I was ashamed by how shallow I had been, assuming that education should cater to my pre-conceived interests. I was changed, and I wanted more.

Terri Jiménez-Sutton, Nan Marie Durst Kartvedt, Sue Sherwood Hastings and Dodge White stand beside a hard day's work of making bricks for houses with Habitat for Humanity in Chichicastenango, Guatemala.

In January, the tour began with host family stays and intensive Spanish language study in Antigua, Guatemala. The Guatemalan government was headed by President Cerezo who had assumed office in 1986. The country was coming out of a long period of government repression and civilian insurgency, but the president was utilizing very controversial methods to put down civilian unrest. Some CAST students witnessed these methods up close and personal. Professor Ron Frase described one such experience:

> In our last week in language school, I was walking along the street in the late afternoon and saw Michael LeRoy and Michael Barram walking toward me. As

we drew closer to one another, I could see that they were quite disturbed. They told me that they had just witnessed plain clothed military people rounding up draft dodgers and forcibly marching them to jail. The Michaels were following them to the jail. Later that evening when they arrived at the jail, they discovered a small crowd of parents had gathered outside the jail pleading for the release of their sons. After waiting for some time, a few of the prisoners were released after the parents paid a bribe. Those whose parents were unable to pay a bribe saw their sons forcibly recruited into the Guatemalan army. This was their first introduction to military injustice.

Years later, Michael LeRoy also commented on the same event:

> I stood in front of a police station and listened to a tearful man tell the story of his son who was abducted by the military for the "draft" in Antigua the day before. He asked me whether I "believed in a God of justice." I told him I did and with my reply, he commissioned me to "then live as I believe and obey and tell the story of God's justice on behalf of those who have no voice." His statement of commission has haunted and compelled me over the course of my life since that time. I was deeply shaken on that day and found it hard to talk about it for many years. I have also tried to keep it before me as I have lived my life, but I confess that I have only done so in a very imperfect way.

The students spent the month of February in Honduras. After a week in the capital city of Tegucigalpa, the students spent the rest of the time in rural areas and participated in service projects. Nan Marie Durst had been placed in the small village of *Cantarranas* to work with children. While there she had an unforgettable experience. Her host mother, Isabela, was more than eight months pregnant. Her host father was working in another town cutting sugar cane. In the middle of the night, Isabela woke Nan up and told her, "I am going to have the baby." Nan accompanied her host mother through the entire process (boiling the water, severing the umbilical cord, burying the placenta to avoid it being eaten by wild animals, etc.) Later that day, Nan wrote the following entry in her journal:

Nan Marie Durst Kartvedt and Michael Barram studying with their Spanish instructors in Antigua, Guatemala.

I went to live in the village of *Cantarranas* (Singing Frogs) for my month-long Honduran service assignment. CODE, the organization that coordinated my placement in this community, had originally intended to send me to San Marcos which is close to the border of Nicaragua, but there had been fighting in that area, and CODE decided it was not a safe time to be there. My departure was delayed by three days as they worked to secure a new location, possibly in Valle de Angeles, which I thought sounded quite lovely. Valle de Angeles did not pan out; however, and I was placed in the community of *Cantarranas*, large and poor, to provide *"educación de salud"* (health and hygiene education) and to distribute basic supplies to the twelve families that have joined together to work with CODE in a cooperative. *Cantarranas* is approximately one hour north of Tegucigalpa. It is hot and muggy with a coating of dust everywhere. It is approximately ninety degrees during the peak sun of the day and remains hot at night making sleeping uncomfortable. Sleeping is also uncomfortable because I'm covered in flea bites. I've been provided a hammock which is strung from one wall of the shack to a pole in the center. It is difficult to toss and turn to scratch one's bites in a swaying hammock, so the first night I fell out onto the dirt floor, awakening all of the family with my shriek and thud. I fell out again the second night, but quieter and only awakened the dog and four chickens that lived in the shack with us. Yes, the chickens live in the one room house with the family, and they roam freely. They are a little intimidating. The home is a twelve by twelve-foot shack of crudely nailed together uneven boards, a tin roof, and a dirt floor teeming with bugs of all kinds. There is no electricity, no running water, no windows; only two doors that can remain open when you prop them with a stick.

My host family members are Isabela (thirty-two years old) and Paco (thirty-six years old). They are Christians and are the only two literate people in the village. Paco works in the sugar cane fields across the river during the week. He returns home on the weekends. Isabela is stout, hardworking and kind. She is eight months pregnant with their fifth child. She worries. They do not have the forty-five lempiras that it costs to go to the hospital, let alone the hospital fee, nor the thirty lempiras the local woman charges to assist with the birth. Their whole life is a struggle. The dog is pregnant too, though you would not know it to look at her; she is so thin. There is not enough food for the dog. She is last to be fed in a family that struggles to feed its own children. Isabela says there are enough beans and rice for all, but the extras like meat, an egg, a cabbage are more difficult to come by. My family appreciated my presence and always insisted I should have the choicest food.

As was the occasion on Sunday evenings, Paco returned to the village on the other side of the river to be up early and work the fields before the heat of the day. The rest of us went to Sunday evening church then returned to prepare for bed. Around 1:00 a.m., Isabela awoke me saying "It's time. I'm going to have the baby." She must have known because earlier in the day she had placed plastic in the bed and had cut up a sheet to prepare. We sent the children to the closest neighbor and I built up the fire to boil water in the family bean pot. It took a considerable effort to get that fire going hot enough to boil the water. While I labored over that, Isabela labored on her wooden bed. The night was long, but the birth progressed naturally. Thankfully Isabela's body knew what to do, and I knew the basics. I did fear there was too much blood, but really had no way of knowing and Isabela was so experienced and doing so well, I tried not to fret about it. Around 8:00 a.m. the baby was born. A boy! It was extremely emotional and incredibly moving. Isabela cried with joy, and I cried with relief and happiness. Using a piece of thread, I tied a knot in the umbilical cord and cut it with the old scissors I'd boiled much earlier. Isabela told me I must dig a deep hole away from the house and bury the afterbirth, so the animals wouldn't devour it. I had just finished reading "The Clan of the Cave Bear" in which they did that very thing, so that resonated and out I went to accomplish that task.

By then the children had returned with the neighboring women to admire the new baby. There was no scale, but we guessed he weighed between 7 and 8 pounds. He was bright pink, had a shock of dark hair, and a good set of lungs. There were no diapers, simply ill-fitting cut up cloths.

Later in the day, I made the following entry in my Spanish journal:

My tears are the only things I have left to give. My body is drained, and my heart has been ripped open. Everything else is choked, but my tears stream on as if they will never stop. The blood is overwhelming. I've never felt so much of someone else's blood on me. I don't know if it is too much blood, so I pray a little more. My head is swimming—maybe it's the blood, but I think it's the whole of the situation. My tears are falling on the head and body of the tiny creature, and each one washes a little of the hideous blood and afterbirth away. I wanted to dance and scream, but the baby is so fragile that I laugh instead. It is as if each tear is crudely baptizing him and as crude as these surroundings are, I know God is here. He is here more than he has ever been before, and I am knowing him, and He is knowing me.

It is sometime after 8:00 a.m. March 16th. Today I delivered Omi Acroli, a baby boy, to my Honduran mother, Isabela. I don't feel like writing, I just want to hold him and be grateful because so many things could have gone wrong. There is so much filth here, so many bugs, so many diseases, so much dust, so very much dust, so much heat and so much pain. Isabela was beautifully brave, and Omi is a healthy and whole baby. The three of us are holding each other and crying. Isabela tells me that had he been a girl, she would have named him Ana Maria (in my honor). I am crying harder now. Though time and distance will separate us only farther, I am linked to my family in Honduras in a way that can never be broken. This little baby, so small and precious, has created a bond that will never break. That bond has wrapped itself around my life, and I wait for the day I can see him again.

I think about the vast differences of access to health care these rural Hondurans have compared to Hondurans of the bigger cities and the communities in North America. I will never take hot water, medicine, and medical care for granted again. It is extremely difficult for these hard-working rural Honduran families to secure the basic necessities of life. Life is tenuous here; comforts are few. I have a better understanding of why people in Central America are rebelling against an unresponsive system in which the ruling elite virtually ignores their existence. Paradoxically, a few miles away, the United States is investing millions of dollars in constructing an airbase. There is money available to invest in instruments of death and military might, but so little for the nurturing of life. How long can we, as Americans, tolerate this inversion of priorities without permanently damaging our national soul? These are the thoughts I take with me from the *campo*.

It was not safely possible to travel by land from Honduras to Nicaragua. The Contras would hide out in Honduras and make incursions into Nicaraguan territory, fight battles, and then retreat back into Honduras. Therefore, the CAST group traveled by plane to the San Salvador airport, and after an extended layover, flew to Managua. The month in Nicaragua began with time dedicated to debriefing the rural experiences in Honduras. Each student was an "expert" on her or his home stay experience and was able to teach the others. Professor Don Liebert has mentioned how fascinating (and humbling) it was to learn so much about Honduras from each student.

Nevertheless, Nicaragua presented its own set of disturbing challenges. One of the most difficult was to discern the truth about the armed conflict going on in the country. On the one hand, the Reagan administration was funding and arming the Contras (in spite of the fact that the US Congress had prohibited the sending of funds to them. Nevertheless, the administration continued to do so through the infamous Irangate triangle via Oliver North). According to Reagan, the Contras were "Freedom Fighters" who were trying to topple the tyrannical, "communist" government of the Sandinistas led by President Daniel Ortega. On the other hand, most Nicaraguans saw the Contras as another example of US intervention in the affairs of a small country. Given that the Contras were made up mostly of soldiers who had served in the Somoza army, they were trying to establish a right wing, puppet government that would serve US interests rather than Nicaragua's. In the din of such opposing interpretations, where was the truth? How could sincere people be lined up on both sides of the conflict? It was common for both sides to accuse the opposition of having been brainwashed, either by the Reagan administration or by Ortega and the Sandinistas. Don[1] and María "Ría" Reasoner, the consultants for the CAST program in Nicaragua, gave some very helpful background information. People were unwilling to consider information that went against their already formulated paradigm. Don told the CAST students that he had hosted many congressional "fact-finding" missions from the US. "Most groups would spend less than eight hours in the country. Although they would speak with personnel from the US embassy, they would not talk with the Nicaraguans themselves."

Don provided another clear example of this "information divide." Back in 1984, Nicaragua's election took place on November 4. The US presidential election happened three days later. In order to make Reagan's anti-communist stance look good (including his support for the Contras), the US administration tried to get major networks to air a story about Russian shipments of MIG fighters to Nicaragua. According to an ABC news correspondent on the ground in Nicaragua, ABC didn't think there was enough factual evidence to justify airing the story. Nevertheless, during the days leading up to the US election, the Defense Department "confirmed" that MIGs were, in fact, being shipped, thus helping Reagan's re-election victory. Later it was acknowledged that what were in those shipments were not MIGs after all, but tractor parts. So, although the Sandinistas decisively won the Nicaraguan election (declared fair by multiple international observers), the false "MIG" story dominated the news in the United States.

Ría told more accounts of the darker side of the Contras. Early in the 1980s, the Sandinista government had launched a massive literacy campaign throughout

---

1. Don Reasoner had been a CAST participant in 1979 and was the Teaching Assistant for the 1981 tour. He therefore had good credibility with the group. They felt that his opinions carried a good amount of weight. The Reasoners had settled in Managua and offered consulting services to "fact-finding" congressional representatives, church groups, academics, and others interested in finding out about Nicaraguan reality.

the entire country. Much of Nicaragua's perennial illiteracy problem was resolved in a year. A few years later, the government sent out high school and college student volunteers to conduct a follow-up literacy program. They travelled to various parts of the country. Ría had met many of these volunteers. They told her horror stories of volunteers who were kidnapped and held by the Contras. Women were having babies from rapes, and men were forced to fight for the Contras or were killed if they refused.

One of the original goals that founder Ron Frase had for the Central America program was that Whitworth students would listen carefully to people's stories and then relay them back to Spokane and beyond. One participant told about his conversation with Bonnie. She was an American nurse who had worked in the small city of Estelí for about a year. Estelí was in a major war zone. She said, "We are beginning to see the effects of the new Contra "aid." Many more civilian casualties are coming in. Also, the Contras have begun to use much smaller mines than before. Their main intent is to cause severe injury—blowing off a foot or half a leg. If this isn't terrorism, I don't know what is! Freedom Fighters??!! Whose freedom??!!"

Teaching Assistant Doug Segur shares from his journal and some of his reflections:

Journal: March 29, 1987. Managua, Nicaragua. Had dinner with Don and Ría Reasoner last night. Wonderful time with fifteen young Nicaraguans, some of them musicians. They talked and sang songs of hope, and of sadness in losing friends to the war with the Contras. I spoke with a young man M . . . . . . who served in the army for two years. A . . . . had served also, as had others. They fought real battles, lost real friends. They all asked us to carry the message home to our people that, "We are not communists like your government says. We are not puppets of the Russians. We are not Cubans. This is Nicaragua and we are Nicaraguans. We want and deserve the chance to see this revolution work and more so, we want and deserve to live in peace."

Reflection: I did take this message home. I arranged speaking engagements at my home church in California and also to some groups in Spokane. The reactions I got were mixed. Some were open to hear the messages that I relayed directly from the Nicaraguans. Others couldn't let go of what they'd been hearing from the Reagan administration as truth and felt I had been duped, had been shown "what they want you to see and hear." It was frustrating and heartbreaking to not have the words and experiences of the Nicaraguans themselves believed more than they were. I remember realizing the Reagan Administration had done a superb job in selling the package they had crafted that made the Contra war palatable to the public. It is frightening the power that exists in being able to affect public opinion this way.

Reflection: I remember our group meeting with one of our speakers—a public leader who had been impacted by the war. His perspective really hit me. His belief was this: "Nicaragua is a threat, and I'm not surprised your president wants to stop us. We threaten the status quo of your country's involvement in, and relationship to, Latin America. It's a relationship in which the US derives most of the benefit. Think about it. If Nicaragua stands up to the US and says, 'No More! We get to decide our own destiny,' then don't you think other Latin American countries will take notice and try to do likewise? No! That is what threatens your country—to not be able to continue as they have for decades using us to derive what benefit they can due to their dominance in the western hemisphere and beyond." This made so much sense to me. The contradictions in what we're being told at home and the reality that we saw in our experiences in Nicaragua, and the reality of our country's history which only backed up what this person was saying. It was impossible for me to not be incensed at our government who spoke of freedom and democracy with their public face while in reality, behind closed doors and through back channels, it practiced a systematic terrorism (providing arms and training to militaries who then used those weapons and training to "disappear" dissidents). It was us on the side of evil, not the Nicaraguans.

Three decades later, Michael Barram shared two additional stories:

We spent a week in Matagalpa where we were divided into two groups. One group ended up helping construct some part of a preschool building. While having lunch at the woman's house who was feeding that group, someone came and told her that her son, who was in the Sandinista army, had been killed during a Contra attack. It was not lost on any of us that the Contras were funded by our own government, so the ironic connections between our group (and our government's role in the death of this woman's son) were palpable and deeply unsettling. The other group, of which I was a part, stayed at what I think was a Sandinista cooperative (farm). We had little to do at that season, but we did stay with them. One of the incredible highlights for me was the opportunity that I had to drive a truck transporting the cooperative defense group from a training day. Basically, most of the men in the cooperative left for the day to go do what I gathered was practicing (exercises? reconnaissance?) preparing to defend the community against a potential Contra attack. Given that we were up in the mountains near Matagalpa, such an attack was not an entirely unlikely scenario. Late in the afternoon, one of the men came and asked me if I would like to go with him (in this large, Eastern European/Russian?) truck (like a large cattle truck) to go retrieve the guys who had been out doing their defensive practice up in the mountains. I was ecstatic! What an adventure! We drove quite a way up into the hills on a very tricky dirt road until we found the men coming down. Then, they all piled into the back of the truck with their guns. The guy who had driven us up into the hills then asked me if I wanted to drive back. I couldn't believe it! I was so excited! Yes, I knew how to drive a manual shift truck. And off we went. Here I was, now a 20-year-old college student, driving 10–20 peasants back from military exercises in a huge, 'communist' truck, through the jungle of Nicaragua. I still can feel the excitement of that drive even now, thirty years later!

1990: A Troubling Transition to Peace in Nicaragua

CAST 1990 COHORT: RONALD Barnes, Sarah Calvin, Michael Cunningham, DeLona (Davis) Campos-Davis, Kim (De Villeneuve) Markillie, Anne Goranson, Kris (Hannigan) Hannigan-Luther, Erik Holm, Julie Holstein, Susan (Hunt) Stevens, Pamela (Jacobi) Jacobi Starbuck, Barbara (Klava) Wilson, Lynn (Liebert) Caruso, Suzanne (Liebert) Marble, Kenneth Meagor, Jeffrey Moore, Patricia (Morita) Morita-Mullaney, Vanessa (Morris) Smith, Karen Murphy, Melissa Poe, Toby Rogers, Jefferson Shriver, Kelley Strawn, Jeffrey Tankersley, Naomi Uchishiba-Inaba, and Robert Wilson. Teaching Assistants—Sharon (Glasco) Bailey and Michael Barram (CAST 1987). Faculty Leaders—Ron Frase, Ed Miller, and Don Liebert.

The 1990 CAST group was facing a Central America that was in the midst of various transitions. In the global setting, the Soviet Union was collapsing with a concomitant decline in the Cold War. President Bush had already begun to signal that the United States would no longer support "anti-communist presidents" in Latin America if their human rights records did not dramatically improve. Violeta Chamorro had won the presidential election in Nicaragua, and the Sandinistas were preparing to hand over power to her new government in a peaceful transition. The devastating decade of armed conflict between the Sandinista government´s military and the US-backed Contras was coming to an end. There was a cautious optimism for peace in most of Central America. Students were excited to see if these visions of peace could really come true. This optimism was tempered by the sad aspects of reality. Civil war continued in El Salvador and, as a result, the portion of the tour that was going to take place in that country had to be suspended.

In the fall of 1989, the group prepared for their learning tour by taking a course on "Contemporary Latin American Problems" taught by Chaplain and Sociology Professor Ron Frase. Students later commented that the time spent in class and reading the long books would prove to be of great help during the trip.

The 1990 tour officially began in January with Spanish language study at the *Centro Lingüístico Maya* in Antigua, Guatemala. Professor Don Liebert accompanied the group during this first month. Students had a deep immersion experience because they spent the entire month living with host families. There were many enthusiastic *fútbol* fans in the group, especially Rob Wilson who was the star goalkeeper for the

Whitworth College soccer team. A special treat was when many of the students were able to watch the national soccer team of Guatemala play against the national team from Argentina.

Due to the schedule change because of the civil war in El Salvador, the students stayed an extra week in Guatemala and worked at Habitat for Humanity projects in Huehuetenango, Rosario, and San Juan la Laguna. Prior to the trip, the group had raised extra funds to support their service assignments. To wrap up their time in Guatemala and to prepare for their next service assignments, the group spent time in the indigenous town of Panajachel on Lake Atitlán. In addition to visiting indigenous villages and sites important to the recently ended civil war, the students also had a chance to rest and enjoy the lake.

The group then traveled by bus to Honduras but had a (funny?) mix-up at the border. The students went to one border crossing, but Professor Ed Miller was waiting for them at a different crossing. So, the students spent a crazy eight hours in the station until Ed could find them. In Honduras the students had the wonderful privilege of living with Honduran *campesinos*. Given that rural life in Central America is quite different from living in an urban center, the students had special assignments to learn directly from these families about rural Honduras.

Playing guitar music makes a border crossing wait more enjoyable

Then the group went to Costa Rica where they visited many sites including the Manuel Antonio National Park, the Monteverde cloud forest, and Atlantic coast plantations. They were accompanied on this portion of the trip by Professor Ron Frase.

Next was an extended time in Nicaragua where the group stayed at an overcrowded youth hostel, the Arlen Siu. Students learned about the rampant inflation and volatile dollar–córdoba exchange rates. Within a decade the córdoba went from being traded at 7 córdobas to one dollar to over a 100,000 to one. While that drop in the córdoba′s value greatly benefitted those who had dollars (including the CAST students), it was devastating for most Nicaraguans. On April 25, the CAST participants witnessed an historic event at the National Stadium, but it was not a baseball game. They had the opportunity to attend the presidential inauguration ceremony of Violeta Chamorro. The transition from a Sandinista administration to hers was peaceful and boded well for the near future.

Naomi Uchishiba on May Day in Nicaragua

An interesting "addition" to the CAST cohort was the presence of two fathers. Long-time Presbyterian pastor Jack Shriver (father of Jefferson Shriver) and Doug Barram (father of TA Michael Barram) joined the group. Years later Michael recalled:

> Our dads came down and spent two weeks with the group. For the first week they participated in our service project in Matagalpa (the project was coordinated by Ross and Gloria Kinsler). Our fathers also participated in a week of the time we were in Managua, including a May Day workers march. It was profoundly challenging and reorienting for both Jack and Doug—as both of them still talk about that trip as changing their lives in radical ways.

Ron Frase describes why those two fathers had such a profound and life-changing experience. He narrates:

> We arrived in Nicaragua on April 16 and traveled to Matagalpa. The next day our group was divided into two work sections. The first section of twenty members remained in Matagalpa, in a barrio named *Reparto Sandino*, with a project to construct a fence for a pre-school. I was proud of our students— they worked under the hot sun from 7:00 am—5:00 pm with a two-hour lunch break. We were in Matagalpa for only a week. I am sure they would not have been able to maintain that pace for many more days.
>
> The second section consisted of eleven students, plus Doug Barram and Jack Shriver, fathers of Mike and Jefferson respectively. This smaller group went to work with a cattle cooperative of nineteen ex-Sandinista soldiers located ten miles north of Matagalpa. Four days after their arrival, they were waiting for the return of Pedro, the leader of the cooperative. He had gone to a meeting of ex-Sandinistas in another part of the country. Pedro finally arrived at 6:30 pm, some three and a half hours late with a truck loaded with stacks and stacks of metal boxes filled with ammunition.
>
> After they finished unloading the truck, they went into the house and Pedro described how they got the ammunition. They had a two-way radio which they used to deceive the hovering helicopter pilots by saying they were Contras and instructing the US pilots where to drop the boxes of ammunition.
>
> Pedro began to reminisce. He was frustrated with the Contras' constant harassment. He and his comrades wanted to farm not to fight. He told us, "There are 500,000 men ready to fight if the Contras don't disarm by May 1." He went on to express the depths of his frustration with the United States government. He lamented, "We can handle the Contras, but we can't take on the whole US."
>
> He expressed his desire for a normal life, but they had to fight for liberty, independence, and sovereignty. These are God's gifts to people—no one had the right to steal these from them.

He then spoke of Jesus' incarnation and how he shed his blood to do this. With the Almighty God there are no boundaries. He was very articulate—the words tumbled effortlessly out of the depths of his being.

He invited our group to go outside and to pray for peace, and for the 70,000 who had died, the 12,680 wounded, and the 50,000 mothers who had lost children.

A campfire had been built and the group gathered around it. Pedro asked Doug Barram to pray for peace in English. The was followed by singing Kumbaya. Pedro asked others to join in prayer. Several stood up and prayed silently. Toby Rogers stood up and prayed out loud. He was in tears and said, "Up until now, God, it has all been a game—we had fun shooting AK-47s. All of a sudden, this is no longer a game. These are real people, real women and children." He prayed for peace—that the Contras would lay down their arms; that the US government would come to an understanding. After he finished, everyone was in tears.

Pedro said, "We will pass the peace by hugging each other. Tonight gives me and my comrades courage and strength."

Another student, Julie Holstein, shared her response to this very emotional experience by writing in her journal:

All of a sudden, I began to cry. The reality of it all began to hit me. I saw for the first time how US foreign policy affected people—their suffering and the prevalence of death. This wasn't a hillbilly fight as the US portrayed it, but an all-out war. I was experiencing guilt for what my country has done and pain for the kind of lives people are forced to live. The whole purpose of the trip was to see how other countries solved their problems first hand and how I was seeing them and feeling them. I was sickened by the whole situation. I felt terrible that I could simply "study" their problems and never become a part of them. I couldn't control my tears, the pain, and the guilt. Everything, all of a sudden, felt real. These are the problems of Nicaragua—war, suffering, anxiety, and death. Pedro told us, "Tonight, we will pass the peace by hugging each other. Tonight gives me and my comrades courage and strength."

A Nicaraguan Senator and his translator, TA Michael Barram

The students were originally scheduled to visit El Salvador, but in the end were not able to do so because they were not able to obtain visas due to the political problems in the country. The tour ended in Mexico where the group debriefed and reflected on their experiences.

Twenty-eight years later, student Naomi Inaba reflects, "Ron Frase, Don Liebert, and Doc Miller were amazing facilitators of what really was a life-changing experience. As we were preparing to leave the US, Ron gave us a quote I have carried in my heart and mind for 28 years—'You will go from seeing to perceiving, and from only hearing to understanding.'"

1993: El Salvador Takes Center Stage

CAST 1993 COHORT: JOY Barton, Stephanie (Boyajian) Dennis, Betsey (Broyles) Moe, Allison (Brumback) Puketza, Kristine (DeCristoforo) Nowak, Amy (Duryee) Oakley, Ryan Frey, Renee (Fritz) Fritz-Cunningham, Julienne Gage, Jennifer Heller, Nhi (Hoang) Irwin, Taudd Hume, Krista (Hunt) Ausland, Tracey (King) Ortega, Alycia (Jones) Krieger-Jones, Christopher Koch, David Lee, Heather (McClure) McClure-Coleman, Courtney McDermed, Christopher Murphy, Jeffrey Phillips, Linda Steen, Dustin Stevens, Karen Stubblefield, Laurie Werner, and Amy (Wood) Wood-O'Cana. Teaching Assistants—Keith and Laurena Ketzel-Kerber (CAST 1990). Faculty Leaders—Ron Frase, Don Liebert, and Jim Hunt.

By 1993 the Cold War was over, and a new world was emerging. The United States was the recognized world leader on the planet and the USSR was rapidly falling. Of course, this would have an impact upon Central America.

There were also new winds on the Whitworth campus. The *Whitworth Today* magazine celebrated the appointment of Bill Robinson to be President of the College by highlighting a strategic goal of the college: "Building a Global Campus for the 21st Century".[1] The first sentence of the issue rightfully affirms:

> *It's impossible* to talk about international education at Whitworth College without talking about Ron Frase . . . . Frase has opened the eyes of so many at Whitworth to the cultural diversity and splendor of Latin America. But a genuine understanding of Latin America and its people can only come about through direct experience. Since he joined the Whitworth faculty in 1973, Frase has led hundreds of Whitworth students on study tours to Latin America. And for many of these students, these trips became life-changing experiences.

The magazine later highlighted the news that the American Association of Colleges and Universities recognized Whitworth "as one of six institutions across the country providing strong leadership in international education."[2] That goal and commitment to "internationalize the campus" would continue for the next two decades.

The students for this CAST program were selected in 1992. During the fall semester, the participants took a preparation class on Central American Studies with

---

1. For further details, see *Whitworth Today: Alumni Magazine.* Spring 1993, p. 1
2. *Whitworth Today*, p. 17.

Professor Ron Frase. Some students seemed somewhat overwhelmed by the quantity of reading required in the course.

The group began their tour in Xela (Quetzaltenango) Guatemala with home stays and intensive Spanish language study. Students advanced rapidly in their linguistic abilities because they had one-on-one instruction with their Spanish teachers and were enveloped in a continuous immersion experience. Ron Frase taught about the historical and sociological aspects of this culturally rich country. Shorter stays took place in Guatemala City and Panajachel.

On their way to Honduras, students formed groups of 3 or 4 for the famous "Plunge." Then they settled down for their month long rural home stays. Students participated with World Vision and other NGOs in service projects. Don Liebert was the professor on this segment and visited the students in their homes. One of the students expressed his admiration of the Honduran people and their hard work ethic, even in the children. He writes:

> While living with *campesino* families in Honduras and helping to build houses, I made the acquaintance of an 8-year old boy, son of a young man, hard-working and humble. (I don't know what happened to his mom). The boy often held my hand as we walked places in the village, which was cool, but what made an impression was that he carried buckets of water as big as he was from the creek to our construction site, and he did it *all day long* without once complaining as far as I heard. Amazing!

Costa Rica was the next destination. It began with a time to debrief the rich and varied experiences that the students had lived with their rural Honduran host families. Then the group studied the differences between Costa Rica and the other Central American countries, especially the economic contrasts. Professor Jim Hunt taught Central American history to the students during their three-week sojourn in Costa Rica. They studied ecology at several national parks, and they visited coffee and banana plantations.

The fab four: Alycia Krieger, Dave Lee, Krista Hunt and Julienne Gage

Jim Hunt led the group during the Nicaraguan portion of the tour. He helped the students understand the history of Nicaragua, including the Somoza regime, the Sandinista revolution, the Violeta Chamorro administration, and US intervention at various times.

Whitworth alum Kay Ekhoff provided guidance in the development of the El Salvador program. In this small country, the students participated in a variety of dialogue and education projects including visits to the US Embassy, seminars from FMLN and Arena political parties; the University of Central America and sites where the Jesuit fathers were killed, and where Archbishop Romero was assassinated. There was also a visit to *El Mozote*—a massacre site in El Salvador's civil war.

Ron Frase rejoined the group in El Salvador and experienced a transformative moment of his own. He wrote about it later that year on Human Rights Day:

> The year 1993 has not been a good year for the United States on the human rights issue which it has championed. The report of the United Nations sponsored Truth Commission in March and the release of 12,000 documents by the State Department, Defense Department, and Central Intelligence Agency at the insistence of our Congress last month made it abundantly clear that people at the highest levels of our government were well informed of the human rights abuses and "death squad" assassinations by El Salvadoran security

forces and their surrogates. Nevertheless, our officials turned their heads the other way while the Salvadoran military we funded killed with impunity.

As I read the above accounts, I thought back to a late afternoon in February of this year when I was led by two former students into a small chapel. It was located in a residential area adjacent to a hospital for the terminally ill in San Salvador, the capital of El Salvador. Leslie Vogel had been on the 1979 Whitworth Central America trip and Karen Murphy on the 1990 one. Both, at that time in 1993, were living in El Salvador. I had often visualized this chapel in my mind's eye, but, as is so often the case, the reality was quite different from what I had imagined. It was smaller and much more modern than I had expected. I was impressed with its simplicity and airiness of its interior illuminated by natural light streaming in through windows and skylights in the "V" shaped ceiling. Its architecture was a pleasant contrast to the heavy dark baroque style typical of Latin American Roman Catholic religious structures.

The chapel was empty except for a middle-aged couple kneeling in prayer who left shortly after I entered. I felt that I had come to the end of a long pilgrimage. I had been taking groups of Whitworth College students to South and Central America for a four-month study/service term since 1975. On several occasions we had planned to visit El Salvador but each time those plans had to be abandoned because of a fresh outbreak of fighting. This year, as a result of the United Nations brokered peace, we were finally able to travel to this tortured country and at last I was able to visit this chapel. It was here at the altar that Archbishop Oscar Romero was shot thirteen years earlier on March 24, 1980, as he lifted the host celebrating the mass. The Gospel passage which he had just finished reading was John 12:23–26, "The hour has come for the Son of Man to be glorified . . . unless a grain of wheat falls to the earth and dies, it remains a grain. But if it dies, it bears much fruit" (NIV). Archbishop Romero is living proof of these ancient words. Adjacent to the altar hangs the only witness to that tragic episode today: a small plaque, donated by a religious order, which cryptically provides the facts surrounding that infamous deed.

As I knelt during the waning daylight hours, I was overcome with the sense that I was on holy ground. Romero, in the tradition of the prophets, had cried out against the violence and injustice which had devastated his people, knowing that in doing so, he became a marked man. Only the day before, in what proved to be his final homily, he appealed to members of the National Guard, police, and military to stop killing their own peasant brothers and to obey the commandment, "Thou shalt not kill." "No soldier," he continued, "is obliged to obey an order contrary to the law of God. No one has to obey an immoral law . . . In the name of God, in the name of the suffering people whose cries rise to heaven more loudly each day, I implore you, I beg you, I order you in the name of God: Stop the repression!" The response to this challenge was a hastily called meeting of top-level military personnel presided over by Roberto d'Aubuisson, a death squad leader and ex-officer in the National Guard.

Lots were drawn for the privilege of killing Romero. The next day the assailant entered the doorway of the chapel, fired one shot, and fled.

As I was praying, I found myself asking questions. First, is my level of commitment to Christ and his Kingdom such that I would be as faithful as Romero if I faced similar circumstances? A second question which has long perplexed me, returned with renewed intensity. Archbishop Romero, a profoundly Christian man, one month before his assassination wrote a letter to another deeply Christian man, President Jimmy Carter, in which he pleaded, "I ask you, if you truly want to defend human rights, prohibit the giving of aid to the Salvadoran government." In the judgment of Jimmy Carter at that time, the best way to reduce the carnage that was convulsing El Salvador was the military option. Earlier in the year he had asked Congress for 5.7 million dollars in military aid to "help strengthen the army's key role in reforms." (In March of this year, the United Nations sponsored Truth Commission report attributed 85 percent of the violence which claimed more than 75,000 lives during twelve years of war to the El Salvadoran security forces.).

It is ironic that Jimmy Carter who succeeded in making human rights a part of U.S. foreign policy unintentionally aided the cause of those who succeeded in stilling the voice of the most powerful defender of human rights in El Salvador. I can only imagine the anguish he felt as he received the news of the assassination of Romero, and later that year in December when he learned of the murder of the four Roman Catholic church women.

A third disturbing question which has long haunted me returned with pressing urgency as I sat there in the gathering darkness. How could my government supply and train such a depraved institution as the El Salvadoran military? As I pondered this question, I remembered an encounter that took place eleven years earlier at the Biblical Seminary in San José, Costa Rica between Whitworth College students and nine students from El Salvador who were studying at the seminary and planning to return to their country to serve in the Baptist Church. When they learned of our arrival, they asked if they could meet with us for a discussion. We met twice in what proved to be a traumatic experience for the North American students coming from relatively affluent, comfortable, and safe circumstances. They were anxious to learn first-hand about the situation in El Salvador after having read a great deal about it in preparation for the trip. After some initial awkwardness, the conversation began to flow in an animated manner as they realized that, in spite of some obvious cultural differences, they shared a common bond—they were all students seeking to expand their understanding. The students from El Salvador shared episodes from their respective church communities involving disappearances, rapes, torture, and murder at the hands of government security forces and related "death squads." They spoke with passion and sadness as they described the cruel fate of family members and friends. They spoke of returning to their homes at the end of the day never knowing for sure that they would find their families waiting for them. The American students had read about this. However, hearing this now face to face from students like themselves transformed these facts into a living tragedy of incomprehensible proportions. The war in remote El Salvador now had human faces.

The critical moment in this exchange came when the Salvadoran students asked us, "How can the United States, a Christian nation, send money and arms to the El Salvadoran government which uses these resources to oppress its own people?" I remember one of our students, a leader who was to become the student body president for the coming year, attempted to give a reply. The longer she spoke, the more frustrated she became as she tearfully realized that she was unable to reconcile the question with the country she loved. The American students felt embarrassment, shame, anger, and impotence—impotence because they felt powerless to influence American foreign policy toward El Salvador.

I was aroused from my contemplation as Karen and Leslie returned to the chapel to take me to my hotel. As I stepped out into the descending darkness I found myself sharing the embarrassment, shame, and anger experienced by my students. I, too, was unable to reconcile this unspeakable violence with the ideals my country professes.

The tour ended with a debriefing time in Mexico at the *Comunidad Teológica de México*, an ecumenical consortium of seminaries next to the large *Universidad Nacional Autónoma de México*.

An essential component of every trip is the dialogue that takes place among the students. They encounter new circumstances and information which challenge some of their previous ways of thinking. All participants process this "challenge of ideas" in their own way. Healthy tension and discussion often arise. Student David Lee shares his perspective about this tension:

While many students had their hardest times facing sickness (their own), rampant poverty, political oppression, or simply being away from home, my personal hardest time came from the political focus of the group, both academic and personal. In a nutshell, I came from 4 years of Marine Corps infantry, so my view of the US was largely positive. In Central America, the predominant view (of those citizens and of our own group) was negative. So, my hardest time came from the complicated muddle of realizing and acknowledging what our country really did wrong there (a lot), and the other members' collective view which I felt (and still do feel) took from Central American history to over-generalize toward certain "left-wing" sentiments like anti-militarism, anti-capitalism, and just general anti-US sentiment. Reality, of course, is probably in the middle somewhere. In any case, that was the biggest struggle for me—the political and philosophical shock. And, while it probably hit me hardest, there were at least a few other students who came from relatively conservative backgrounds who struggled too.

The 1993 CAST group had an epilogue shortly after the program ended. After a dozen years of civil war, on March 20, 1994, the small country of El Salvador held elections for the office of president, for members of the National Assembly, and local offices. Three members of the CAST cohort (Tracey King, Julie Gage, and Dustin Stevens) traveled to El Salvador as part of a contingent of international observers to monitor the elections. They were stationed at the little town of San Simón, four hours outside of the capital city of San Salvador.

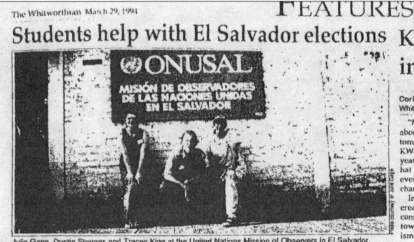

The Whitworthian March 29, 1994

FEATURES

Students help with El Salvador elections

Julie Gage, Dustin Stevens and Tracey King at the United Nations Mission of Observers in El Salvador.

Todd Orwig
Whitworthian Staff Writer

While most students packed their bags to go home for Spring Break, three Whitworth Students prepared for a 10-day trip to El Salvador.

Juniors Dustin Stevens, Tracey King and Julie Gage travelled with a Presbyterian delegation active in Latin American relief programs to monitor elections in El Salvador. They joined six others from the group in Houston, and headed to El Salvador. There were more than 3,000 international observers monitoring the elections.

Although the election only lasted one day, the other days were spent learning the history of the war in El Salvador, getting educated about political problems of the country and the election process.

"We were busy every day, listening to different speakers and getting information about the election guidelines," said Gage.

In the past, elections have been marred by corruption with the military standing over voters with machine guns forcing people to choose a certain candidate. In an attempt to change this practice, the international observers were brought in to help stop the corruption.

Thousands of Salvadorans braved 100-degree heat to place their votes in the country's first full election after 12 years of civil war. The students were there to resolve complaints, help voters find their names on registration lists and ensure the election ran smoothly.

"It was hard to see people stand in line for hours in the heat and then not be able to find their name on the list," said Gage.

"People were glad to see us because they knew that meant the elections meant a great deal," said Stevens

The three students, who also spent last spring in Central America on the Whitworth sponsored study tour, received donations from the Inland Empire Presbyterian peacekeeping committee. Overall, though, the trip was financed primarily by the students.

The group was able to meet a lot of people, not only from El Salvador, but also from different parts of the United States.

"The people we met were great. Both the Salvadorans, and the observers," said Stevens.

The international observers tried to stop any voting irregularities that occurred. The A.R.E.N.A. party, the ruling party, handed out free lunch tickets to voters as an incentive to vote for their party, and some people voted more than once. The observers realized that they couldn't catch everything. According to Gage, there were several small problems she observed throughout the day of elections.

The students understood that, although they could not stop all the corruption, their presence was felt. They are unsure how much of a difference they made in the election process, but are glad they had the experience. "Even though we were neutral participants, it was good to let the Salvadorans know we were concerned," added Gage. "It was rewarding to help the Salvadorans who had never voted before to participate in the election."

Ballot theater is in the Fieldhouse

1996: A Powerful Encounter with the Only Survivor of the El Mozote Massacre

CAST 1996 COHORT: BETH (Anderegg) Paez, Anna Atkinson, Kelli (Borden) Cable, Amy (Clark) McNelly, Alissa Diehl, Timothy Evans, Kresha (Frankhauser) Faber, Nyla Fritz, Christina (Grissen) Burch, Ryan Hawk, Heidi Hiatt, Si'Imoa (Iata) Galoia, Christine Ingersoll, Stephen Jost, Rachel (Karr) DuPont, Kari (Longmeier) Hammond, Nicole Marcovchick, Jeremy Nelson, Tami (Nida) Arntzen, Mary Penninga, Daniel Plies, Andrea (Read) Joachim, Carianne (Smith) Sherwood, Michelle Stupey, Julie (Taylor) Venegas, Daniel Wartman, Jennifer (Widrig) Widrig-Hodges, Nicole (Windhurst) Nelson and Matthew Yeoman. Teachings Assistants—DeLona and Martín Campos-Davis (DeLona, CAST 1990). Faculty Leaders—Sonja Hokanson, Don Liebert, Jim Hunt, and Ron Frase.

In the mid-1990s Central America was coming out of the long, dark night of civil wars and conflicts. Peace accords had recently been signed in the region, and there was hope for an enduring peace. Nevertheless, the peace agreements were tenuous, and that hope was interspersed with a good deal of anxiety.

The CAST participants were selected in early 1995. During the fall semester, students took two Sociology courses that would prove to be quite useful on the trip, "Social Reality" and "Latin American Problems."

From January 2 until February 11, 1996, the students lived in Quetzaltenango, Guatemala (also known as Xela) and studied Spanish intensively at the *Casa Xelajú* language institute. Spanish professor Sonja Hokanson accompanied the group during this segment. Much more than mere Spanish study took place in Guatemala. Student Carianne (Smith) Sherwood narrates in her journal a spontaneous episode:

> As an option at *Casa Xelaju*, some of us took a weekend trip to the *Finca Chaculá's* second anniversary of the refugees' return to Guatemala from Mexico. The day after the party, as my journal reminds me, "I was walking down the road and, at the next-to-last house there were three girls washing the laundry. I felt bad for them, because it was so cool, and they were out washing; I figured they must be freezing, but they were having a great time. They all said hello to me and asked me where I was going. I told them I was walking and taking pictures and asked if I could take one of them, which they agreed to. I ended up joining them, and though I didn't wash any clothes, I did discover that the water was warm! I was surprised and told them that in Quetzaltenango I only had cold water to wash my clothes." I vividly remember these girls all laughing and splashing and chatting away in Mam but stopping to greet me in Spanish as I walked by. Surprised by my revelation that I washed clothes, they asked, "Don't you have any daughters?" To be unmarried at the age of 20 was almost beyond their comprehension! I enjoyed a long conversation with them and an older sister who eventually emerged from the shelter nearby. Like so many

Carianne Smith's new friends

others we encountered in Central America, they impressed me with resilient cheerfulness that belied their circumstances.

A most difficult event took place back in the United States which deeply impacted the group. On February 2, Arnie Fritz, the 14-year-old brother of participant Nyla Fritz, was killed in a school shooting in Moses Lake, Washington. Nyla's close friends on the tour accompanied her to the airport to fly home for his funeral. Tracey King, from the 1993 group, immediately flew to Guatemala City in order to be with Nyla on the difficult flight home. A few weeks later, Nyla bravely completed the study tour by joining up with the group in Honduras. Laurie Werner, also from the 1993 group, arranged special host family accommodations in Honduras, so that Nyla could maintain contact with her family back in Washington during this mourning process. The cohort became a "community of grief" and was able to help the Fritz family transform this terrible tragedy into seeds of hope. Since graduating from Whitworth, Nyla has dedicated her life to the education of America's youth. Her sister Renee (from the 1993 group) has become the leader of the Alliance for Gun Responsibility, which strives mightily to reduce gun violence.

For the next month, the students were in Honduras and were led by Sociology Professor Don Liebert. He helped prepare the students for their home stays by teaching them how to make a social/political/economic map of their rural villages. For three weeks students lived separated from each other with their peasant host families. When they gathered together again, the students interviewed each other as sources for their research projects.

The students were able to debrief their deep Honduran experiences at a Costa Rican camp owned by *Vida Joven* (Young Life). During their three-week sojourn in Costa Rica, History Professor Jim Hunt taught a course on Central American History. The students also learned a lot about tropical plants at several national parks, and they visited coffee and banana plantations. It was evident that ecological issues were at the forefront of Costa Rican concerns. The students saw this first-hand when their bus was delayed for a demonstration against a garbage dump.

Then the group traveled to Nicaragua for three weeks. One week was dedicated to working on service projects under the direction of *Vida Joven*. Some students helped out at a camp, while others worked clearing a plot of land that had recently been donated to *Vida Joven*.

Chaplain Ron Frase and Professor Jim Hunt accompanied the students during their last days in Nicaragua and then on to El Salvador. War and peace dominated the teaching sessions and discussions. A very unique interview took place in El Salvador. The group met with the sole survivor of the *El Mozote* massacre. That conversation had a deep impact upon the students. Ron Frase describes that powerful experience and provides some of the context about the massacre:

The monument in memory of the victims of the massacre of El Mozote

On December 11, 1981 the village of *El Mozote* in El Salvador was attacked by an elite force of the Salvadoran army known as *Atlacatl* that had been trained at Fort Bragg, North Carolina. The citizens of *El Mozote* believed that they were safe from attack by the military because it was a community of Protestant evangelicals with its own pastor and a staunchly anti-communist reputation. To their dismay, the army did attack and destroyed *El Mozote* and several nearby villages, killing approximately one thousand people. It was briefly noted in the *New York Times* and *Washington Post* but dismissed by the Reagan administration as leftist propaganda. The *El Mozote* massacre could not have occurred at a more inopportune time for the Reagan administration. Congress was involved in a debate concerning the certification of a renewal of aid for the government of El Salvador by stating that, "It is making a concerted effort to comply with internationally recognized human rights and is achieving substantial control over all elements of its own armed forces, so as to bring to an end the indiscriminate torture and murder of Salvadoran citizens by these forces." Without this certification, all assistance to the government of El Salvador would be suspended. There was no attempt to verify the report by the US Embassy in San Salvador. One person, however, survived the massacre, Rufina Amaya. She spent the next eleven years telling her story, but no one took her seriously until an article about her finally appeared in the *New Yorker* magazine.[1]

On April 30, 1996, I visited *El Mozote* with a group of Whitworth students. Our guide for the trip was Katherine "Kay" Eekhoff who had gone on the Whitworth Central America trip in 1984. After graduating from college, she moved to Los Angeles to attend UCLA where she earned a master's degree in Urban Planning. She also became active in the Central American community where she met Oscar Andrade, a Salvadoran who worked with *El Rescate*. This organization provided aid to Salvadorans who had fled from their homeland and were seeking help as they attempted to navigate the US legal system. Kay and Oscar returned to El Salvador where they were married and have raised their three children. Today Kay works with Catholic Relief Services. Kay had organized our twelve days in El Salvador by finding us a hotel, making travel arrangements, and setting up meetings. She had become acquainted with Rufina and invited her to speak to our group. Rufina agreed to meet with us and share her experience. We arrived in *El Mozote* after a four-hour bus ride from San Salvador, the capital city. The town was a scene of mass destruction. Only fragments of destroyed homes remained as silent witnesses to the massacre that had occurred fourteen years earlier.

Kay located Rufina and her daughter, and we began our journey through the destroyed town as we navigated around 500-pound bomb craters. Rufina told us that it was a miracle of God that she was still alive. She was 39 years old when the massacre occurred. A majority of the victims were children. As we continued walking through the town, she declared to us that her hope had always been to live in a community, to help children, and to ensure that this would never happen again. "Where we are standing," she said, "is holy ground."

We stopped in front of what was at one time a church. She told how she was able to escape by hiding in the thick underbrush of a culvert opposite the church. Her children were forced into the church, and she could hear their cries calling for her to help them as the soldiers fired their guns and killed everyone.

She remained hidden in the culvert from five in the afternoon until one in the morning, weeping over her three children who were killed. She passed the next eight days lost and without food. She staggered around the hills until she stumbled upon a family. They lived together in a cave while the bombardment continued, and she kept on sobbing for her children. She said that she still had nightmares about them. As we listened to Rufina's grief, there was not a dry eye in our group.

Rufina remarried and has two children. One of our students asked, "Do you ask why this has happened to you?" She replied, "God gives faith and hope to continue. By God's grace we are protected. I am discouraged, and I read the

---

1. Mark Danner, "The Truth of *El Mozote*" in the *New Yorker*, December 6, 1993: 50–133.

Bible for encouragement. My hope is to live for my two children. God chose me for something."

As we continued walking we came to the memorial to *El Mozote*. It consists of a cross with a mother and a father and two young children at the foot of the cross and an engraved marker inscribed with the words:

They did not die,
    They are with us, with you and all humanity.
    El Mozote, December 11, 1981

Before getting on the bus for the return trip to the capital, Marta, age eleven, Rufina's youngest daughter, beautiful and very shy, spoke with us. She said that she was the treasurer of her school, and they were going to do something special for tomorrow, Mother's Day. She wondered if we could help them. We collected an offering from our group to take to their school.

Rufina Amaya, the sole survivor of the El Mozote massacre, and one of her children

The ride back to San Salvador was very somber. We had been overwhelmed by what we had just witnessed. We were greatly troubled by the role our government had played in funding the Salvadoran government at the rate of one and one half million dollars a day, of training Salvadoran troops and of tripling the size of the Salvadoran army. This seemed so contrary to what we have been raised to believe—that the US defended people struggling for freedom. The students were beginning to see the ambiguity of this issue. The United States didn't always stand with the oppressed—that in El Salvador, Guatemala and Nicaragua, we defended ruthless, totalitarian regimes, because the US foreign policy was built on maintaining stability in the region, which was more important than supporting the desire of oppressed people. We have forgotten that during the Revolutionary War, we did not opt for stability. We revolted against the British in order to achieve our independence.

To end the program, the students went to Mexico City for a week to meditate and reflect upon their experiences.

The crucial role of the TAs on the CAST program cannot be overestimated. They do much more than merely assist the professors. According to Ron Frase, this tour was blessed with "extraordinary TAs" in the persons of DeLona and Martín Campos-Davis. One student's photo album appropriately recognized their importance. Next to the picture of DeLona and Martín she wrote, "In this case, T.A. is not just Teacher's Aide but also . . . travel agent, tour guide, translator, mediator, counselor, nurse, and *friend!*"

1999: Rebuilding Lives after Hurricane Mitch and the Creation of the Krista Foundation

CAST 1999 COHORT: JEFFREY Aitken, Robin (Boddy) Plies, Nathan Distelhorst, Haley (Gold) Townsend, Christin (Hinman) Saugen, Jeremiah Howe, Amber (Isaac) Ziring, Kate (Isenberg) Parker, Catherine (Klein) Hannon, Carlee (Klingeman) Howie, Jacob Meadows, Beth Poteet, Susan Powell, Kami (Roth) Meadows, David Saugen, Sonya (Schaumburg) Kostamo, Carly (Schwarmann) Frizzell, Kristina Solum, Julie (Strong) Tedford, Tethra Wales, and David Werner. Teaching Assistants—Alycia Jones and Laurie Werner (CAST 1993). Faculty Leaders—Ron Frase, Jim Hunt, Conny Palacios, and Don Liebert.

The program began in the fall of 1998 with a special preparation class taught by Professors Don Liebert and Ron Frase. The main goal was to equip the students for their Central American adventure. Their studies took on an even greater importance during the end of October, as Hurricane Mitch hit the Central American isthmus and stayed over Honduras and Nicaragua. It was one of the deadliest and most destructive Atlantic hurricanes on record. Students wondered how the people of Central America, especially the poorest ones, would be able to recover. Two books used in the course proved to be quite helpful to the students: *Understanding Central America* by John Booth and Thomas Walker and *Inevitable Revolutions: The United States in Central America* by Walter La Faber.

Ron Frase led the early portion in Guatemala followed by Don Liebert who accompanied the students through their homestays in Honduras, time in Tegucigalpa, and homestay debriefing in Costa Rica. Conny Palacios then joined the group in San José, Costa Rica and worked alongside the students at a Young Life camp in Matagalpa, Nicaragua. Jim Hunt met the students in Matagalpa, Nicaragua and accompanied them to Managua and El Salvador, and eventually Mexico City where the group debriefed their experience.

In January the participants met at the Los Angeles airport and from there flew to Guatemala City. They then traveled by land to Quetzaltenango for intensive Spanish language study. Quetzaltenango is the second largest city in the country and is more commonly known as Xela. Their Spanish abilities improved greatly from the intensive classes with Guatemalan professors at the *Casa Xelajú* Language School and during the weekend "plunge". The group ended their time in the country with a few days in

Guatemala City. Student Dave Saugen has shared a special journal entry that he wrote in the capital city:

> We met with Julio Quan in Guatemala City on February 9, 1999, a *very* inspiring man. When asked what his hopes were for Guatemala in the next twenty years, he said, "Personally, I want to know more about this country." This coming from a Guatemalan man who has had family in the running for President, whose uncle is a Chief Justice and who was the President of Congress in the 1950s, whose aunt influenced the women's rights reforms in the constitution, whose family includes a *comandante* in the URNG. He was heavily involved in the Peace Accord actions for two years. This man should know Guatemala, yet he is humble, so humble when he says he wants to know more about his country.

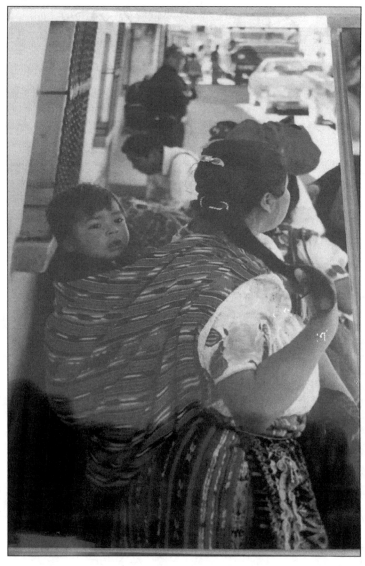

A Guatemalan mother and child in Xela

The group was able to hear first-hand from mothers whose children had "disappeared," former guerrilla leaders, former army generals, the whole gamut of society from some very wealthy citizens to the poorest *campesino* farmers. A powerful experience happened in a presentation with FAMDEGUA. Ron Frase narrates:

> We had an afternoon appointment with an organization known by the acronym FAMDEGUA (Families of the Detained and Disappeared of Guatemala). Thousands of Guatemalans have disappeared, and the organization is dedicated to locating them. The government opposes them—the locating of clandestine cemeteries is an embarrassment. They were currently excavating thirteen clandestine cemeteries. In 1994 an Argentine forensic team began exploring some of these sites. They explored an open well and recovered 162 bodies. The average age was seven years old, and there were very few adults.
>
> In 1982 the counterinsurgency reached its height under Ríos Montt's scorched earth policy. The army occupied the village of *Dos Erres*. They showed us a video of the community which had been totally destroyed. The carnage was unimaginable. The woman who was leading this session asked us to send a letter to the US Embassy in Guatemala urging it to support the *Dos Erres* investigation. She concluded with a powerful challenge:
> > Love is stronger than death.
> > We can't lose hope, we can't forget.
> > We have to overcome obstacles so that hopefully,
> > Future generations won't have to go through this.
> > Love is what keeps us going.
> > After thanking them, we filed out of the office stunned by what we saw
> and full of admiration for these brave people.

The group then traveled to Honduras where the students were placed one by one with rural Honduran *campesino* families. Millions of people had been left homeless by Hurricane Mitch. Many washed out roads had not been rebuilt. The CAST students were able to feel some of the pain of rural peasants. Although this was a lonely and emotionally challenging time for some, all agreed that they had learned some important, difficult lessons. Student David Saugen remembers, "This was a magical time. I cherish these three weeks as some of the best days in my college experience." The students and their rural *pueblito* placements were as follows:

Julie Strong in San Miguelito
Tethra Wales in Aluvaren
Robin Boddy in San José de Pane
Dave Werner in Tornabe
Catherine Klein in Yamaranguila
Jeff Aitken in San Isidro
Haley Gold in Guascotoro
Christin Hinman in Quebrada Honda

Kami Roth in Togopala
Jacob Meadows in Tranquititas
Carlee Schwarmann in Confradía
Amber Isaac in San Marcos
Susie Powell in El Obraje
Sonya Schaumburg, Cololaca
Kristina Solum in El Pinal
Kate Isenberg in Conguacota
Beth Poteet in La Majada
Carlene Klingeman in El Sitio
Dave Saugen in El Rodeo
Jeremiah Howe in Olosingo
Nate Distelhorst in Tofino

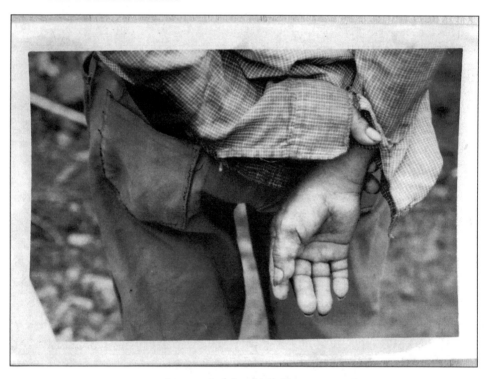

A campesino's hand tells his story

There was a significant time of reflection about their Honduran homestays when they arrived in Costa Rica. This took place at a camp along the coast. Spanish Professor Connie Palacios led the group throughout Costa Rica, where they visited places like San José, coffee and banana plantations, sweatshops, Parque Manuel Antonio, and Afro-Caribbean communities.

In Nicaragua, the students worked on a service project at a Young Life camp in the highlands around Matagalpa, and then traveled to the capital city of Managua. History Professor Jim Hunt led this part of the trip. The national government had recently raised the university tuition by 6 percent As a result, many Nicaraguan students marched in protest. The CAST group was impressed by this "democracy in the streets." The students met with Sandinista leaders, young environmentalists, current political leaders, a women's co-op, youth in recovery for substance abuse, and staff at the US Embassy.

On April 20, 1999 the Columbine massacre took place in Colorado, in which twelve high school students and one teacher had been killed. Dave Saugen later wrote in his journal:

> Nauseous. Rage. Helpless. Injustice. Integrity. Simplicity. Joy. Agape . . . my feelings today. What do I do with the pictures, the graphic nauseous images that I will carry with me for life? Jeff saw Romero as a modern-day Jesus parable. Beth felt anger and hope. Amber saw more clearly that nowhere is safe (yesterday's Colorado school shooting).

When the news reached the group, many Central Americans consoled the students. Some in the group were amazed that these people who themselves had suffered so much were able to offer so much consolation.

In San Salvador, the students did homestays with former gang members, met with former guerrilla leaders, and visited the US Embassy and the University of Central America, where six Jesuit priests, their housekeeper, and her daughter were assassinated in 1989. Traveling outside of the capital, the students visited the massacre site of *El Mozote*, spent time in resettlement communities, and unwound at the beach. After visiting the memorial to Archbishop Romero at Divina Providencia, Jim Hunt decided to start the Krista Foundation to honor the life of his daughter Krista Ausland-Hunt.

The group then traveled to Mexico City where they did a week of debriefing their experiences and visiting museums and the indigenous pre-Columbian city of Teotihuacan. Before flying back to the US, the group closed out their time together with a final "Coffeehouse." The following fall semester, the group shared about their experience during a Forum presentation, complete with photos, stories, and reflections.

One student has recalled that the event that makes the 1999 trip unique is that it was the last one before 9/11. She writes:

> I know that many of us felt out of step with our friends, coworkers and neighbors when 9/11 happened. As a group, the way we all had received the experience of the 1999 trip made us less shocked by 9/11. That people out there in the globe would be very angry at and target Americans did not shock us. The reactionary patriotism and the rush to the Iraq War also fell on us differently. I wish that that whole period had been more self-reflective for the US and that everything had moved much slower. But that is not what the majority of Americans wanted at the time.

2002: New Life Emerges from Destruction

CAST 2002 COHORT: DANA Boddy, Heather (Bupp) Larsen, Stephanie Cotton, Tarah (Eaton) Leung, Rebekah Fite, Stephanie (Frederick) Fevergeon, Rebecca (Hyder) González, Joel Gaffney, Lisa (Gavereski) Hatchell, Katelin (Hodge) Simons, Chris Irvine, Margreta "Greta" (Isaacson) Cheney, Matthew Kaemingk, Katherine King, Coral (Langton) Haslet, Jacob McCoy, Addi (Norman) Assi, Lars Olson, Matthew Ridenour, Adam Roberts, Amy Robinson, Benjamin Robinson, Caleb Stewart, Sarah (Stocks) Edmonson, and Stacie (Wilson) Webb. Teaching Assistants—Amber (Isaac) Ziring and Jeremiah Howe (both CAST 1999). Faculty Leaders—Jim Hunt, Esther Louie, Don Liebert and Terry McGonigal.

This was a traumatic period in the history of the United States. It was during the fall of 2001 that New York City, Washington, D.C. and the entire country felt the terrorist attacks of September 11th. Our government reacted vigorously (some would say overreacted) and, in order to protect citizens against terrorism, began to reduce individual freedoms with increased screenings at airports and other public venues. The relative decade of peace after the end of the Cold War gave way to a new war, a more ambiguous war on terrorism. Of course, this had many impacts upon CAST. The schedule was originally planned to include a few weeks in Cuba, but this segment was changed due to a fear for student safety. In addition, leadership of the CAST program had now been passed on to a new group of professors.

The group members were selected in 2001 and spent the fall in preparation and orientation sessions with Jim Hunt, Esther Louie, Don Liebert and Terry McGonigal. Professor Don Liebert also taught a course on the history of Central America that was required of all the students.

Students traveled to Xela (Quetzaltenango), Guatemala in January for intensive Spanish classes at the Casa Xelajú Language Institute. Students were housed in local nearby host homes which supported the students' language skills while learning to live with a Spanish-speaking family. Intensive language sessions (five hours each day) were geared toward the language level of each student. After lunch time, the students participated in cultural learning and volunteer service. The students learned about local skills such as making chocolate and corn tortillas and cooking a typical Guatemalan meal. Cultural excursions took the students to the language institute's sponsored after school program, area historical sites, and other important venues in the community.

Following the end of the language school experience, the Teaching Assistants and Chaplain Terry McGonigal organized the "Plunge" wherein groups of three to four students would travel to outlying areas for the weekend. Their task was to explore the assigned village, learn and meet local community members, and finally to travel back to an appointed meeting place to join the full group. They were given an allowance to cover transportation, meals and lodging. The Plunge was designed to develop teamwork with their small group and to improve their Spanish speaking skills and interactions with locals. Often the students spoke of the Plunge as one of the most exciting and among the most memorable CAST experiences.

In February, the students traveled to Honduras where Sociology Professor Don Liebert joined the group. He helped students begin to understand the challenging differences between Latin American indigenous and mestizo cultures. Each student was placed in a rural home setting with Honduran NGO partners. Students were usually not in proximity to each other to allow for greater immersion and participation with their host families. During this period the faculty and the teaching assistants would periodically visit each student in their homestay community to connect with them and to offer support and guidance. Jacob McCoy shares the downside of being a tall man:

> The home stay in Honduras was definitely a singular experience. I lived with coffee farmers in the northwest of Honduras for 3 weeks. It felt like a lifetime unto itself. I slept in a bed that was far too small for me (I'm 6'5" and my bed

was 4 feet long), ate nothing but beans and tortillas, and tried to keep pace picking coffee with my gracious and tireless hosts.

This rural Honduran adventure was when some students "hit the wall" with culture shock. Culture shock is a phenomenon that affected some participants in deep ways. Nevertheless, these "trials of our faith" can produce good fruits. Stephanie Frederick shares about her experiences:

> During the five months of my tour, God broke down my protective walls and guided me into a new stage of emotional health and transparent relationship. I spent the first two months in undetectable yet absolute culture shock. My head lied to my heart as my fascination with experiencing everything new, submerged my rolling emotions like waves engulfing an inexperienced swimmer. Guatemala was excitement and exploration, exhilaration by day and weeping into my pillow at night. No one knew I was drowning that first month, not even me.
>
> The second month, in Honduras, I went into full shock. Emotional and mental numbness. I followed my training and said yes to every opportunity. Yes, I will gladly go to the most remote and inbred village for four weeks alone. Of course, I would love to teach school to their forty students, six days a week. Sure, I'll get up at 4:00 am to make tortillas with smoke watering my eyes and Ranchera music blasting in my ears. Yes, I can handle not hearing my name or being touched by another person for thirty days. Certainly, I can embalm that dead body shot on the mountain pass I just traveled yesterday . . . Wait, what? The shock ended abruptly after I returned to Honduran civilization, received scabies medication, ate at Pizza Hut, and called my mother to regale her with my adventures. When I started laughing hysterically as I described children defecating in the village street, I understood I was in culture shock. I finally knew which way was up.
>
> I slowly resurfaced over the last three months. Joy returned as I began to open up to three close friends. When half the group contracted head lice, we spent hours picking nits and bonding with peers that I had always kept at a friendly arms-length away. Demonstrating that vulnerability is a strength, the Holy Spirit took me to the next step, convicting me to share my internal struggles with the whole group. Their shock and embracing reactions were all the confirmation I needed that my pain had been secret too long. I had finally reached the shore of community and belonging.

After the rural home stays in Honduras, the group traveled to Costa Rica where Professor Don Liebert led various sessions about Latin American societies. Assistant Dean of Student Life for the Intercultural Student Center, Esther Louie, and her husband Wayne Beymer, joined the group. Esther facilitated intercultural training and reflection exercises to support and encourage the students to process the first half of their CAST experiences. Through various exercises and discussions, the students examined what they had learned from living and learning in their language school, host families, and all aspects of the cultural, social, spiritual, and personal engagements up to that point. The group then traveled to Puerto Limón on the Atlantic Coast of Costa Rica and celebrated *Semana Santa* there as well as joining in the Easter Sunday pageant in Cartago.

The group then traveled by bus to Managua, Nicaragua. This portion of the study program was organized by Augsburg College. Anne McSweeney, representative from Augsburg, had arranged multiple visits with speakers and organizations. The group met with representatives from three Nicaraguan political parties and received a briefing at the US Embassy. Esther Louie narrates a very powerful visit to an orphanage for girls:

> The experience at the orphanage had a huge impact upon the students because this orphanage housed young girls who had been sexually assaulted and raped. The guide from Augsburg apologized when she told us that this was an orphanage that took in girls who had been sexually violated. You could hear a pin drop as our shocked students learned of this. The youngest girl, who was a bright exuberant child, quickly became a favorite of our students with her outgoing demeanor. The reality of her experience shocked us all to know that she had been sexually assaulted. Students started to cry, and the men in the group were speechless. All of us were quiet.

That night, Esther Louie led a reflection and discussion for any topic that the students wanted to discuss and share. This was one of the most moving activities that helped the students to work through their experiences and emotions.

A highlight in the country was an afternoon spent with Fernando Cardenal. He was a Jesuit priest and a liberation theologian. In 1980 he led the Nicaraguan Literacy Crusade in which half a million people learned how to read and write. During the Sandinista government he served as Minister of Education from 1984 to 1990. Both he and his brother Ernesto Cardenal had to leave the priesthood by a direct order from the Pope. It was claimed that this was due to their serving in the cabinet of a national government (a task supposedly not appropriate for priests), but most observers agree that this suspension was due to their left leaning ideology, which could not be tolerated by Pope John II. Although not all the CAST students were convinced of the tenets of liberation theology, most admired the depth of Fernando Cardenal's convictions and actions.

Professor Jim Hunt joined the group in Managua, from where Esther Louie and her husband returned to the States. The group traveled to El Salvador where they studied social issues and politics. The group ended the semester with a debriefing week in Mexico City where Esther Louie rejoined the program. She, together with the TAs Amber and Jeremiah, led the debriefing sessions. These debriefing and re-entry sessions were designed to help guide the participants through self-reflection and assessment of their learning and growth through the semester-long study program.

Esther Louie wrote a letter to the parents of the CAST cohort in April.[1] We have chosen a portion of that letter to include here in which she comments on her perceptions of the students in the group:

- They all cared for Matt K. when he was so sick in Guatemala.

- Greta, Stacie and Matt slept close together and took turns to keep guard for the rat that haunted their room on the plunge.

- We all cried together with Katie as we tried to understand the mystery of death and why a father is taken from his family.

- Worried and prayed all day as Sarah and Jero (TA Jeremiah Howe) went in quest of her lost backpack, and then celebrated when it was found.

- We watched out for each other on the beaches of Costa Rica as the riptides were fierce.

- We laughed heartily and sung loudly at the "coffee houses" where we watched in amazement of each other being funny, clever, talented, and used humor to help us understand our lives.

- Watched as Adam, Caleb and Amy shaved their legs in solidarity, or was it about gender equity?

1. See the remaining content of Esther's letter to the parents in the Vignette section of the book.

- Matt R and Adam for writing and playing hilarious songs to memorialize the group's experiences and their own.

- Coral French braiding Lars' hair, and so lovingly braiding anyone else's hair which went beyond beautiful braiding to Coral giving us comfort by her gentle touch.

- Hours of ultimate Frisbee on the beach where to just run and play was the best medicine for being apart for a month in Honduras.

- Becky organizing early morning devotionals and the prayer bag helping to remind us how to keep our spiritual focus.

- Adam keeping us all on our toes through his games and announcements—no one knows where they come from—we just accept them because it's Adam.

- Katelin in her quiet and gentle spirit for always supporting us and being there to listen.

- Jake for his thoughtful and inspiring writing, and for the questions that he asks that cause us to pause and wonder.

- Dana, the Kitchen Queen, and her gift of making meals that pleased and comforted us. The wonderful and delicious meals that cost next to nothing that she and the food committee could whip up faster than any chef.

- Chris for giving us a sense of safety and showing us all how to defend ourselves from unwanted attention. He will be known forever in *El Sontule*, our *campo* home stay in Nicaragua, as the Karate Kid of Central America.

- Ben for making the ultimate hygienic sacrifice of having his head shaved so he wouldn't spread head lice.

- Tara, Stacie and Addi for their angelic voices that uplifted us and many a congregation here in Central America and helped us in worship.

- "Nurse" Lisa for showing us what a successful Whitworth graduate can do, and we would have been lost without her rock-steady, can-do attitude.

- Heather for being dubbed the Trump Queen for the ability to name trump in pinochle, only to immediately forget what trump is. For her smile that could light up any room.

- Stephanie C. for always being accused for not shuffling the cards in pinochle. For her honesty and forthright way of stating her observations and saying the things that some of us didn't think to say.

- Stephanie F. for her friendly smile and wonderful way of providing introductions to our speakers in her wonderful and charming Spanish.

- Jero, Caleb, Ben, Katie and Greta for logging marathon mileage on this trip and showing us what great athletes we have among us.

- And for Joel, who in his quiet manner impressed us all, as all people who met him and wanted to take care of him. He may win the award for owning the most machetes.

A boat ride on a lake

A very powerful event for the group was a visit to *El Mozote* where the group heard the testimony of the sole survivor of the massacre. Teaching Assistant Amber (Isaac) Ziring relates the impact the visit had on her:

> It was a great privilege to have Rufina Amaya join us for our visit to *El Mozote*. Having been there in 1999 as a student, I had seen the efforts to bring *El Mozote* back to life were making progress in 2002. There was more development; there were increasing efforts to teach the lessons of this massacre; life was recovering and thriving. Translating Rufina's story was a defining moment in my life. I knew the facts as they have come to be understood from Don Liebert's class and from visiting with a tour guide three years earlier. There is something visceral and life changing about translating the horror of the death of an entire community in the first person voice of the sole survivor. We stood at the wells, now providing life sustaining water, and heard of how Rufina's friends and neighbors' bodies were used to poison it. We stood by the bushes that kept Rufina alive and heard of the hours of listening to murder. I cannot imagine the decision to return to the place where the unspeakable happened to me and speaking that truth, yet that is what Rufina did. As I translated, I tasted Rufina's story in my mouth—and I know that taste was far from the bitterness of her reality.

Some students struggled—we were in a time of turmoil and absolute American devotion at home—and Rufina's story was hard to swallow given its implication for the US. How could we possibly imagine such a thing happening in this beautiful mountain village, let alone embrace the possibility that the US had played a role? She was patient and answered questions. She explained that she tells people like us the story, over and over, not because it's gotten any easier over time, but because of the promise she had made to God. She promised if she survived, she would denounce what happened to ensure it would never happen to anyone else. Rufina said with confidence that we, Whitworth College students, would be able to keep this from happening again—because if you knew this truth, how could you not work to stop it? What a tall order for such young people.

2005: CASP—A Change in the Program Name and Permaculture in Punta Mona

CASP 2005 COHORT: MELISSA (Binford) Beck, Jonathan Brewer, Molly (Bruner) Carlson, Lora Burge, Mark Chapman, Bethany (Dufault) Harmon, Hannah Dufford, Aaron Fishburn, Emily (Fletcher) Schuldt, Jacob Grady, Kirk Harris, Clinton Lipscomb, Michael Marchesini, Teranne (McComas) Arentsen, Ryan Niemeyer, Yori Okada, Allison (Oyster) Cummings, Chelsea Peterson, Kathryn (Robinson) Townsend, Katie Stephans, Katie Stewart, Laura (Thaut) Vinson, Jennifer Thomson, Crystal (Viken) Ben, and Danielle Wegman. Teaching Assistants—Dan and Robin Plies (CASP 1996 & 1999, respectively). Faculty Leaders—Terry McGonigal, Esther Louie, Michael LeRoy, Jim Hunt,

The long-standing, transformative program that had been taking Whitworth students and faculty to Central America since 1975 adopted a new name in 2005. Instead of referring to the trip as a study "tour," the faculty leaders decide it was more accurate to call it a "program." Afterall, the challenging travel and living conditions and demanding academic components, were nothing like a tourist experience!

During the selection period in February of 2004, students underwent a rigorous interview process in a pool of over fifty applicants. In the Fall, those selected took a new Latin American Politics course taught by Professor Michael LeRoy. The Assistant Dean of Student Life of the Intercultural Student Center, Esther Louie, had developed two new courses. "Maximizing Study Abroad 303" was a prep class in the fall, and "Maximizing Study Abroad 304" was a debriefing and re-entry class the guided the students' processing both during the trip and upon their return to Spokane in May. In the fall prep class, students worked through a number of exercises and reflections on cultural awareness. They also began to learn the responsibilities and privileges of being members of a team; lessons that would come in handy on the trip.

Flexibility has always been a cherished (and very needed!) virtue in the CASP program. Modifications need to be made based upon the changes taking place in the host countries. Although students were scheduled to take intensive Spanish courses in Guatemala during Jan Term, certain modifications had to be made due to the political unrest happening during the fall semestser in the country. The leadership team scrambled and found a suitable alternative in Nicaragua, first in Granada and then in León. Chaplain and Theology Professor Terry McGonigal led the program this first month. One of the students described a "paradise" experience:

> I think one of our most memorable Nicaraguan outings was out of the port in Granada. One afternoon we got into a small boat which brought us to a tiny little island in Lake Nicaragua covered in the most delicious mangoes, recently fallen from the trees. The island was so small we could walk across it in a couple of minutes. I think the consensus was that we were in paradise.

During the spring semester, the students spent time in four Central American countries. In February participants were placed individually with host families in rural Honduras. As in the previous study programs, students were placed with non-governmental organizations (NGOs) in a wide array of social, religious, and educational service programs. For many students, staying in the individual homestays for three to four weeks was one of the most challenging parts of the semester. Students were visited periodically in their host stays by Esther Louie, her husband Wayne, and the TAs, Robin and Dan Plies. Dan had previously met with each NGO to set up the service activities and family stays. As a result, this part of the program went very smoothly.

The next country visited was Costa Rica where Michael LeRoy taught about ecotourism, universal healthcare, and living in a country without an army. The group visited the US Embassy, a coffee farm, and the town of Manzanillo. For the next week the group headed to the Punta Mona Center, a new study location for this group. Backpacks and luggage were ferried to the Center via powerboats while the general access to the Center was a five-mile hike led by Garifuna guides. This retreat and workshop center offered instruction in the study of permaculture. Permaculture is a multidisciplinary study, set of principles and ethics that offers a guideline and methodology to conserve and regenerate natural systems, intentionally design human settlements, and maximize efficiency while using less energy. It seemed like a second paradise. The group next traveled to Monteverde and their beautiful cabins. The group loved the zipline experience and the guided tour during which they learned about the plants, animals, and insects of the cloud forest.

Fun time in the water

The students arrived back in Nicaragua on April 3. History Professor Jim Hunt taught about primary and secondary sociological research. His rigorous assignments gave the students direct experience in interviewing and compiling questions that would yield a variety of data—what factors influenced the growth of the community, how did the community govern itself, who were the leaders current and past, what role, if any, did religion play in the community, etc.? Students had to gather the information, analyze it, and then present the history of their homestay community.

One student even recalls the precise history project that Professor Hunt assigned:

> Our history paper for Jim Hunt was to write the history of our Honduran host villages and families. We had to draw a map locating as much as we could within our villages, touch on the religious backgrounds and dynamics observed in our villages, and investigate whatever we could about their histories.

Students had brief, but significant, home stays in Estelí, Nicaragua. Assistant Dean Esther Louie recalls:

> The homestays in the Estelí area were well designed. The students were divided into two groups to stay in two different communities. One community was developing an eco-tourism focus, so the students helped to build nature trails in their area. The second community that Wayne and I stayed in was to help the local interest of their women's organization to start a coffee cooperative. Our students helped to dig and prepare soil and to plant coffee tree seedlings.
>
> Many of these host homes had survivors from the civil wars. Family members spoke of the invasion of the Sandinistas, even displaying gunshot wounds. A strong development program had been organized by *UCA Miraflor* which included the building of outhouses at each home, and at the time of our stay, building cisterns to capture rainwater for household use.

The group then entered El Salvador. A highlight was the homestay experience. The students stayed with the families of former gang members who were part of an organization that was developing safe alternatives to participating in gang life. The group had a fruitful debriefing time in Chalatenango, El Salvador.

Several new components were added to the program, including a debriefing period in Spokane. A new activity was to invite CASP parents to join their students on Whitworth's campus for the final debriefing. Parents and family members were invited to the last CASP luncheon, and to participate in brief activities (during and following lunch) to support their student in the re-entry process together. This was based upon Esther Louie's utilization of best practices in how to process such an experience for sojourners and reentry to their home base. Additionally, a new event followed the luncheon. The Whitworth community was invited to gather for the CASP presentation. The students had previously formed country committees during the Honduran segment. Each committee presented summary learnings and experiences at this public campus-wide presentation.

As Professor Jim Hunt later reflected about the program, he acknowledged that music, arts, and Protestant/Pentecostal churches were not given the attention that they deserved. He did recommend the continued use of the Bryant Myers book, *Walking with the Poor*, for future CASP groups. This volume has been a godsend to the program for over two decades. Students have found this book helpful to understand the many dimensions and levels of poverty and suggestions on how to respond.

2008: Intensive Spanish and Powerful Plunges in Guatemala

CASP 2008 COHORT: SARAH Bratton, Shiloh Deitz, Christopher Dennis, Emily (Dufault) Lazuhrcatt, Ashley (Ernst) Deitz, Gillian (Goodrich) Cleary, Anna Gray, Derek Gruen, Glen Guenther, Laura Hickey, Michael Johansen, Kristina Kielbon, Allyn Kryzmowski, Jeremy Molinaro, Amanda (Moos) Wall, Erik Nilson (Jan Term only), Kelsey (Orr) Pell, Richie Ressel, Caitlin Risk, Ryan Sobotka, Diana Stapp, Ashley Thalmann, Joseph Tobiason, Cheri Torrence, Travis Walker, and Jeff Wilson. Teaching Assistants—Ryan Niemeyer and Emily (Fletcher) Schuldt (both CASP 2005). Faculty Leaders—Kim Hernández, Terry McGonigal, Michael LeRoy, Jim Hunt, and Karla Morgan.

By 2008, Central America was enjoying the beneficial "dividends" of the peace accords of the 1990s. In particular, Nicaragua enjoyed relative stability and a growing economy, especially in agricultural exports. Nevertheless, the neighboring countries of El Salvador, Honduras, and Guatemala, saw increased rates of violence, particularly due to gang activity.

In the spring of 2007, another large pool of applicants showed interest in the program and participated in an intensive selection process. During the fall semester of 2007, the selected students took two courses on the Spokane campus. Esther Louie taught the Prep class that covered the range of nuts and bolts items like passports, packing, and the itinerary. Nevertheless, the class went much deeper than that. Esther helped the students explore their "cultural selves" and how the overseas experience might affect them "educationally, personally, spiritually, and professionally." She also mentored new CASP faculty leader, Kim Hernández, on the important techniques of intercultural training and many details about the preparation for the work with students on the program. Provost Michael LeRoy taught the course "Latin American Politics" and delved into important themes such as the military, peasants, US foreign policy, multinational corporations, urbanization, and education.

On January 8, 2008, excited and nervous CASP students arrived on the Spokane campus for a few days of orientation with Esther and Kim. Then the group flew to Guatemala for intensive Spanish language learning, cultural exploration, and community engagement. From January 12 until February 2 they had five hours of one-on-one instruction daily with Guatemalan teachers at the *Casa Xelajú* Language Institute. Kim, together with her husband José, led the group in Guatemala. A student recalls:

Diana Stapp with her language school teacher at Casa Xelajú in Guatemala

97

During the first week of our semester in Central America, I sat in a small plain room with off-brand Sesame Street characters painted on the yellow walls trying to explain in broken Spanish that I wasn't feeling very well. Every traveler will recall a time when they have been ill during their trip, whether it was making an adjustment to the food, or catching something much more malevolent. The first time I got sick during the Central America Study Program, I did so splendidly.

My teacher at Casa Xelajú was quiet and patient, but I was poorly trying to describe my symptoms. Not wanting to miss a fun outing, I gingerly walked along with her to the open-air market in the center of town to see the labyrinth of vendor stands and speak with some of the sellers. Weaving through narrow aisles and brushing past tables groaning under fat carrots and heads of cabbage, we suddenly turned a corner into a new section of the market. It took a moment for me to register, but I realized we were wandering through the meat section when I almost kicked the face of a cow's head sitting on the ground with my bare, sandaled toes. My stomach lurched and suddenly the humidity under the market tarps was suffocating. Embarrassed and not wanting to seem like an "ugly American" grossed out by a decapitated cow's head, I suffered through the remainder of our market tour and barely made it to my bed in my host family's house, near the school.

Past that moment is still mostly a blur in my memory. I spent a night (and a day? Two days?) in and out of fevered sleep with my host mom shuffling in and out of the room to take care of me. My only memory of that day is that somewhere in fever dreams, the title song from Forrest Gump floated in through my bedroom window from the neighbor's yard for what felt like the entire day. Over and over and over, it played on repeat. I thought, "No one can like this song that much...can they?" To this day I'm still not sure if it was actually being played on repeat, or if I only heard it one time and in my addled state imagined it played the whole day. Fortunately for me, two wonderful healers came to my aid. Profe Kim Hernández and her husband José rescued me from my amoebic state to bring me back to good health. They brought me tonics and cures, and most importantly, anti-nausea medications. José expertly prepared the medicine in a syringe provided by the clinic, while Kim comforted me. They helped tell me what foods to eat to get better and talked with my host mom as well. Being so sick and such a long distance from my own family had been an emotionally and physically exhausting experience, but the care and love I got from my teacher, my host family, my classmates, and from Kim and José, was restorative.

Ten years later whenever I hear that title song, I think of that little yellow classroom and my healers—my teacher, my host family, and Kim and José.

One of the more powerful experiences was a weekend trip to Lake Atitlán to meet indigenous groups that had suffered oppressive persecution from the Guatemalan government in the 1980s and 1990s. During the first days of February, the group divided into smaller teams for the infamous Plunge, where they had to put their newly acquired Spanish skills and street savvy into action and discover Guatemala for themselves by talking with the people.

Ashley Ernest, Kristina Kielbon, and Christopher Dennis on the Plunge

Participant Kristina Kielbon shared this Plunge story:

> Ashley (Ernst) Deitz, Christopher Dennis, and I boarded a chicken bus early in the morning in Quetzaltenango, the air still cool and misty. This was the start of our Plunge, which during our preparation for CASP was talked about with bemusement and warning—just about anything could happen. The Plunge was our initiation into the rest of the semester, putting to the test our weeks of language school and learning how to navigate new surroundings. The three of us were headed to *Mazatenango*, several hours directly south of Xela. The area surrounding Xela is more mountainous, and the roads bend and wind wildly down into the lower valleys we were headed to. Not long into our trip our bus stopped suddenly in the middle of a curve and all the men on the bus flooded out the back-emergency door in an instant. Sitting in the middle of the bus I hadn't seen that the bus in front of us had tipped over sideways because they had taken the corner too fast. Now with half the bus cleared out I had a clear view of why all the men had jumped out of the bus. About forty to fifty men

were now pushing and pulling the bus to upright it! And they did! It only took them about five minutes, and the bus was back on its wheels, driving away again. I sat shocked, praying that our driver was more cautious on these roads than that other bus driver had been!

The last few days of this segment were spent in the city of Antigua where the students gained more historical perspective on the country. The group stayed at a colonial retreat center and focused some time on debriefing this first life-changing month in Central America.

Professor Karla Morgan traveled from Tegucigalpa to Copán, a small town bordering Guatemala and Honduras to welcome the CASP group to the Honduras portion of the trip. Students were tired but excited to be placed in their homestays in rural Honduras.

All of the team leaders, including Kim, Karla, former TA and Consultant Dan Plies, and the TAs, had a meeting to discuss the strategic matching of the students with a host family. The host families were located throughout the north, east and west of rural Honduras.

After a few days of exploring the ancient Mayan ruins and receiving final preparation for their rural homestays, Emily, Dan, Kim, and Karla drove throughout different locations to drop each student with their homestay families. Professor Morgan wrote:

> It was hard to let go of my CASP students into such precarious environments. Three of the homestays were more than two hours away from the small town of Copán. The problem was not the long distance, but the poor infrastructure and almost nonexistent roads adequate for a vehicle. I left them all at the side of a dirt road, outside their homes, always surrounded by kids. Some of my students just went on playing soccer with the boys, on the dirt road, with a ball made out of rags. Ten days later, TA Emily and I initiated our journey to visit each CASP student and to meet with the host families again. We had problems with our initial transportation, thus, at the last minute, we found a new driver. In 2008, few of the host families had phones, therefore, it was impossible to call in advance to indicate the time of our arrival. One of our students was out in the coffee field with his host father, and we had to wait for approximately six hours until his return. In another town, we arrived at 8:00 p.m. This community had no electricity; thus, most of the town was in the dark at our arrival. The student and all the members of her host family were sleeping at the time of our visit. Overall, every CASP student was well adjusted and happy to be there, loving their experiences with their host families and new friends. All of them talked to me about their culture shock during the first few days, but also about their fairly fast adjustment to daily activities. Some of them traveled every day to the coffee fields; some others went to the only school in town to teach English; and some spent their time in the kitchens of their neighbors.

During this period in Honduras, the students threw themselves into a variety of service projects with groups like the Center for Christian Development, World Vision, and Habitat for Humanity. Throughout their rural experiences, they reflected on their work and service through an experiential learning course, "Development Strategies in Central America," led by Michael LeRoy in which they explored the positive as well as the not so helpful aspects of "development." The group finished the Honduran segment with a few days in the capital city of Tegucigalpa.

One student shares her memory about food:

> One of the first things I remember when coming to Tegucigalpa after our month-long homestays in the *campo* of Honduras, was greedily eating a small plate of salad on the rooftop deck of our hotel. The food in the *campo* had been simple and heavy—not a fresh vegetable in sight for an entire month and my body was in pain. Most days I had eaten stacks of fresh tortillas, beans, and a dense, salty cheese. The only times I did get vegetables they had been boiled within an inch of becoming mush to ensure that any possible parasites were killed, so I didn't get sick. I haven't taken the abundance of fresh, crisp vegetables for granted since! I still remember my month without the crunch of raw vegetables every time I make a salad and say a small 'thank you' in my heart.

Jeremy Molinaro shares quality conversation with a boy in Guatemala

The group spent most of the month of March in Costa Rica. First the group traveled to the capital city of San José. Then they spent a week at the "free-spirited" permaculture ecological farm of Punta Mona on the coast. They were both frustrated by the devastation that humanity was causing to God's creation, but also inspired by the small, yet significant, practices developed on the farm. During the rest of the time in Costa Rica, special attention was given to the place of religion in the Latin American culture as observed in Easter Holy Week. The Easter weekend was designated as "Family Weekend," and many parents and siblings visited the CASP group and were able to learn about Latin American Catholicism and ecotourism.

The Nicaraguan experience began with a week in Managua, followed by two different homestays. First, students lived with rural families for four days. Then they traveled to another rural area outside of the city of Dario for an additional stay with the group Seeds of Learning. Dan Plies also arranged for the excellent host family stays through his work with Seeds of Learning in Nicaragua. Professor Jim Hunt taught a course on the history of Central America. He urged and taught the students to have "historical mindedness" and to practice "appreciative inquiry." This last concept is "the asking of questions without rendering moral judgments or asking a question to seek information rather than to evaluate." Students had to produce five historical narratives on what they had observed on the program:

1. The Indigenous Heritage of all Central America, especially Copán

2. Spanish Colonial Influence, especially in the cities of Córdoba, Cartago, and San Salvador

3. The Formation and Development of a Nation

4. A Host Family's History

5. A Village History

During the El Salvador portion, the students took the course "Globalization, Ecology and Gender in Central America" taught by Economics Professor Karla Morgan. The group spent most of the time in San Salvador, where they visited several organizations such as the National Entrepreneur Center for Small Businesses, The Center for Women and Business Development, the House of Deputies, and The Central Bank of El Salvador. Students had the opportunity to discuss issues on foreign investment, the new role of female participation in the labor force, monetary policy in a dollarized economy, and business development using remittances from immigrant workers. The group also heard the sad but courageous stories from many poor Salvadorans who shared about their lives and struggles.

This group returned to the US with more questions than answers on a variety of issues from politics, to justice, to foreign policy, to faith, to vocational calling. After an intense week of debriefing back on campus, faculty leader, Kim Hernández, led the students in a reflection on Monseñor Oscar Romero's legacy in Central America that wrestled with the injustice and powerlessness of the present and aspired to the hope of the future in God's hands.

2010: CASP Gives Birth to Whitworth's Costa Rica Center

FOR MANY YEARS THERE was a growing desire to increase the opportunities for Whitworth students to study in Central America. CASP was usually offered on a three-year cycle, which did not meet the increasing demands of a growing student body ever more desirous of studying abroad. The CASP experience had been so successful in transforming students' lives that Whitworth's leadership explored the possibility of developing a campus in Costa Rica. Provost Michael LeRoy took the initiative to present the proposal to President Bill Robinson and the Board of Trustees. After considerable prayer and discussion, the decision was made to move forward with the project. A suitable property was found in the cloud forest above Heredia, Costa Rica.

Whitworth University's Costa Rica Center

Classes began at the Costa Rica Center (CRC) in the fall semester of 2010. Professor Lindy Scott was the Director of the Center and Professor Dinorah Scott taught many of the Spanish courses. Each semester students were not only able to take Spanish classes at their specific level, they could also take Core 350 (*Corazón 350*) and a Creation Care ecology course that met general education requirements for Whitworth. Professors from the Spokane campus came down on a rotating basis for short-term or semester-long stints and offered special courses that combined their areas of expertise with the Costa Rican reality. For example, Patrick Van Inwegen taught his Non-Violent Defense and Conflict Resolution course with an interesting focus on Costa Rica's unique status as a country without a military, and Art Professor Katie Creyts taught classes on Latin American muralism. The town of San Rafael, Heredia even allowed Whitworth students to paint a mural around a brand-new park. To this day, people admire the beauty of that art! Excellent Costa Rican professors like Fernando Montero intertwined their deep, Christian faith with their areas of specialization such as Spanish, ecology, music, culture, and literature.

Key components of CASP were incorporated into the Costa Rica Center's program. The Center's staff included graduate teaching assistants who partnered with Lindy, Dinorah, and the other faculty and staff onsite to create excellent programming and accompany the students well. These TAs were CASP alum or Spanish majors with other Latin American study abroad experience, who knew the area, not to mention the cultural immersion experience, very well.

Although students would study at the campus during the day, they lived with host families around the town of San Rafael. Professor Dinorah Scott and the graduate assistants set up excellent host family relations, and as a consequence, the experiences gave students the chance to become part of their new community. Even years later, some students and their host families maintain frequent communication.

Every student had the opportunity to work in an internship one day a week. Some of the favorite internships included medical clinics, local schools, the Roble-alto farm, and bakeries. Semester long programs included one-week trips to both Nicaragua and to Cuba so that students could obtain a broader understanding of the region. Significant differences between the neighboring countries of Nicaragua and Costa Rica led to fabulous discussions on history, politics, war, and US relations with nations in the region.

The Costa Rica Center offered a special Jan Term course for Whitworth freshmen who had been admitted with honors. Theology professor Terry McGonigal offered his Shalom course and Biology professor Grant Casady created a course on Creation Care. Summer courses were also offered. A total of sixty-three students took classes at the CRC that first year. Enrollment increased every year to over one hundred students in Academic Year 2013/2014.

Provost Michael LeRoy teaching the first cohort of the CRC in the fall of 2010

A significant drop in enrollment back on the Spokane campus in the fall of 2013 caused the administration to make tough decisions on budgetary cuts. Provost Michael LeRoy had left Whitworth to take the president position at Calvin College, and without his strong support for international studies, it was decided to close the Costa Rica campus. As a result, the number of Whitworth students studying abroad generally, and in Latin America specifically, began to drop. The number of students majoring or minoring in Spanish has also notably declined.

2011: The Enduring and Inspiring Example of Archbishop Romero

CASP 2011 Cohort: Annie Aeschbacher, Peter Bratt, Katie (Carlson) Bratt, Bryce Covey, Sagen Eatwell, Stacey Eyman, Stephen Eyman, Breanna Feddes, Kylie Grader, Ali Johnston, Aaron Korthuis, Taylor (Faranda) Korthuis, Andrew Lewis, Lars Nelson, Laura Reardon, Alex Spencer, Catherine (Cook) Tobey, Erica Yoder, and Jennifer Zavala. Teaching Assistants—Danielle Wegman (CASP 2005) and Travis Walker (CASP 2008). Faculty Leaders—Kim Hernández, Lindy Scott, Terry McGonigal, Michael LeRoy, and Karla Morgan.

During the month of January, the CASP students spent one week in Spokane in an intensive orientation course with professor Kim Hernández and Assistant Dean Esther Louie. They then flew to Guatemala to do advanced language and culture study at the *Casa Xelajú* Language Institute in Quetzaltenango. In addition to their five hour a day individualized classes at the Institute, the students participated in many extra-curricular activities and ministry outreach projects led by Kim and her husband José. Highlights included traditional Mayan weaving, cooking with local friend Isabel, and serving at Xelajú's after school center, *La Pedrera*.

Xela children on the way to La Pedrera

CASP 2011 established a ministry partnership with InnerCHANGE (*Cambio Interno*) in Xela. This organization is an apostolic order among the poor under the leadership of CRM: Church Resource Ministries, which establishes communities of missionaries living in poor, marginalized neighborhoods around the world—places most people want to avoid or ignore. Their teams seek to live out the good news of Jesus among the poor, both with words and deeds. The team in Xela is led by local residents who are family members of Doña Olga, who has hosted Terry McGonigal, Kim Hernández and her family, and several CASP TAs for many years. InnerCHANGE in Guatemala focuses on street kids, tutoring, bible studies, women's prison visitation, and deported immigrants. InnerCHANGE allowed the CASP group to serve in their outreach to shoeshine boys who live on the streets of Xela, and also gave invaluable talks to the group about the social realities of the poor in Guatemala and the missionary experience of doing incarnational ministry. Since 2011, every CASP group has served with InnerCHANGE in Xela.

The next month was spent in Honduras. Each student lived with a rural *campesino* family separated from the other students. The goals included: learning about rural Central America, depending upon God's provision through one's new host family and community, and growing in one's practical Spanish skills. Other than a brief visit of the students in their homestays by TAs Danielle Wegman and Travis Walker and Professor Lindy Scott, the students were "on their own." Throughout the many generations of CASP, some students have found that the Honduran rural homestay segment has been the hardest, yet most transformative, component of the CASP program. Participant Stacey Eyman describes the month's experiences quite well:

Stacey Eyman toasting tortillas

After leaving Guatemala, our group spread out in separate host families across the country of Honduras. For me, it was lonely to be separated from my travel partners, but I quickly became integrated into a supportive host family. My family appreciated that I was there to learn and wanted to provide every experience they could for me to understand life in their town. They included me on trips to get *leña*, sent me to grind corn into *masa*, shared how to bake in an earth oven, and fed me more than I could hold! All of my needs were met although I could barely communicate. I am forever grateful for their acceptance and guidance at a time when I was so dependent and vulnerable. When our group finally reunited in Tegucigalpa, we had different stories to share.

Some people brought back head lice (which would later be shared throughout the group), one of our group members left the program to return home, one member brought back a sampling of arts and crafts her host neighbors had taught her to make, my brother (whom I had the privilege of sharing this trip with) had been to the hospital with dehydration, others lost weight, and we all had bug bites—including ticks. Everyone took away something different from their month in Honduras, both physically and personally. The take-away I still treasure most is the relationship that was formed with my host family.

The Honduran rural experience has had long range effects on the participants. Andrew Lewis described that impact over five years later:

> The CASP program was part of why I chose to go to Whitworth, and it has been formative for me in more ways than I can count. The most important phase of the trip for me was my time in a homestay in rural Honduras. There, as a ninteen-year-old on my first trip to a non-Western country, I was able to learn lessons beyond the "pinecone curtain." The simple everyday interactions with members of the community were an important part of my personal formation. I learned how to bridge cultural divides and how to better empathize with those of different backgrounds than my own. In this time, I gained a new understanding of the Holy Spirit's work in my life and engaged in discussions of faith and hope, politics and suffering, and everyday joys and pains. I now carry their stories with me as they help me navigate through whatever culture I find myself immersed in. My experience has given me tools to see through cultural barriers and look to the heart of what God is doing in unique corners of the globe. In my travels since graduation, I have had the privilege to travel to Guatemala, Palestine/Israel, Western and Central Europe, and now to Brazil. I am touched by my CASP experience to seek to understand people's stories and to address others' deepest concerns through everyday interactions and as a part of God's great work of justice and salvation.

Whitworth's Chaplain and Theology Professor Terry McGonigal led the next segment in Nicaragua on Latin American Theology. Students were challenged as they realized that the Bible not only teaches personal salvation, but also emphasizes social justice, structural sin, and communities of faith. Years later, Terry described the life-changing experience which was the catalyst for the group in Nicaragua:

> A tragic event deeply affected the group in the first few days in Nicaragua. The day after the group arrived in Managua, we received word that Peter Bratt's mother was gravely ill. When we received this news, we suspended all activities for the rest of the day and returned to our hotel where we gathered for prayer, small group discussion, and most of all tried to support Peter in the best way possible. That night we received the dreadful news that Peter's mother had died. Peter received the news via a phone call from Michael LeRoy,

Whitworth Provost and member of the CASP teaching team. Freddy Méndez, our Nicaraguan liaison, arranged immediate transportation to the Managua airport. Terry McGonigal and Aaron Korthuis accompanied Peter, along with Freddy's brother who stayed with us all night as we made flight arrangements for very early the next morning.

After saying goodbye to Peter, Aaron and Terry returned to the hotel where a theological firestorm was raging. Basic questions were at the forefront of everyone's hearts and minds: "Where is God in the midst of such tragedy? Peter's mom was a translator in a health clinic for the rural poor. Why would God take her? Why weren't our prayers answered with miraculous healing? "How do we make sense of the unexplainable suffering in our world?" Some students had prayed ceaselessly since the moment we heard about the illness. Others had scoffed at the efficacy of prayer. The group splintered into two distinct camps of believers and skeptics (some switching sides), and the divide influenced the rest of the CASP experience for every one of the students.

Looking back now eight years later, many of those same questions remain, because they raise issues about which we humans are so limited and finite in our understanding of God's ways. And the lessons of time and distance still work their way into the story. Peter's father has recently re-married. Peter and Katie (Bratt) were married and now live in Colorado Springs with their first child. They use their intercultural skills in teaching and ministry. Aaron and Taylor (Faranda) are also married and pursuing their legal careers, still seeking justice in the face of seemingly incessant injustice. I had the joy of officiating both ceremonies, and truly experienced how our sorrows can be turned into dancing as those celebrations became CASP 2011 reunions. The conversations with so many CASP alums were rich in meaning and connection as vocations continue to be formed.

The community we experienced together during CASP, especially after this life-transforming experience of tragedy, molds every one of our lives to this day. None of us can endure alone, and in the worst of circumstances, it is community that carries us. Suffering is the crucible in which our souls are refined as we are cared for by others when we have no capacity to care for ourselves. What this group has gone on to do since CASP 2011 is testimony to the relentless and mysterious work of God!

During the El Salvador portion, led by Economics Professor Karla Morgan, the group completed two brief homestays. First, the group stayed five days in the small town of *Suchitoto, Cuscatlán*, thirty-seven miles from San Salvador. There, students stayed with host families, and interviewed several women who were owners and managers of small businesses in the downtown area. All the activities and homestays were organized by the "*Escuela Pájaro Flor.*" The second homestay involved four days in *San Pablo Tacachico, La Libertad*, twenty-two miles from San Salvador. This is a new settlement of less than 100 families developed after the Civil War. Most families in town were exiled in Honduras since the 1980s, and the students had the opportunity to hear about their lives and struggles in exile, and their journey to return to El Salvador and to gain access to land. The rest of the time, the group stayed in San Salvador, where they visited the Center for Women and Business Development, the US Embassy, the House of Deputies, and the Central Bank of El Salvador.

Students learned about foreign investment, gender issues in economic development, and business development using remittances from immigrant workers. Students also met with leaders from ARENA and FMLN, the two largest political parties in El Salvador.

Lake Atitlán

Participant Kylie Grader aptly summarizes the experiences of this group:

> When Terry McGonigal told the CASP 2011 group, "This experience is always hard, but this group is experiencing devastation unlike I've seen before," I knew we had a real opportunity to be shaped and formed for the rest of our lives. Not only did this group of twenty students experience the joy and turmoil of life in Central America, we also were subjected to personal grief from family losses, as well as losses and reshaping of faith at every turn. The group that eagerly boarded the flight to Guatemala City in January, was forever changed as we returned to the comforts of Spokane in May. For better or worse, life seemed to hit us all at once and without apology. Michael Leroy

was able to capture this bizarre experience in a phrase I've held dear—"We live between a curse and a promise"—and since our CASP journey, we've all had to understand how to navigate the in-between, having seen what we've seen and knowing what we know.

Discernment of God´s will and the honing of one´s understanding of vocation have been hallmarks of CASP for four decades. Participant Jennifer Zavala describes this process in her walk with God:

> Although I am constantly learning more about God's purpose for my life, my time on CASP is a fundamental piece of who I am today. When I first came to Whitworth, I had a basic understanding of what my passions were—Spanish, Latin America, my faith, and helping others. However, I was unsure of how to engage those passions in a degree program at Whitworth and, eventually, in a career. Although I was settled in my chosen degree programs as a junior at Whitworth, CASP gave me the opportunity to better define my calling and to turn my passions into actions. Through CASP I gained insight into the lives of both rural and urban populations, political history, current events, theology, and international development in Central America. For the first time in my life, I was surrounded by a group of peers and mentors who were passionate about the same issues and who challenged me to live in solidarity with the poor, fight for social justice, and work to make the world a better place. There is rarely a day when I do not think about the people I met, the places I went, and the things I learned during my CASP experience. Today, because of CASP, I get to continue building on my experience in Central America in my day-to-day job at an international development company.

2014: A Shift to Vocational Training through Internships

2014 CASP Cohort: Niko Aberle, Melissa (Andrews) Abbott, Eli Deitz, Kelsey Grant, Dana LeRoy, Mirra Matheson, Lizzie Williams, and Ben Wiseman. Teaching Assistant—Sagen Eatwell (CASP 2011). Faculty Leaders: Terry McGonigal, Lindy Scott and Kim Hernández.

A significant decision was made regarding CASP after the return of the 2011 group. The positive fruits of CASP were readily recognized: a growing awareness of Central American realities, improved Spanish communication abilities, an increasing appreciation and love for Central Americans, a recognition of the impact, all too often negative, of the Christian Church and the United States government in Central America. Many students wanted to return to Latin America, or work in Hispanic communities in the US, after their graduation. There was a realization that students had increased in their "academic" knowledge of Central America, but this was not always accompanied by a similar increase in their practical skills. It was decided that an in-depth internship program in Nicaragua would enhance the students' experience and prepare them better for their vocations, careers, and service, whether that be with Latin Americans, with Hispanics in the United States or with whomever else God would put in their paths. To accomplish this, students would be required to spend a summer or semester at Whitworth's new Costa Rica Center prior to their participation in CASP. A name change was also needed to better capture this change in the program. CASP became the Central America Study *and Service* Program. It was recognized that this greater time commitment would reduce the number of students who could fit the program into their four-year Whitworth experience. Nevertheless, those who could only spare one semester would still have the opportunity to study at the Costa Rica Center. The first cohort under the new format consisted of eight students.

Niko, Melissa and Ben chose to spend the summer of 2013 at Whitworth's Costa Rica Center. They spent the entire summer with Costa Rican host families and took courses in Spanish, Latin American Culture, and a course on Latin American Short Stories. They also had the opportunity to participate in internships. Ben describes his summer internship as follows, "I interned daily at the *Clínica Bíblica* in Heredia. I shadowed the family practice physician and assisted in the pharmacy. The experience gave me confidence to participate in Costa Rican life instead of simply observing the country I was studying." Melissa appreciated various aspects of her summer experience. She writes, "During the summer that I was at the Costa Rica Center, I interned at a local elementary school, being a teacher's aide, instructing an English class, and doing a sociology independent study on the education system in Costa Rica."

The other five CASPians (Eli, Kelsey, Dana, Mirra and Lizzie) participated in the CRC's regular fall semester, making their study abroad a full-year experience. The home stays were an essential component of their experience. For example, Dana LeRoy lived with Antonio and Silvia Benavides. Antonio is a Costa Rican who went to Nicaragua in the 1980s to participate in the civil war. There Antonio met Silvia who was a commander of the Sandinista rebel troop, and later, they got married. After the war ended, they returned to Costa Rica and pursued justice through their jobs and their service to the indigenous populations.

Weekly internships were also a significant part of the fall semester program. These were helpful in the vocational discernment process. Some internships had unexpected results. Dana LeRoy served Nicaraguan immigrants together with Whitworth student Erica Ramos-Thompson in La Carpio, a poor neglected area of San José. Their ministry together later developed into a deeper friendship and romance. They were married in 2016. Both work in aspects of international education, social justice, and advocacy.

Some of the most helpful courses were Latin American Culture taught by Costa Rican adjunct professor Fernando Montero and Latin American History taught by Whitworth history professor Rafaela Acevedo-Field. The CRC students also took week-long trips to Cuba and Nicaragua where the CASPians gained helpful insights about the politics and people of the region prior to their CASP experience.

Cerro de la Cruz overlooking Antigua, Guatemala

During January, the CASP participants went to Quetzaltenango, Guatemala (Xela) to study language and culture at *Casa Xelajú* Language School and take part in a variety of community service activities. Graduate Assistant Sagen Eatwell ably supervised the students with support from the *Xelajú* staff and local ministry friends. Both professors, Lindy Scott and Kim Hernández, had medical emergencies that kept them from traveling in January.

Here is an excerpt from Sagen's letter to parents near the end of the month in Guatemala:

> Each morning the students begin with five hours of individual, conversational Spanish class. For our students, who are high-level speakers already, this time is not only focused on grammar and vocabulary, but is intentionally very content driven. Though each student's learning experience varies, all the lessons go beyond normal classroom Spanish. On weekdays after class and a walk home for lunch, we have visited the "miracle city" of Almolonga, met with the local branch of an incarnational ministry named InnerChange that works primarily with shoe-shine boys in the Central Park, learned to salsa dance together, and shared conversation about the Mayan traditional worldview over a ceremonial fire with a local spiritual leader. Last weekend we made an excursion to Lago Atitlán, a primarily indigenous area drastically impacted by the 40-year civil war, where we met with a women's textile cooperative and visited

what is traditionally one of the most important locations of the semester, Santiago de Atitlán. As of today, everyone is healthy and becoming well-adjusted to the cultural and academic differences of immersion/situational learning. We did have one case of amoebas last week, but with the correct care, the student recovered within a day of diagnosis. Based on my group observations and individual conversations with students, it has taken a week or so for everyone to get in the groove of being in a new Latin American culture, using more Spanish than ever, and being bombarded by an incredible amount of new information. We are truly asking a lot of the students, and they are commendably getting very good at the practice of working hard to get the most out of this unique time.

Student Niko Aberle wrote a powerful reflection after Lago Atitlán:

> This evening at dinner, we found out that Pope Francis officially recognized mass as it has been conducted in two Mayan languages in the Mexican state of Chiapas for the past seven years. For us, this was a timely coincidence. Earlier today we learned and celebrated the martyrdom of Stanley Rother. "A'plas," as he was referred to in the indigenous Tzutuhil, was a Catholic priest from Oklahoma who lived for many years among the Mayan people of Santiago, on the shores of Lake Atitlán. This is the place we visited today: the Roman Catholic Church in Santiago. On the morning of July 28, 1981, soldiers from the US-backed Guatemalan military shot and killed him as he was praying in a side room. I cannot speak for all of us when I say this, but the heartless irony of these events grew a sadness inside of me. Gratefully, the shadow of irony was dwarfed by the light of this man's life and the strength of the Mayan people around him, the people that we saw today.

From February through early May, the CASP students each had a full-time internship and homestay placement in Nicaragua that had been set up by our Nicaragua In-Country Consultant, Freddy Méndez. He had worked for many years as a staff worker and then as the Director of the Nicaraguan student ministry associated with the International Fellowship of Evangelical Students (IFES). He then worked for the Centro Nehemías in the area of microfinance. As a consequence, his network with Christian ministries and other NGOs was an incredible resource that he used to place CASP students in internships nicely connected to their major fields of study.

Kelsey Grant shares about her work with children at the *Hogar Puente de Amistad* (The Bridge of Friendship Home):

> I interned at *Hogar Puente de Amistad*, a nonprofit organization in Managua, Nicaragua that provides a home and resources to children who were orphaned, abandoned, or mistreated. It also provides additional resources to children who live with their families but face social and economic hardships. When I arrived in the morning, I assisted Maria Alicia, the lead caretaker for the

youngest children, in preparing the children for school. After we walked them to class, I cared for the two one-year-olds, as Maria Alicia washed clothes and cleaned. Our typical activities included learning to walk, reading Dora in English and Spanish, and interacting with the adolescents. I occasionally assisted the older children with homework, English practice, and hair braiding. After Maria Alicia and I picked up the children from school, we served them lunch, assisted them with homework, and left plenty of time to play.

My most treasured memory from this experience came from three siblings who were brought to us from an abusive situation. They stayed with us for two weeks before they were adopted by their aunt. During those two weeks, I was in charge of welcoming them to the Home. The first few days, they expressed the trauma they had experienced through aggressive actions and painful words. But I only endured the hitting, kicking, and name calling for a few days. In the Home, they quickly picked up on the fact that the adults and other children loved them and were there to care for them. When they realized this, they were able to be vulnerable children again. They became attached to me, as I was to them. A group of students came from the US on a mission trip while they were there, and the students took us all to the beach for a day. As I sat on the beach, the youngest of the siblings sat in front of me. As the waves rolled up, she would run behind me and scream, grabbing on to me for protection. Then she'd giggle and sit back in front of me to repeat it all over again. In this moment, I got to share in the joy of a four-year-old girl who had faced enormous cruelties but was given new hope by a community who cared.

Kelsey Grant with some of the children at the Hogar

Ben Wiseman connects his internship with changes that have happened more recently in his life:

> During my Nicaraguan internship, I worked with *Fundación San Lucas Nicaragua*. The organization was based in Jinotepe, Carazo, and coordinated public health efforts in the rural communities of Carazo. I worked with an engineer to survey the condition of latrines, water filtration systems, and wells in the rural communities. I also accompanied the engineer as he worked towards completion of two solar-powered water distribution systems. These projects involved work in the office and the field which helped me understand the extensive coordination of communication, funding, and reporting needed to complete projects in the rural communities. My co-workers at the organization encouraged me to look at the sociological aspects of water and sanitation issues: Why do some families use their latrine as a tool shed? What are essential elements of a community water commission? These questions fascinated me and contributed to my shift away from technical sciences and into community-based work. Four years after my internship in Nicaragua, I am working with an agricultural development program in Haiti. The job challenges me to look for the cultural and social aspects of the work I do, a skill I first honed during my CASP internship.

Melissa (Andrews) Abbott describes her internship in the following way:

> I spent my internship working at *Villa Esperanza*, a residential treatment program for at-risk adolescent girls that had previously lived in and around the city of Managua's main garbage dump. These girls came to the Villa seeking refuge and education, escaping forms of unhealthy and dangerous environments where they had experienced or were at risk of physical abuse, sex trafficking, rape, drug abuse, and malnutrition. During those months, I spent every one of my days with the thirty or so girls that called the Villa their home. It was one of the most difficult, exhausting and, at times, discouraging, experiences of my life, but the joys and the lessons I still carry with me far outweighed the difficulties. If I had been given a specific job title, it likely would have sounded something like personal tutor, English teacher, group translator, constant playmate, kitchen aide, assistant to the psychologist or *'mejor amiga'* to all the various girls I interacted with. While my specific intern duties successfully provided me with a challenging and vocationally discerning experience that confirmed my desire to pursue a career in social work, what proved to be the most significant aspects of my internship were the relationships that I formed with both the young girls who lived at the safe home and the staff that I worked with. The people I came to know and friendships I formed helped remove some of the gloried aspects that I previously had of "callings," "dreams," or "desires." These people taught me that living passionately and faithfully is a

lot simpler, a lot harder, and yet a lot more life giving than I had ever imagined. Three years later, and rarely a day will go by that I don't think of all of them.

Melissa Andrews and a young resident at Villa Esperanza

Eli Deitz reflected on his experience during his time in a remote rural area on a coffee farm:

My routine has been good on the farm but sometimes it's difficult to incorporate myself into the daily work of the farm. Sometimes Don Moisés insists that I don't have to work and that I should go study and rest. Sometimes Doña Carmen feels bad as a host mom when she sees me working so hard. This family still doesn't see me in the way that I see myself—as one who has come to work like everyone else who works on the farm. For them, it makes them feel bad to see me as a laborer. Maybe because I'm a foreigner. Maybe because they know I'm rich. Maybe because they are such kind and loving hosts. But this ambiguity has been difficult. I want to work, and they don't want to see me as a worker. But I just keep on working, and I keep assuring my hosts that I am very happy working; that's why I came to Nicaragua. And there is so much work to be done by everyone on the farm. That excites me. And despite the ambiguity, I will maintain good communication and show a good work ethic, and that way I will keep working hard.

Over spring break, students participated in an academic retreat in the historic city of Granada. Chaplain Terry McGonigal taught sessions regarding the Central American Church and Professor Lindy Scott led various classes about Latin American Studies. Sufficient time was given for sharing and prayer. Some modifications in the internships were implemented and time for reflection and input was organized by Freddy Méndez.

During the first ten days of May, the students went to the Costa Rica Center to debrief and to finish their academic coursework. They also gave a special presentation at the CRC for the Whitworth students who were studying there as well as for their previous host families. A special part of their presentation was a comical monologue by Eli Deitz in which he encouraged a general reconciliation between Nicaraguans and Costa Ricans, by pointing out specific prejudices between them and how to overcome them. The CASPians also had the privilege to interact with Professor Emeritus Jim Hunt and his wife Linda who were teaching at the CRC that spring. Jim had taught Latin American history for several CASP programs.

The student evaluations of the new internship model were overwhelmingly positive. Although there were the typical wrinkles that needed to be ironed out, students unanimously recommended that the internship format be continued. It was also decided to put CASP on a two-year cycle so that more students could have the opportunity to experience it.

2016: Going Beyond Our Comfort Zones in Guatemala and Nicaragua

2016 CASP COHORT: MICAH Allred, Dakota Bauman, Jessica Baumgartner, Karli Charlton, Rachael Eaton, Camina Hirota, Hannah Howell, Grace Klinkhammer, Morgen Layton, Hannah McCollum, Anne Marie Noll, Katie Noll, Emily Teeple and Katrina Ulnick. Teaching Assistant—Dana LeRoy (CASP 2014). Faculty Leaders: Lindy Scott and Kim Hernández.

Given that the Costa Rica Center's activities had been suspended by the university, students did their fall preparation work on the Spokane campus. All of the students had a strong background in Spanish. Most of them took the course on Latin American

Culture and Civilization (in Spanish) taught by Lindy Scott, while others did independent studies on aspects of Nicaraguan society. All of the students participated in the Prep Course taught by Kim Hernández, which provided intercultural competency training, team building activities, and a variety of academic and personal preparation topics. Students were able to meet with Ron and Marianne Frase, the founders of CASP, in order to get some historical perspective regarding the program. Some also met with CASP alumna Leslie Vogel to understand the recent elections in Guatemala.

CASP 2016 began in Guatemala with the traditional month of intensive language and culture training at *Casa Xelajú*, along with host family stays, community service projects, and many cultural activities. Lindy Scott accompanied the group and arranged many guest speakers for the group. One poignant reflection on the group's time in Guatemala was shared by student Morgen Layton:

> Xela, Guatemala is one of the most historically rich places I have ever visited. Every corner I turned, new stories awaited me. Beyond what I could see, there was even more to be learned. The Catholic church buildings tell stories of the past one cannot fathom from merely reading a history book. And so, the journey through Xela began January 3, 2016, as we CASPians were exposed to a new culture and a new way of life. Little did we know what the following three and a half weeks had in store for us. Xela is not a town I would consider a tourist attraction; at least not for those looking to enjoy a beachfront view. However, for fourteen students looking to learn, Xela was just the place to be. Hiking a volcano at 3:30 am, traveling, and experiencing the culture with our host families left an imprint on my heart I will carry forever. I think my group members all feel the same. Education through living in Guatemala helped equip CASPians of 2016 for tomorrow, by the experiences of today.
>
> Two thirty in the morning comes early, even after a good night's rest. One Saturday morning, part of our CASP group began the climb to reach the top of Volcán María. Walking a narrow path with headlamps was not something I had anticipated taking part in on this trip. It was well worth the view! During the entire climb to the top, we encouraged one another, and even with sleepy eyes and fatigue, managed to engage in deep conversation and reflect on what we were feeling after the first week in Xela. Reaching the top was like no other accomplishment in my life. Tired and exhausted, the answer written on my fellow CASPian faces was one of disbelief and complete astonishment that we had arrived. From the top we could see beyond to another volcano that was actively spewing out red beauty. I must ask, God, how did you image to create such a beautiful place such as Xela? From the top of the volcano we could see in every direction, as if the sky had no limit. Merely seeing other people who had made the trek up was a site. A three-and-a-half-hour hike takes commitment, especially when the descent is still to come. The morning frost had been warmed by the sun's rays and the descent was rather slippery. Also unexpected was seeing women trek up the steep volcano in sandals, with

chickens, and some carrying infants. It was explained that these Mayan women believed they could be closer to God, the closer toward the sky they moved. The chickens were for sacrifices. Upon arriving at the bottom, I thanked God for our safe excursion.

Yesterday was all I knew before today arrived. When arriving in Xela, I was overwhelmed by thoughts, feelings, and emotions due to the quality of living. Traveling exposed our group to the reality that there is far more than what we see in the US. It is not that I was oblivious, rather my imagination of what Guatemala might be was very off. How can one imagine more than what they know? Prior, I was not accustomed to seeing people urinate in the street whenever and wherever or dodging dog feces on every sidewalk. Being guided through the city streets, we arrived at a cemetery one afternoon. We were greeted by the site of fabulous, intricate, hand crafted . . . dead people homes. These tombs, some the size of small homes, were decorated with flowers, some painted, and many accompanied by cement, 3-feet-tall or taller angels. Our guide informed us the angels without heads (all the angels) many people believed were headless due to the work of Satan, as it would have taken someone with a very tall ladder who was extremely strong to break the cement sculptures. This gave us a lot to ponder!

Living with our host families allowed us to learn by action, emotion, and feeling. Mi compañera de casa and I had a unique situation; we had the opportunity to live with two different host families. We were deeply culturally enriched in the last two weeks of our trip. Our second host family consisted of our host mom and four sons. Her eldest two children were married with children and lived elsewhere. It is interesting that in many Latin American homes, it is not uncommon to have the children live at home, even into their late twenties and early thirties. Our new family was welcoming. They demonstrated love of a different magnitude, and we were even invited to attend *Inicio de la novena* the first night we stayed with them. This is a Catholic tradition; whereby family members unite to celebrate the life of a family member on the one-year mark after their death for nine evenings. The last night of the event which marks one year since death is celebrated in a church with mass. During *Inicio de la novena* songs are sung, a sermon is given, prayer is said, and morning comes. This was a beautiful reflection on the meaning of life and death.

I have much to be thankful for regarding the time spent in Xela. Exposure to the language, meeting new people, hearing real life stories, that while extremely sad, shed light on how to make a better tomorrow. There was not a single day I would have wanted any other way. Learning about Catholicism, for me, was the most powerful piece of new education I obtained. It had a very profound impact on the way I see religion, which affected the perspective I had on being in a relationship with Christ. It all changed for me because I realized regardless of language, belief, religion, culture, or skin color, God created us all. Each human life has the same value as another. It was no longer, in my mind, two groups—those going to heaven and those going to hell. Human life had the meaning it was meant to have. I know Jesus used my time in Xela to help me grow. Our encounters with the most exquisite Catholic churches was one of many ways. Looking in awe at the work that went into making such beautiful structures, I could only imagine the hard work and sweat that was required. Their brilliant colors made them stand out, unable to be missed. We could have stood outside the church all day and still not noticed every detail. There were more stories to be told from inside the churches, too. Statues of Jesus and Mary and other figures lined the walls. They were like glass boxes within the walls that we were able to look into. One must only look to know Jesus once lived, flesh and bones, for Christ. This was an unexpected confirmation of the realness of Jesus Christ that has been the foundation of my faith for many years.

Hannah Howell and Grace Klinkhammer with their host family in Xela

Light shining on Guatemalan artisanship in Momostenango

The Nicaraguan portion began with an orientation retreat in Managua led by CASP consultant Freddy Méndez. He led sessions on Nicaraguan culture and church life as well as suggestions regarding living with host families and working in internships for three months. Freddy told the students that Nicaraguans have a big sense of humor, and therefore, the students should not take jokes personally.

The internship experience was the heart of the program, and students participated in a broad array of opportunities. Micah Allred describes his internship like this:

> I worked as a legal scribe for a volunteer lawyer in El Tuma-La Dalia, a rural municipality northeast of Matagalpa. The organization that I worked for is called *Centro Cristiano de Derechos Humanos* (affiliated with the Nehemiah Project), and my work involved accompanying families to court proceedings, meeting with the local police, helping mothers petition for alimony, and facilitating mediations between conflicting parties.

CASP internships frequently placed students outside of their "comfort zones" and required them to learn new roles. Emily Teeple writes, "My work at *Clínica Vida* mostly focused on lab duties such as drawing blood, doing microscope work, and preparing/running blood tests; however, I also got hands-on practice with ultrasounds, running EKGs, and aiding in patient evaluations with the general doctor. "

Katrina Ulnick describes her various tasks and opportunities with the *Fundación San Lucas*:

> As a Cross-Cultural Studies (Political Science emphasis) and Theology (Environmental Studies track) double major, I would say my internship experience was the ideal mix of both of my fields of study. I worked specifically in the Food Security sector, cooking with families in the community, attending conferences on sustainable agriculture, and helping my bosses run seminars on nutrition and ways to maximize their resources against the negative effects of climate change. In addition to a mixture of those jobs, I also had the primary task of planting corn for the organization. I planted two beds, one with compost and one without, and measured their growth. This data was then brought to the surrounding communities in hopes that they would be more encouraged to try out compost as a new technique. As a Cross-Cultural Studies major, planting corn for a job, not simply for leisure, was completely out of my comfort zone. I was afraid I would not be able to produce the results they wanted. To my ease, the beauty of nature is that it does most of the work for you. I got great hands-on experience with the help of my co-workers and was able to take in invaluable data for San Lucas that my other team members did not have time to carry out. My interest in creation care as part of my calling as a Christian was strengthened through the environmental awareness the organization was committed to and spread to neighboring communities. I was able to observe the insides of how a non-profit was run. And finally, I was sustained by the faith of both my Catholic and Protestant coworkers each Monday, when we gathered for team meetings with updates on work, a bible study, and prayer.

At times, students were placed in internships where they were stretched beyond what they thought they could do, but they grew to the challenge. Camina Hirota shares her experience:

> My internship was at the *Colegio Público Chiquilistagua* in Managua, Nicaragua. I worked as a school counselor at this public school with about 1,200 students. This was my first time gaining experience as a school counselor, and when I first heard about this internship opportunity, I thought maybe I would be shadowing their school psychologist or counselor. However, this position did not exist. I was introduced as "*la psicóloga*" to everyone and felt super terrified in the beginning. I was at the school Monday through Friday from 8:00 am to 4:00 pm and in between seeing individual students or working in groups, I focused on journaling to make sure I was debriefing and reflecting on self-care.
>
> When I got to the school first thing in the morning, I would take a few laps around, passing each classroom with the intent on smiling through the windows and waving at students who smiled back. I wanted to make sure that

127

they knew I was there for them. I wanted them to know my role and I wanted them to feel comfortable talking to me. Students would ask their teachers if they could leave their classroom to come talk to me, and other times teachers would send students to me if they weren't doing their homework or if they were misbehaving in class. On rare occasions, I even had sessions with parents of students who happened to hear about my role at the school.

Camina Hirota and some of her school kids in Nicaragua

I was exposed to problems that I would have never known existed had I not been placed at this school. If a teacher doesn't show up to class, the students are expected to sit in the room all day alone and miss out on a day's worth of education because there are no substitute teachers. If a student cannot afford to pay for transportation and they have to walk a long distance to get to school, uncomfortable or broken shoes could keep them from coming. During sessions with students, I would learn in extreme cases how they deal with physical abuse and sexual trauma outside of school. With these serious circumstances, I had to be honest with the students and tell them that I did not have the power to change what had happened to them, but I could help with how they feel about their self-worth and help get them back on track academically.

I was able to use what I learned from the psychology courses I took at Whitworth and personally what I had learned from my own therapy experiences to guide me at my internship. I was able to help students learn more about themselves and how they could change their attitudes and see that they could have a bright future despite their hardships. Besides improving my Spanish, I was able to build relationships, learn more about Nicaraguan culture, and discover that school counseling is the career I want to pursue in my future.

A great amount of flexibility was frequently needed. For example, Karli Charlton served at three different internship sites. She writes:

> My first internship was in the *Clínica Merced*. Inside the clinic was a private laboratory that ran basic health tests such as, glucose and cholesterol levels. Two days a week I went to a private school called *El Colegio Eben-Ezer*. Part of the time I observed and assisted various teachers with their classes. Other days I acted as an impromptu substitute teacher for a variety of subjects including science, English, math and art. I was also on several occasions a judge of school wide competitions. My third internship was at *Fundación Coen*. This organization offers affordable consultations to people who are unable to afford going to a hospital. On any given day I would shadow an orthopedic doctor, a pediatrician, a doctor who specializes in chronic illness, or a general practitioner.

Anne Marie Noll writes about her internship at the *Centro de Nehemías, Programa de Desarrollo Comunitario*:

> I worked as a transformational community developer through the integral mission department of the Nehemiah Center. While I spent the majority of my time in León and surrounding towns, I went back and forth to the Center in Managua a few times a week to participate in meetings with the directors. My main responsibility in León was helping community leader Doña Cruz prepare and serve meals in a nutrition program every Tuesday, Wednesday, and Friday in the emerging neighborhood of *Anexo Arrocera*. I spent my time cooking and chatting over a wood-burning stove with Doña Cruz and developing relationships with the children who came every week to her front patio. As well, I would travel with my boss Roberto, in his truck or on the bus, to visit five underdeveloped urban and semi-urban communities in the León and Chinandega regions. We would meet with and listen to leaders in the community who were part of the Urban Transformational Strategy where projects were in various stages of development. At the end of my internship, I was able to take part in an official evaluation of the community development programs in each neighborhood with the directors of the Nehemiah Center and invited development specialists from all over the world.
>
> I also had another unofficial internship where I would take a bus thirty minutes out of town to work with a family at their plant nursery and farm. While there, I helped restore and expand their plant nursery, harvest watermelons, and cultivate fruit trees, while focusing on sustainability. Through my experience as an intern at the Nehemiah Center, I was able to observe an organization that was made up of different groups that work collectively for a common purpose. It was a strong example of biblical community in a professional field. The most rewarding part of the internships was learning to understand the significance of developing relationships and listening to the

personal stories of community leaders and members. Both of my internships helped me to develop personally and professionally in fields that I had been studying and was passionate about.

Katie Noll followed her passion for animals by working at the national zoo.

A community development meeting in Nicaragua

Katie Noll with two of her patients

She tells us about her daily tasks:

> I interned in the rescue center at the *Zoológico Nacional* outside Managua, which is the only wildlife rescue center in the country. My main job was to assist a few volunteers in organizing and running a neonatal clinic, since the staff often didn't have time to give the young animals the multiple daily feedings and constant attention they needed. Many of the animals we received were seized from the illegal pet trade or surrendered once their owners realized they were too much to handle. It was difficult to watch when animals would succumb to illness or complications from malnutrition due to the lack of funding, veterinary equipment, and other resources at the rescue center, but it was immensely satisfying to watch our baby monkeys, opossums, foxes, and other animals as they learned and grew with the care we provided.

There were many other internship sites where the 2016 CASP students served:

- Jessica Baumgartner worked with a doctor and a dentist at the *Clínica Mi Crédito.*

- Dakota Baumann served at Faith in Action Ministries.

- Rachael Eaton ministered at the *Centro de Protección Hogar de Fe.*

- Hannah McCollum worked as an assistant at the Nicaragua Christian Academy in Nejapa. She also did translation work for the Nehemiah Center.

- Morgen Layton served at the *Comunidad de Estudiantes Cristianos de Nicaragua* (*CECNIC*, Nicaragua's affiliate of the International Fellowship of Evangelical Students), an evangelism and discipleship ministry to university students.

- Hannah Howell worked with the *Asociación AFIMANIC.*

- Grace Klinkhammer served at the *Clínica Médica Carlitos* in Los Cocos, León.

Host family stays and participation in a local church were also life changing. One student noted the diversity of church experiences:

> Dakota attended overnight vigils and was impressed by the harsh physical-spiritual dualism that he encountered. Micah chose to attend Mass every Sunday and the priest celebrated Mass at his host family's home as part of a goodbye party. Hannah McCollum's family held church services in their garage/courtyard multiple evenings a week. Hannah Howell's room opened to the worship space, meaning that she heard the loud music whether she was attending or not.

The group gathered for the academic spring break retreat in Granada, led by Lindy Scott, TA Dana LeRoy, and Freddy Méndez. During this week, the group shared times of reflection and prayer, celebrated the Holy Week festivities of colonial Granada, and enjoyed some time to relax, cook, and kayak together. The week also included academic intensives to cover material related to the CASP coursework on politics, theology, and history.

Emily Teeple shared some final thoughts on her CASP experience:

> Something that I really learned to appreciate during my time in Nicaragua was the slow-paced way of life—also called "Nicaraguan time." I began to learn how important it is to be present in each moment and not to waste time thinking or worrying about what is going to happen later on down the road. I saw people in Nicaragua put friendships and people before work and other responsibilities and because of this, I felt that they made very rich connections with each other—something that would not have been possible if they were always focused on keeping a schedule. The best example of this was when my host family took me to Matagalpa to spend the day with the rest of their extended family. I knew that both my host parents had many things to accomplish while we were away, like helping run their family store, but instead they took me and their nieces and nephews to the border of Jinotega to watch the sunset. We spent about three hours sitting on the side of the road on a big hill waiting for the sunset and enjoying each other's company.

Emily Teeple and her friends

> I also think my time on CASP has changed the outlook I want to have on life. I met people in both Guatemala and Nicaragua that live with so little compared to me, yet they seem to have a deep joy and thankfulness that I have never seen so abundantly. I think they have a pretty good sense of what's important in life and they look at life through a different lens. This was most evident for me in the clinic because we spent so much time laughing and joking with each other even when the work we were doing could be stressful and unenjoyable at times.

My host mom also showed me this deep joy when she would come home from work exhausted, sit down at the table with me, and burst out laughing at silly little things like the way our dog would bark at squirrels outside the house or the way my host dad cooked *gallo pinto* with the wrong ratio of rice to beans. I know our society can value the serious and down-to-business mindset at times more than the importance of finding little joys in each day, and that is something I have taken away from living in Nicaragua. By taking time to be present and living with a deep joy, I hope my experiences in Central America continue to allow me to change my own outlook on life to one that celebrates the little victories and simple moments more.

The group returned to the Whitworth campus in early May to debrief and make a campus presentation. The group invested significant time and energy to self-reflection and the process of beginning to find meaning and next steps related to their transformative experience in Central America. Their campus presentation made strong emphasis on their wide range of experiences and how these encounters with cultural differences, social injustice, political turmoil, and spiritual formation had impacted their lives as Whitworth students and global citizens.

2018: The CASPians Witness Democracy on the Streets in Nicaragua

2018 Cohort: Erik Blank, Hope Gerdon, Katelyn Granum, Vanessa Heller, Natalie Karcher, Jessica Langdon, Lindsay Lassiter, Kamryn Laurence, Amanda Llorens, Morgan McKeague, Maddi Rinehart, and Anna Waltar. Teaching Assistant—Micah Allred (CASP 2016). Faculty Leaders—Kim Hernández and Lindy Scott.

The CASP 2018 journey began with a month in Guatemala. In roommate pairs, the students lived with host families in Quetzaltenango, Guatemala for three weeks and spent weekdays attending *Casa Xelajú*, a Spanish language school to help boost student language ability and confidence. They received two-on-one instruction from Spanish teachers that have worked with Whitworth students for many years and regularly took field-trips to the (delicious!) Mennonite bakery, local museums, markets, or the nearby cemetery that is home to the body of Vanushka the gypsy, a Guatemalan "Juliet" who tragically died of heartbreak when forced to part with her lover.

Hope Gerdon, Profe Henry Estrada and Amanda Llorens at Casa Xelajú Language School in Xela, Guatemala

On weekends and weekday afternoons, students learned how to make chocolate, participated in Mayan ceremonies, took part in various community projects, and ventured out into the city. The group made visits to Lake Atitlán, hiked Volcán Santa María, and partook in the famous CASP "Plunge," where four groups of three students traveled to different cities in Guatemala. One Plunge group traveled to Nebaj, Guatemala, an indigenous town in the northern mountainside of Guatemala that was devastated by the Guatemalan civil war in the 1980s. This group coincidentally stumbled upon an event in the small town: a debut of the documentary *500 Years,* which recounts the story of the Nebaj Ixil people fighting for long-sought after justice by charging Ríos Montt, former general and the man responsible for the slaughter, of genocide. In the small hotel, the three students sat in a small room crowded with Ixil people witnessing their story on the screen for the first time. It was in Nebaj that these students experienced great tensions and wrestled with their national identity. After their individual adventures, all Plunge groups arrived at a hotel in Antigua where they had a 5-day retreat to debrief their experiences in Guatemala, to complete some academic work, and to do some final preparation for their internships in Nicaragua.

After a short two-hour flight, the students arrived in Nicaragua where they would begin their three-month, second phase of their Central America adventure. Freddy Méndez and Lindy Scott picked up students from the airport and drove them to a hotel on the outskirts of Managua where they would be prepped on the details of their individual home stay and internship placements. With anticipation, and notable sadness at the inevitable group separation, students traveled to their individual locations and were welcomed by their new host families for the first time. With a handful of students in Managua, four in León, and others in Rivas, Los Brasiles and Diriamba, the students were able to fully immerse themselves in Nicaraguan culture and put their Spanish to the test in a professional work environment. Internships ranged from assisting in an ecological museum, to aiding doctors in a health clinic, to single-handedly creating and implementing a nutrition program in a Nicaraguan school system. Other students helped teach classes for children at schools and participated in activism against gender violence in feminist organizations. For the next three months, students developed their daily routines, discovered the *correct* bus routes, and created lasting friendships. The TA, Micah Allred, organized a group trip to a waterfall in mountainous (and relatively cold!) Matagalpa in April. Many traveled to visit their fellow students in León, the hub of the revolution, to learn more about the history of the country's civil war. While the heat was often suffocating (and hot soup was still served!), students discovered how to navigate new cultural situations and came to wrestle with even more trying issues—corruption, injustice, health, wealth and everything in-between.

The internships in 2018 continued to focus on giving students an opportunity to gain experience in their area of academic and vocational interest. The twelve placements represent a wide range of experiences:

- Erik Blank worked in León with the *Asociación Mary Barreda Proyecto Mujeres,* an organization that was founded on the principles of liberation theology and serves women who are involved in prostitution. Erik focused on the department that fights violence against women.

- Hope Gerdon worked with *Mujeres con Ministerio Cristo para la Ciudad*, traveling around the country to prepare and facilitate ministry workshops for women. She was based in Nejapa, outside of Managua.

- Katelyn Granum taught English classes and served as a classroom assistant at the *Escuela Faro de Luz*, a private Christian school that serves all grades in the town of Los Brasiles.

- Vanessa Heller worked in Managua at the *Clínica Vida*. She got hands-on experience alongside a number of medical specialists.

- Natalie Karcher worked with a doctor and a dentist at the *Clínica Mi Crédito*, in Managua.

- Jessica Langdon worked in the violence prevention sector of a women's group called *Xochilt Acatl* near León.

- Lindsay Lassiter worked in Rivas with the Nicaraguan chapter of *Living Water*, an organization that attempts to provide both physical and spiritual water to needy communities around the world. She also accompanied North American short-term mission trips to a variety of communities.

- Kamryn Laurence worked primarily with *Clínica Carlitos*, one of Nicaragua's leading rural clinics, located thirty minutes outside of León. She spent multiple weeks in a number of rotations, including working in the pharmacy, doing tests in the laboratory, receiving patients in the reception area, and accompanying her supervisors during patient consultations.

- Amanda Llorens worked in Nejapa, with a home for at-risk girls, called *Villa Esperanza*, a ministry of Leading Edge International. She formed intentional relationships with girls and led small group bible studies, in addition to assisting with a variety of administrative tasks.

- Morgan McKeague worked part-time at the *Museo Ecológico de Trópico Seco*, where she led student tours and worked on research relating to the region's history of coffee cultivation. She also taught English and helped with a social studies class at *Colegio Bautista Emanuel de Diriamba*.

- Maddi Rinehart developed and implemented a series of school workshops designed to teach children about healthy eating and exercise. She taught at schools along the southeast perimeter of Managua. She worked under the care of *Cristo para la Ciudad*.

- Anna Waltar worked outside León at *Casa El Refugio*. She taught English to a class of young boys who are at-risk because of poverty and domestic violence. She also assisted in other classes and aspects of the youth center.

The 2018 CASPians in their iconic Guatemalan stoles

Many members of the cohort were eager to share reflections on their experiences in Guatemala and Nicaragua:

Hope Gerdon: My CASP experience was incredible. The opportunity to travel to another part of the world and experience different cultures, meet wonderful people, and learn new things was something that I will always be grateful for. I am thankful that my time on CASP did not feel like a vacation, but rather a time to live a real life in Central America and form lasting friendships. I also grew a lot academically during CASP. During my time in language school in Guatemala, I learned about the history, politics, and indigenous culture of the country. I also studied in depth about theology with my language school teacher, Henry, who is also a university theology professor. I was amazed at how much I grew in confidence using my Spanish, even when I didn't feel like I was doing it perfectly, in just one month. Before CASP, I did not have much confidence in my Spanish speaking abilities, but throughout my time in Central America, I became much more comfortable speaking with native Spanish speakers and using my language skills spontaneously.

My internship experience working in a women's ministry in Nicaragua really made me evaluate my vocation. I often felt like I didn't have all the necessary skills to do my job perfectly, however, I realized that I have a strong passion for working with and caring for people on a personal level. My work with *Cristo para la Ciudad* helped me discover that my vocation needs to focus on working with other people, as well as contribute to organizing and creating systems to expand projects and organizations/ministries to serve others well. I am so thankful that my CASP experience confirmed and expanded my vocational calling to work in the social work/nonprofit ministry field in the future.

Katelyn Granum: I worked in a private Christian school called *Faro de Luz* in Nicaragua. This school truly was a lighthouse during my time there. I learned so much about my future vocation as a teacher, and I was finally able to grow in my ability and confidence to use my Spanish. It's incredible to think about the amount of growth I was able to achieve with my language skills between the first month in Guatemala and the three-month period in Nicaragua. I knew I had learned a lot and was speaking much better by the end of the month in Guatemala; however, at the beginning of my time in Nicaragua, I wasn't sure I could be successful as a teacher and the new member of a family speaking only Spanish. However, I realized that I was participating in an exchange of language and culture with my students, their families, and my own host family every day. It was almost funny for me to realize that at the end of my three months in Nicaragua, I had actually acquired a Nicaraguan accent! That was an exciting sign of my progress—I started out thinking I could not understand anything, and I ended up speaking just like a local community member! When I returned from CASP, I took the national foreign language proficiency rating exam and received an advanced rating! I am very encouraged by this confirmation of how much I progressed in my language skills during CASP, and I can't wait to become a teacher in the near future and share my excitement for the language and culture with my students! All in all, my CASP internship experience completely confirmed my vocational calling to be a Spanish teacher or dual language elementary teacher. This is an experience I could not have had any other way. I am very grateful for CASP!

Vanessa Heller: During my time in Nicaragua I had the opportunity to work alongside Nicaraguans in a local clinic and a hospital. This experience was more than I could have ever imagined! I learned so much about medicine and improved my Spanish far more than I ever thought possible in just four months in Central America, and I can now see my future career as a doctor working in the US and Latin America! My internship allowed me to work with patients, get trained to work in the lab, and observe a wide variety of procedures and surgeries. When I applied to go on CASP, my biggest hope was that I would be able to do something significant during my internship. I can say that this is how I would describe every day during my three months in Nicaragua, as well as the month of language training in Guatemala. I acquired more hands-on skills than I thought possible, became comfortable speaking Spanish, and got to become a member of two families and communities in two countries that I now consider like other homes to me. I had also never really been interested in topics like politics, the environment, and immigration.

Thanks to CASP, not only did I get the chance to study these topics, but I was able to learn about them firsthand from the people I was living and working with in Central America. I also came to realize that my interest and knowledge in these topics is an important part of my vocation as a doctor, because I need to understand the realities of my patients and the places they come from. I am very grateful for my time on CASP and how it will impact my future.

Morgan McKeague: During CASP I grew in my understanding of the Body of Christ. What prompted this extension was being welcomed to participate in worship with a faith community of Catholics of the Franciscan order, quite different from my own Protestant tradition. This community extended their love to me as a sister in Christ and challenged and inspired me. I became thankful that I was part of their context as a Christian and felt the unity of Christ. This community was known for cultivating a socially aware congregation and I think that is what attracted me initially. Although socially aware, the commitment to the Gospel and preaching the good news in the context of the city of Diriamba was not compromised and was evident in how they responded to issues in their community. My love for the Church as a whole on CASP was affirmed and gave me hope that I will continue to be a part of the Church even though it can be messy. I have found that my commitment to the Church is sustained by communities of believers who preach and practice the good news in their context.

Relationships are humanity's lifeline, and as a Christian, I believe in the incarnate God, who seeks relationships with us. We know who we are in relation to others, the things that pain or bring us the most joy in our daily lives are because of relationships. The gift of God to connect with others across language, culture, and interests is special and what makes us human. Reflecting on my time on CASP I realize how my identity is formed through my relationships with the Body of Christ, especially those who holistically seek the Kingdom and welcome difficult questions. To have seen how the Body of Christ operates in a new setting and to have witnessed the unique gifts of others is a privilege and I give thanks to the Lord that these themes were visible during my time on CASP. Welcoming new growth, I look forward to continuing being challenged and renewed by the Church.

Amanda Llorens: In Nicaragua, people spent more time together talking and enjoying each other's company around a table. Some of my best memories are of watching a movie with my host parents after dinner, or them taking me new places and introducing me to new people. For my internship at *La Villa Esperanza*, my primary role was to be a friend to the girls who stayed there. This is a rescue home in Managua for girls who have either been in domestic abuse situations or have been sex-trafficked. Being shy, this was a challenge for me. However, I was able to make connections with some of the girls who had just come to the Villa, and one girl who had been there for many years. I led daily devotionals and helped them with homework, and I think I was able to set an example when it came to the importance of prayer. Most of the time I felt unsure about what I was supposed to be doing. However, looking back I feel as though I did more than I realized. I grew a lot in my faith and my self-confidence from my CASP experience. I can't wait to see how God uses this time in my life to equip me for future ministry opportunities.

Anna Waltar: CASP, more than any other experience of my time at Whitworth, has completely shifted the way I think about the world and how I understand my sense of purpose within it. It's taught me how to struggle with the harsh realities of poverty, privilege, marginalization, and corruption that have dominated so much of Latin American history and society—and it's challenged me to engage more actively with those same issues back in my own country, where I so often turn a blind eye. CASP has helped me learn how to be a guest in another culture—to approach situations and people I encounter with a posture of humility, sensitivity, and gratitude. Above all, this experience has challenged me to hold on to hope even when I'm tempted to say there is none. God is continually at work bringing reconciliation and justice to this world, and I've gotten to see powerful glimpses of that during my time here in Central America. Who am I to give up hope when I've had this chance to witness such resilience and dedication in the lives of so many I've met here? I know my life will continue to be shaped by CASP as I keep seeking out ways to live in solidarity with these friends I've made and strive to learn what it means to take up my own role in seeking the coming of the kingdom of God in all its fullness.

Maddi Rinehart: My CASP experience helped me confirm my vocation and taught me ways I can continue to grow spiritually and mentally. My internship with *Christ for the City International* had me designing a nutrition program for local schools, which I then enacted by giving short lectures, leading a salad-making workshop, and teaching the students ways to exercise. This helped strengthen my passions for preventive health care and speaking Spanish, which I hope to pursue for the rest of my life. Spiritually, I gained a deeper appreciation and understanding for the history of the Christian faith in Central America (including its imperialist beginnings), as well as its many distinct manifestations, including Catholicism and Pentecostalism specifically. I also learned a great deal about indigenous culture and religion in Guatemala, which CASP helped me approach with an open mind and heart. The theology class and required journals have translated into my openness to new ways of worshipping and following Christ, and a deeper curiosity about others' expressions of faith. The journaling we were required to do has impacted me much more deeply than I expected. The way of describing an event objectively, thinking of multiple interpretations for what could be going on, and then evaluating what was happening has become how I process the world around me. It has encouraged me to have an even more open mind to the possibilities of what I experience in my daily life, rather than becoming stuck in one (potentially incorrect) way of viewing the circumstance. Finally, my experience with my host family in Nicaragua opened my eyes to how I respond to cultural differences and how I can be more self-aware in my responses to them. I learned to advocate for myself in situations in which I felt I was not being cared for well, and to communicate my needs effectively. I also realized the value I put on independence and the ability to travel from A to B easily. I am extraordinarily privileged to have these freedoms as a twenty-two-year-old woman in the US. CASP inspired in me an interest in history that I had never experienced before, and I now feel competent and able to express my frustrations with how my country has approached Central America through our foreign policy and otherwise.

Maddi Rinehart teaches about health and fitness in Nicaragua

Natalie Karcher: I had the opportunity to work in a medical clinic associated with a bank where medical care is linked to loan services and general bank services. People who apply for loans are required to get medical checkups as part of their approval process, and general bank clients are also given access to women's health and dental care in an affordable way. The clinic also offers health and wellness classes on a variety of topics.

During my internship, I learned a lot about medical care, but the most important training I received was how to treat patients as important and highly valued individuals with feelings, opinions, and rights, and not just treat their medical needs. It is essential to establish trust with the patient before any medical care can be offered, especially for women who may not have ever had access to gynecological examinations or talked about topics that may be sensitive for women in their culture. In this way, I was able to learn important aspects of Nicaraguan culture and connect with people in ways that I may not have understood without my clinic experience every day. I am also very grateful for the medical training I received in taking patient histories, assisting with checkups, and learning how to use ultrasound equipment. The anatomy and physiology class I studied at Whitworth gave me highly applicable knowledge and understanding as to what I saw on the ultrasound equipment and helped me to explain what I saw to patients.

As a result of my CASP internship, I am confirmed in my vocational calling as a healthcare professional and love of learning from cultures other my own.

On April 18, 2018, the students were finishing up their final week and a half in their internship placements when political unrest suddenly shook Nicaragua after the current president, Daniel Ortega, passed a controversial social security reform. Protesters took to the streets to show their resounding disapproval; however, pro-government groups and police actively pushed back with force, only to aggravate more unrest. After four days of increasing violence, CASP leadership decided to pull students from their homestay placements, as the US Embassy had started to order non-essential dependents of embassy employees to leave the country. Although no students were in imminent danger, and some were upset about the surprise early departure, the group recognized the need not to burden their host family members and decided to return to the United States early. Travel plans were changed, and the group got their flights booked to leave one week earlier than expected. After an emotional, quick separation from a much more unsettled Nicaragua than when they had first arrived, students transitioned back into US life with more tough questions to ask themselves, their community, and their country. CASP 2018 undoubtedly witnessed a unique ending to their CASP experience and the participants will be processing the history they witnessed for many years to come.

SECTION II

Testimonies from Individual Participants

Betsy Brownlee Gano (1975)

This vignette is taken from a letter that Betsy wrote to Ron and Marianne Frase on June 10, 1986, eleven years after that first Latin America Study trip. Her trip classmates were having a reunion that summer, and Betsy sent this letter to be shared with the group because she could not attend the reunion. At that time, she and her husband John were living in Tokyo, Japan.

As I REFLECT BACK on our Latin America trip, what sticks in my mind most are the poignant encounters we had with such a variety of people. Sure, we saw some beautiful and unusual sites: the sunrise at Machu Picchu, the gorgeous beaches in Rio and Salvador, an aerial view of the Andes, the skeletons in the cathedral in Lima, the drive along Lake Titicaca, the Indian markets in Cuzco and La Paz, the favelas, a boat ride on a tributary of the Amazon, the machine gun toting guards and military police in Santiago, to name a few. But it is the people we met, whose names I've long forgotten, that made that trip so rich and impressionable.

I'll never forget that Sunday afternoon in Santiago, with all of us crammed into his small apartment, when Señor Cortés related the suffering that he and his family endured as his wife was quietly weeping in the corner. Nor will I forget the afternoon we spent out in a satellite town (a shanty town) of Brasilia where a friendly old lady insisted that we come in for a cup of coffee. But Mrs. Reasoner, who had accompanied us, politely refused the invitation for us, and later explained how this poor woman could hardly afford food for herself, let alone use up a week's supply of coffee for hospitality's sake.

In my idealism, I had gone to Latin America with preconceived ideas of how bad and oppressive the governments were, how any sensible person would stand against this injustice, and how I was going to make some contribution to this process of justice. Well, I found out that issues were not so black and white. There were many hazy, gray areas where no really "right" solution existed. I found that people my age were far more politically aware and mature and were trying to do their best under difficult circumstances. And besides, those who were wealthy (i.e. most of our host families) and were supposedly on the side of the oppressors, were some of the warmest, generous and loving people. What contribution did I make? Really very little. I received so much and gave so little.

And how about now? Does this close encounter with Latin America still affect my life today? I think I can honestly say yes. First, the trip was my first real encounter with suffering and poverty. In rereading my journal about the trip, throughout my entries, I seemed to ask the question, "What do these people live for?" Perhaps, this question was really being directed toward myself at the time. I never answered it in my journal, and I'm still working on the answer.

Secondly, as a result of this trip I am more historically and politically aware of the situation in Latin America. I think I am more discerning. So, I am happy to read that democratic processes seem to be working in Brazil and Argentina, yet I am saddened by the situation in Chile and especially in Central America. I see that the present US administration has been so bull headed and wrong with their policies in Nicaragua. I want to cry out "Give those people a chance at governing themselves." And what is this business about the Contras being freedom fighters? They are more ruthless terrorists than the government troops they are opposing. It's an insult to our founding fathers to compare them with those who fought for America's independence.

Lastly, I ask myself the question, "What am I doing to further the causes of justice in the world today?" Well, in truth, I'm not doing much at the moment. There is as much, if not more, injustice and certainly poverty and hunger in the world today as compared to eleven years ago. I live each day mothering my child, caring for my husband, and trying to make a happy home. My worries are not about hunger, unemployment, secret police, torture or war. Sure, occasionally I feel pangs of guilt at my plenty when I see or read about the famine in Africa. I vicariously suffer with the poor mother who has to waste away for lack of food, for my child is so precious to me. Or I am grateful that my friends or my husband aren't being whisked away by secret police in the middle of the night because of their political views. I am complacent, and I am generally happy.

So, I'm not doing much now, but I see there will be opportunities in the future. John and I have been active with the Democrats Abroad in Japan. We helped over five hundred US citizens register to vote in the last election, and most of those were Democrats. My "neighbor" here in Japan isn't Latin America. It's Southeast Asia. Japan's borders aren't being threatened by "communist insurgents," but it has become smug in its affluence and stability. Japan is currently facing an identity crisis about its role as a world power. By being here, we hope to influence its search.

In conclusion, I'd like to say this letter has been a good exercise for me. It's jarred me out of my complacency somewhat to try and answer that ever-present question, "What am I living for?" The Latin America trip was one very important part of my education, and it opened my eyes to many things. As I grow older, mature somewhat, and try to gain some wisdom, the answer to this question seems to change. In the end, what gives me the courage to go on is my faith in God and believing He is working out His will in my life and in the world.

Also, I'd like to once again thank you, Ron and Marianne, for having the vision that inspired this trip. You were wonderful leaders. Your patience, endurance and loving concern added a dimension to the trip that I nor the others, I'm sure, will forget. There are so many, many more events, feelings, reactions, etc. about the trip that I'd like to share. I'm sure at the reunion, you'll have many things to reminisce, laugh, or even cry about. I wish I could be there.

Dixie Reimer Marshall (1979)

THE WHITWORTH CENTRAL AMERICA Study Tour continues to have a profound impact on my life journey. An objective of the Whitworth Contemporary Latin American
Problems course taught by our beloved professor Ron Frase in 1978 prior to the trip
was "to develop the attitude of empathy for the people of other nations—that is, the
ability to see and understand the problems sympathetically from their point of view
and to see the interrelatedness of the problems of both developed and developing nations, and the necessity of creating a global response to these problems." As a science
teacher of thirty-five years, I was so excited to look back on the syllabus and be able to
say that yes, this experience did open my eyes and heart to the people of other nations
and has deepened my own understanding of the interrelated nature of our lives.

Just two years after our shared Whitworth trip, Tim Marshall and I were married.
Tim was in seminary and chose to do his final internship in Mexico at CCID-Cuer-
navaca Center for Intercultural Dialogue on Development. Our Spanish became very
good as we worked with faith and university groups that came for a week of immersion and experiential learning experiences. Tim and I helped at the center in many

ways—leading groups, hosting local speakers, translating, building relationships with local families and making connections to bring our groups into their homes. We continued to be immersed in the politics of the time-with civil wars in Nicaragua and El Salvador, and the struggle of deep-seated poverty in Mexico. In a journal I wrote, playing hopscotch with the children on the hillside dirt, they are laughing, so pleased with their success. We scratched out a game board on the dirt area of the front door . . . tonight in the ravine, where the sewage water from rich homes nearby breeds a blanket of flies in its feces. I think of these young girls' futures as I climb out of the ravine, to a car, a hot meal waiting, and not one fly in the kitchen. They wave goodbye as they huddle together on the floor, on the edge that hasn't collapsed with the rain.

Upon returning home we settled in Olympia, Washington, where I took a job as a middle school science teacher. I did everything I could in that role to develop an experiential program and weave in the real-world issues of poverty through the lens of nutrition and the environment. I had a strong commitment to outdoor field—based experiences and involved my students in water quality testing, observations in their local ecosystems, and many environmental service projects. I was able to develop strong community partnerships that have carried over into my current role as the district secondary science specialist where I am able to advocate for real-world problem-solving and hands-on science in all of our North Thurston Public Schools.

With the civil war in El Salvador intensifying in the early 80s, thousands of refugees were seeking safety in nearby countries and Catholic Relief Services was requesting an international peacekeeping presence in the camps. I was able to volunteer during the summer and again would find myself deeply connecting with the families and their stories and finding ways to come back home to be their voice. While in the camps I reflected, looking into the mountains that divide the people from their homelands, living from the dead, mother from father and sister from brother, shades of blue watercolor sky descends to meet the rugged peaks. Laughter of children playing soccer, hammers working, guitars strumming-noises full of life and love. Moments splattered by a memory of the cold, stab wound, blood, death-echoing through the hills is the distant sound of the helicopters. How ironic it is—such magnificent beauty, God's spirit present, such giving people gripped by such a brutal and inhuman war whose military is being supported by my own government.

During one of the summer trips, I became very close to a young couple, Jilma and Avilio, whose safety in the camp became compromised due to some of Avilio's leadership activities. We worked closely with Catholic Relief Services to secure their safe passage along with their 3 children to Calgary, Canada. During one of our early Whitworth Central America reunions in 1994, the family came to share their story with our group—their struggles escaping the war in El Salvador to safety in Mesa Grande, as well as the cultural barriers and post trauma difficulties of day to day life in a new country. We have stayed closely connected to their family, and a few years ago when twenty-five-year-old Dixie Carolina married a young man from Paris Mina,

Costa Rica, they asked if Tim and I would come to the remote island where his family lived and had founded a non-profit turtle sanctuary, to perform their wedding ceremony.

In 1988 I had the opportunity to help lead a delegation of seven people from Washington State sponsored by Going Home, an Interfaith Foundation. In a letter to family and friends, I shared how my life had been very influenced by the profound faith, courage, and generosity of the people I had lived and worked with throughout Central America. We were planning to escort food and medicine to the farming community of Las Vueltas, an area that Salvadoran refugees had repatriated in 1987 from Mesa Grande. Although they had been guaranteed in the Central America Peace Plan the right to return home and farm in peace, there had been numerous harassments by the governments' military. The presence of international visitors had provided needed security for these people and it was our hope to escort food and medicine into their community. We had several supportive letters from our local St. Placid's Benedictine Priory, the Washington Association of Churches, our State Senator Brock Adams, and Congressman Don Bonker. The support proved critical as we faced denied permission to travel but managed to connect with a colonel willing to only speak with myself and Sister Andrea, requesting that if we were able to get the local bishop to assume responsibility, we could continue. After hours of waiting and negotiating, we were ultimately granted passage. Our truck was halted at the last five miles due to the washed out road, so we hiked in on foot with mules carrying the supplies. The evening's mortar fire and strafing by helicopters could be heard on the outskirts of town, and I can still vividly recall the building we were sleeping in was shaking with debris crumbling off the walls. We listened to stories of war and loss, hope and new crops, stories from the Madres group who had found strength in working together as a community, of starting a childcare center and a Health Guardians program. We talked with teachers who were proud of their schools and a Spanish volunteer working with them to write their own math and reading curriculum. We were inspired by their deep-rooted faith in their community and in God who pushed them forward. They did believe that peace would come.

In the early 90's Tim and I were blessed with two sons, David and Michael. The war in El Salvador had ended with many efforts to rebuild communities. We connected with a project called the Foundation for Self-Sufficiency in El Salvador through the invitation of Doctor Diane Dakin who had delivered both of our boys. Headed by Chencho Alas, a priest who had worked closely with Oscar Romero, they were dedicated to creating zones of peace, sustainable organic agriculture and environmental protection in the lower Lempa area of repatriated Ciudad Romero. I first went with a colleague, Vicki Leonard, to bring what their teachers requested of us—their first computers, and to teach them how to use them. We also scoped out the safety and potential for bringing down our children to volunteer in classrooms, which we did, and made community connections to bring back to our own science classrooms.

When the boys were in their early teens, it was time to organize a family delegation from Olympia to Ciudad Romero. Twenty-five people joined us for a service learning experience where we responded to the requests of the community and provided an art workshop for preschoolers through adults, sports equipment, and a fruit tree revegetation project around the soccer field. This also involved homestays for families in Isla de Mendez where we joined a local Coordinadora project, helping to plant mangroves and releasing baby sea turtles.

In our boys' busy teen years, our service focused closer to home on migrant families in the Granger area. With youth from our local church, we worked on building houses with Habitat for Humanity. Each of the 3 houses was for a young Hispanic family that was a first generation to enter post high school education. Tim was our lead, using his excellent skills as a teacher, carpenter, and house builder. He has continued his career gifting and inspiring high school students in technical and architectural drafting at North Thurston High School in Lacey, Washington.

The experience of sharing in people's lives—students in Olympia Washington, our own family and friends, Central American families that have shared their stories, culture, faith, and perspectives with us—continue to inspire in me a commitment to serve others, to have empathy and compassion, and to walk gently on this earth that sustains and connects us all. Just as Ron Frase so clearly said to me in his wise age of ninety-two—That experience touches your heart not just your mind. It changes your life!

Liz Raymond Schatz (1981)

M<small>Y SERVICE ASSIGNMENT IN</small> Honduras was through CEDEN (*Comité Evangélico de Emergencia Nacional*). Ellen Skillings and I were sent to a small village in the mountains east of Choluteca called Las Casitas. There we were to set up and run a preschool for the children of the village. We did accomplish that task.

Through CEDEN we were introduced to an American Peace Corp nurse from Chicago who told us she wished she had access to all those supplies, like Band-Aids, she had merely tossed from her pockets at the end of each shift at the Chicago hospital she had worked at. She took us on a tour of the Choluteca hospital.

In the nursery, the children and babies were laid out on child-sized beds. Each of the beds, some without mattresses, most without rails, were elevated so that the staff could attend to the child without bending over. Each child was on their back, splayed out, some with protruding malnourished bellies, their wrists and ankles tied with gauze to the four corners of their bed. None appeared comfortable or comforted. Their expressions were lifeless and so deeply sad.

She showed us the small room with a janitor's sink, mop bucket, a small table, and a most uncomfortable looking bed. This is where, she explained, babies were delivered. Most babies were birthed at home, but if there were complications and the mothers were brought to the hospital, this was the room that was available for them.

As we walked the long hallway with its large windows looking out into the trees, I felt trapped and faint. I could feel my shirt begin to cling to my body and my head begin to spin. The air was so still. I was desperate to get out!

We were to return to that hospital a few weeks later. While sitting on the veranda of the Las Casitas home we stayed in, doing our afternoon studying for Dr. Hunt, Esteban, a young man from the village, appeared. He was panicked and pale. As he had been working in his field, his machete had slipped and severely cut the front of his leg just above the top of his cowboy boot. By the time he reached us his boot was filled with blood. Both our family and Esteban were begging us to do something. Neither Ellen nor I had any medical experience, nor the supplies needed! Just then, as though a miracle from God, our CEDEN contact came driving up in a Jeep! (There were no vehicles or roads in our village!) He took the three of us to the Choluteca hospital, which was an hour's drive away. Esteban did not want to go, but we insisted that we would pay for his treatment. At the hospital, they took him in immediately. Ellen and

I arranged the payment. It was then that I remember seeing the long line of sickly people waiting, for what must have been hours, to be seen. I wondered if Esteban would have been one of them if we had not had the funds to pay.

Years later, as I lay in the adjustable bed, in my private room with private bathroom, after the cesarean delivery of my first child, I thought about that janitor's closet in Choluteca. And once, when volunteering at a local food bank, I happened to wander out into the hallway where some of my fellow Spokanites were standing in line for food, and I was reminded of that line at the Choluteca hospital.

Those three and a half months on the study tour were filled with so many experiences, but I find that I think about the events surrounding my home stays the most. My husband and I have continuously supported a child (four so far) through Child Fund (formally Christian Children's Fund) since the first month of our marriage thirty-three years ago. Each girl has been from the San Pedro Sula region of Honduras. I have tried to be sensitive to the vast differences in our lives as I have communicated with each of them and have found they help me stay grounded.

A look that penetrates your heart

Laurie McQuaig (1981)
and David Ramaley (1982)

DAVE RAMALEY, WHO PARTICIPATED in the 1982 Whitworth trip, returned to Nicaragua to work with Witness for Peace in 1984. The purpose for this organization was basically to keep a U.S. civilian presence in Nicaragua in order to deter attacks and to get affidavits from people who had been victimized by the war, either by the government and/or by the Contras. This was also during the MIG crisis and the fear that Reagan was planning an invasion of Nicaragua. Throughout Nicaragua there were signs saying in Spanish, "*No pasarán*" (The [US troops] will not pass [through our country]). Dave returned to Seattle in 1985 for a brief period.

He and Laurie McQuaig, who had gone on the 1981 Central America trip, resolved to return to Nicaragua together in the early part of 1986. They settled in the town of *El Cua* in northern Nicaragua. This also was the time when US newspapers carried stories of Ben Linder, a North American, who worked with the Sandinistas.[1] He became famous for dressing like a clown and riding a unicycle through town. He was followed by adoring children to the local medical center where they received their injections. In El Cua he was helping to build a small hydroelectric project for the town. In 1987 he was shot by the Contras. Laurie was there to identify the body (Dave was not available to identify the body as he was in Managua that day). She then had to fly with the body in a helicopter for its autopsy.

Dave said that the funeral for Ben was one of the most memorable experiences of his life. He can remember looking out of the house where Ben's body was kept and seeing thousands of Nicaraguans standing outside in a show of respect. "I always try to remain as objective as possible, but when asked 'Aren't there some good aspects of the Contras that helped change the country?', I find none. Schools, teachers, health workers, etc. were all targets and we saw first-hand the death and destruction. The Contras would have failed miserably without the backing of the US"

At the conclusion of their year, they returned to Seattle and were married. They spent the next two and a half years in chiropractic school. Dave continued his education by getting a naturopathic practice degree at Bastyr University. In 1996 they opened their practice "Seattle Natural Health" in Seattle.

1. For more information about the life of Ben Linder and his work in Nicaragua, see http://liberationtheology.org/library/ben_linder_remembrance.htm.

Linda Gillingham Sciaroni (1982)

TURNING POINTS IN MY life:

Summer of 1982 I was an innocent college kid traveling through volatile Central America. There are a hundred strong memories from my trip, and it has become the foundation for so much of my life going forward. I currently work at Marco Antonio Firebaugh High School. Most of my students' parents ran out of Central America in the 1980s. I use my Spanish every day, but more importantly I use the values I witnessed to meet my students half way.

When we were traveling, I was the student body president of the Associated Students of Whitworth College. I was admonished by Ron Frase to never tell a soul while we are traveling that I had this honor, it might endanger me. As we traveled we learned of student leaders who had been murdered for their advocacy and because they were seen as a threat. I thought a lot about the difference in the passion and respect felt by different cultures towards their leaders.

When we came back, we learned that war issues in El Salvador had removed the scholarships to seminary our friends had come to count on and we had two fundraisers to help replace some of that revenue. I wish I could have done more. I wonder where they are now.

The two incidents that have completely shaped my understanding of my privilege as an American are these: I was living in Honduras with a strong souled woman named Sonia and her two children. We lived in a two-room adobe house; I slept in the corn shed. Her husband was away a lot as he was a foreman at a farm in another town. She had the only refrigerator in the entire town and had a little store in the front corner of her home. This refrigerator allowed us to sell beer, milk and homemade popsicles. We were a favorite treat-day stop on the way home from the fields. Many men stopped by to greet Sonia, some could afford a beer. I would sit on the bench in front of our home writing in my journal and shooting the breeze with these guys. Many would playfully ask Sonia for my hand and she would rebuff them with a litany of how useless I was as a wife. I could not make a soft tortilla, nor turn it with my bare fingers. I could not get the clothes clean, as I valiantly struggled to master the technique of beating my clothes on a rock. I spilled more water than I fetched, on our trips to the river. If they wanted to marry me for my pretty face, they needed to know that they were in for a life of suffering, as the chores would not be done well. I would laugh with her, adding a story from my latest episode of "Home Ec Honduras." One time I told an old man that I delighted in this opportunity to learn about how it is to live in Honduras. A dark shadow crossed his face, and he scolded me. "You will *never* know what it is like to live in Honduras. As long as you have your plane ticket and your passport in your backpack, you are only playing at living our life." He was absolutely correct, and I think about it every day. I think about this, as I compare my temporary unemployment to many of my students' long term multi-generational poverty. I think about this when I think about the difference between having my first child at thirty-five and a student's pregnancy at 15. It just ain't the same, because I have many privileges that smooth my path.

Linda and some of her friends in Guatemala

After I returned, I was working in East LA as a science teacher, and I would have parent conferences for some kids where their life was in so much danger. I would present all my concerns to the grandma, who showed up at the school, and she would listen with lots of worry and concern in her questions and tone. At the end of the conference, we always discussed next steps with the family. Often the grandma would get a serenity on her face and she would mention stopping by Our Lady of Guadalupe on the way home and petitioning the Virgin for wisdom and strength. She would say that she would put this young man's care at the feet of the *Virgencita*. At first I was shocked at this detachment from activity. But as I have grown, I have realized that you can either pray or you can worry. You cannot do both, and I have worked hard to get what these grandmas modeled for me—an active and trusting prayer life.

Craig Dander (1982)

As STUDENTS BEGAN TO be placed for home stays in the days after our arrival in Honduras for the service portion of our tour, we noticed Israeli C-130 military transport aircraft were landing at the airport with increasing frequency; at one point, we observed them arriving every seventeen minutes on one particular day and then taxiing all the way to the far end of the airport to disgorge shrink wrapped pallets by the hundreds that were then forklifted inside hangar bays. We had no idea that we had arrived quite literally in the midst of the military ramp up/arming of former Somoza soldiers now based in southern Honduras that Oliver North would later become infamous for orchestrating.

The organization who was placing most of us was an aid group indigenous to Honduras named CODE. One particular day, Sue Cerutti, Pam Hudspeth, Cynthia Huggins and Sally Scrivner were all scheduled to depart for their individual assignments. A doctor associated with CODE was supposed to pick them up at our hotel and drive them to their respective communities where each would stay. He did not arrive as scheduled nor did he call. Dr Frase spent time on the phone trying to sort out what was taking place and when he might actually arrive. He did not show up the following day either, and so it was all chalked it up to Latin time and folks being in no particular hurry to be anywhere on time, although being two days late without notification seemed really odd. On the third day, they learned that the doctor along with two nuns had been murdered two weeks earlier and their mutilated bodies dumped in Copán. We did not know anything further. It was like a lightning bolt passing through the group. We had no idea if he was in the wrong place at the wrong time and murdered by thugs and thieves; or, if something more sinister had taken place that tied back to his work with CODE or as an activist . . . speculation amongst the remaining students at the hotel was rampant.

Abductions in Honduras that summer were happening almost daily during our time there. Saul Godínez, an elementary school teacher and union activist was abducted on July 22, 1982. Manfredo Velásquez, a graduate student, teacher and political activist was abducted on July 25, 1982. Eduardo Lanza, medical student and general secretary of the Honduran Federation of University Students, was kidnapped August 1, 1982. Germán Pérez Alemán, leader of an airport maintenance workers union, was abducted on August 18, 1982. Hector Hernández, president of the textile workers union, was abducted on December 4, 1982. By the end of 1982, one hundred eighty-four Honduran citizens had been abducted or kidnapped, and only the remains of Nelson Mackay Chavarría and our doctor friend found near Copán tortured and mutilated, have ever been found.

Just prior to the girls finding out about the demise of their doctor escort, I had been placed for my service assignment in the very small community of Las Trojes quite literally on the southern border of Honduras adjacent to Nicaragua. I was placed with a very affluent family which appeared to own all of the agriculture land in the region. There were women and girls who were clearly related to the man who owned the farm and the spiraling estate in the center of it. I ventured into the small town center of Las Trojes with my host father one afternoon, and I noticed a small market with a pool hall/bar inside it. There were young men everywhere, just hanging out, doing nothing in particular both inside and out of the building. The ranch owner brought me along for the short drive into the town from his home and took me into the pool hall. He seemed to know everyone and commanded great respect as he held informal meetings with several groups in the building. At one point three men who were older than most of the others in the room walked over to me by the front doors, and one asked in perfect English what my name was and where I was from. They were taller and more European in their physical features and they were dressed in slacks and penny loafers. I learned that they were from Argentina and actually were also visiting the area for the summer. They called my patron "*tío*" and told me they were blood relations to him . . . every evening, the dinner ritual was always the same. The ranch owner presided over a huge gathering of men. At least thirty to forty dined at the ranch each evening and were served by the girls and women who lived there. It was not a family meal, just men at the table. I was not seated with them. My dinner was served to me in the little room I'd been given to sleep that overlooked the front porch of the ranch house. On the third night of my stay very late, maybe around midnight, the Argentinian men and several others came to my room and woke me up. They wanted my backpack, the books and written documents I had in it including my passport. They wanted my diary too. There were loud voices mostly speaking Spanish with each of them telling me in English that I needed to get those items out for them. There was another faction amongst them that seemed to be against the whole idea, and they were trying to get the others to stop. A very loud debate ensued amongst them in my room. One group wanted me to be left alone, while the other led by the Argentinians wanted all my gear and specifically my passport and diary. Evidently one of the Argentinians could also read English, and they wanted him to look at everything I had written. Amidst the yelling, the woman of the house came to the door in a nightgown and admonished them all that there were children sleeping elsewhere in the house, and she literally pushed them all out of my room and pulled the door shut behind her. I sat on my bed and listened to the conversation between her and them that followed . . . something else was happening, and what had just taken place terrified me. I realized that everything I had seen in the previous couple of days was not as it had seemed. The conversation outside my door calmed, voices became lower and eventually lights were shut off and the house was still. I had not moved from where I sat on my bed. Eventually, I quietly packed my backpack, put on my clothes and crawled out the window of my room which overlooked the courtyard. I walked across the yard to the gravel road leading north off the ranch. And once I was away from the house, I began to run. About 5:00 pm that same day, I found my way back to Tegucigalpa and the hotel Centenario, where by then most of the group was now gone and on their respective assignments. Reid Ziegler recalls:

> Me, Ron, Marianne, and Susan were all just hanging out on this one floor where the hotel had a dinner area with lots of seating when Dander came through the door. We could tell right away there was something wrong. Besides being filthy and smelling pretty bad, he looked like he'd been to hell and back. Then we heard what happened. After he finished answering questions, I told him about all the stuff that had taken place with the people from CODE. So yeah, I think it's safe to say the stress level at that moment was at an all-time high.

Today it is common knowledge that a US trained intelligence group called Battalion 3/16 became the name of the Honduran army unit responsible for carrying out political assassinations, abductions, and torture of suspected opponents of the government during the 1980s. Battalion members received training and support from the United States CIA in the form of funded programming provided by the Argentine Anticommunist Alliance, the Pinochet government, and the School of the Americas. It is also worth noting that a church-sponsored college student from Goshen, Indiana, would pass through Las Trojes, Honduras just three months after my hasty departure. The student's burned and mutilated body was found days later just inside the Nicaraguan border adjacent to Las Trojes.

Days after my return, I was placed in another part of Honduras where I completed my service assignment and ended up having a life changing experience. Weeks later, all of the other students in the group gradually trickled back into Tegucigalpa without further issue. Our TA, Susan tells of a moment on a bus outside of Tegucigalpa on one of the many trips she took to go out and personally escort students back in from their service assignments. Susan recalls:

> Several military and civilian vehicles had been set up as barricades across the highway and our bus came to a stop. Three men boarded the bus. Two in military uniforms carrying rifles, and the third was just in front of them in tan chinos and a blue short sleeve collared shirt. He was wearing a black leather holster that contained an electric cattle prod on his right hip. He asked everyone to get out their identification and travel documents. The bus was quiet, and inspection of documents went at an orderly pace. When he arrived at my seat, he examined my passport and travel documents and without looking

up asked about my extended stay at the hotel Centenario in Tegucigalpa. He knew who I was, where I'd come from, the institutional backing we had, and where I was living in a city about three hours away from his location!

From Tegucigalpa, the group boarded a plane and headed for Guatemala City and ultimately Antigua, Guatemala for a week of recovery, downtime and debriefing. Our routine changed. We had breakfast together each morning followed by single group breakout sessions discussing our individual service assignments in Honduras. In the afternoons we walked the cobblestone streets of Antigua, often dining in open air restaurants during late afternoon/early evening rain showers surrounded by hills, volcanoes, and a lush tropical beauty that is unique to the highlands of Guatemala. Ríos Montt had recently come to power after rendering official election results fraudulent and appointing himself president. Our group was unaware of the political assassinations that were also taking place in Guatemala.

We were days from the end of what had been quite an ordeal. The group was exhausted emotionally and many of us showed outward signs physically of a summer's worth of stress and anxiety. The military was present everywhere we went just as they had been in Honduras. Banks were sandbagged and had troops deployed in front of them as if they were defending a fortress from an impending attack. The soldiers stoically stood expressionless as we passed by brandishing automatic weapons and often *technicals* (Toyota pickup trucks with fifty-caliber machine guns mounted on posts in the truck bed). And predictably, once we passed, the catcalling would start, except these guys were armed.

Beth Kinsler, the daughter of Guatemalan missionaries, fluent in Spanish, about five feet tall and maybe a hundred pounds, was, to the naked eye, the proverbial middle class, suburban American college student . . . affable, generous, funny, and polite. An easy target for a catcalling Latin man or even a group of men at first glance. Today, it could easily be said that Beth Kinsler was actually the matriarch and founder of the #metoo movement. Craig Stein recalls:

> I really kind of felt bad for the guys who tried to catcall Beth. I remember her spinning around one time after it happened and walking back towards maybe six soldiers, with weapons in hand, absolutely dressing them down verbally. My Spanish was practically non-existent, but you didn't need to speak a word of the language to know that Beth was verbally putting her whole foot up somebody's butt! Disrespect in the form of denigration like that was not something she tolerated. Even with weapons drawn, I felt like Beth had them outgunned and cowering in a corner like house broken puppies who had just been caught urinating on the carpet in the front room. Though tiny in stature, she is a formidable opponent and more than makes up for her size in personality, charisma, and bravery!

After a few rest-filled days in Antigua, we boarded another plane and flew to Mexico City and split our remaining days between it and Cuernavaca, south of the capital. We became tourists for the most part taking in tours, viewing ruins, museums, and historical landmarks. But there was one final, lasting and poignant moment as we visited *La Estación*, which is a community of several hundred Mexican families living alongside the railroad tracks in mud covered Nissan car parts cardboard boxes fashioned into homes. There were trenches dug around the perimeter of the encampment, and the people there built makeshift privies (toilets) over the top of them. Trash, sewage, and the fragrance of rotting garbage permeated the air. It was yet another reminder of the abject poverty, malnutrition, lack of employment, and economic opportunity that had such a stranglehold on whole regions and nations throughout all of Central America.

We had no last meal or formal ceremony while in Mexico to conclude our adventure. It had been an incredibly long and difficult journey for all of us. In the months and years that followed, many who were not amongst us would say of our group that "we did not grow close." They believed we did not develop an appropriate or profound set of ties to one another as a result of our time in Central America. But the fact is, we were just kids who'd run an almost four-month long gauntlet that we all knew instinctively would change us profoundly and forever. We just had no idea how it would all unfold.

Thirty-five years on, it's easy to see that in spite of the stress and trauma that visited our group as we moved northward through Central America, we allowed what happened to change us. In a day in an age when it's almost fashionable to declare oneself a victim, we were and have never been victims of our experience. To the contrary our group has become a breeding ground for compassion, tolerance, devotion, and love for one another.

Did we change the world in 1982? No, not even a little bit.

But what we did change, was our minds about one another. Maybe that was the whole point! We left Spokane believing we might make a small difference down there and returned home realizing that the only thing that had changed was us.

These stories and thoughts are dedicated to the twenty-two souls who had the courage to allow this event to transform them and change their lives. Bless you all!

Erasmo's Story (1982)

We have three versions of this remarkable and fascinating story. First, we present you with Ron Frase's version. Then we have Craig Dander's personal take on what happened, and finally we hear the awesome version by Erasmo, the goat herder whose life was changed forever.

Here is Ron's perspective:

Marianne and I went to visit Craig Dander, who with Erasmo, a fifteen-year-old boy, was taking care of a herd of goats. We traveled by bus which let us off at a deserted bus stop and then we walked about twenty minutes to a fragile shack where Craig and Erasmo took shelter. It was a very lonely setting where Craig had lots of time to think about his life. He talked very freely about his spiritual struggle and that he hoped that he would keep his priorities straight when he returned to Whitworth.

Marianne and I noticed that the isolation and solitude of their home stays gave students the opportunity to reflect on their lives in a way that had been impossible with the relentless pace of life and the countless distractions at Whitworth. Erasmo was only fifteen and had a full-time job, herding goats. Their different lifestyles also gave Craig food for thought.

Upon graduation from Whitworth, Craig moved to Seattle and started an industrial janitorial business. One day, his receptionist said she had someone on the line from New York City who wanted to talk with him. Craig wanted to dismiss the call and told her it was probably someone who had been trying to sell him some stock. The receptionist said, "No, the caller said he personally knew you from years ago." Craig picked up the phone and nearly fell off his chair when the voice said, "I am Erasmo from Honduras." He continued by saying that he was in New York City with his wife and a son. He had left Honduras to settle in the States. After a series of phone calls between them, Craig arranged for the family to fly to Seattle where Erasmo secured a job as a chef in the Washington State Convention Center.

In July of 1997, Craig purchased a multi-store commercial office and interior company in the Bay Area near San Francisco. This meant moving from his Union Bay Maintenance Company in Seattle to the Bay Area of California. He arranged for Erasmo to buy his company, which he operates up to this day. What an incredible upward social mobility jump for a former Honduran goat herder. Craig had taken pictures of Erasmo and his family when he was on CAST in Honduras. A couple of weeks after arriving in Seattle, Erasmo asked to see the pictures. Craig had not realized that Erasmo had never seen a photograph of himself or his family. When the Whitworth Central America Program holds a reunion on campus, Erasmo, his wife and their three children are always there.

Craig, reflecting upon his relationship with Erasmo says, "Without sounding overly dramatic, I doubt very seriously whether I could have been equipped to handle all this had I not gone to Whitworth—and more specifically, my time in Central America. Not an hour passes when I don't think of Erasmo and my home stay out in the middle of nowhere in Honduras. That single experience keeps me very well grounded and has been the basis for most of the significant choices I've made over the last several years." In an email Craig sent to our daughter Shelly, who was on the same Central America trip, he made a very astute observation, "I don't know that the program at Whitworth is *really* about Central America—it seems to me it has become a vehicle where young people develop character and life skills, where one can learn about what's really real—and how you know."

And now for "the rest of the story," as told by Craig Dander:

Our "work" home stays were going to take place in Honduras. My first home stay lasted three days. A young guy from CODE came to pick me up in a jeep. We drove for hours back towards the Nicaraguan border and to a small village. This guy took me there and literally drove to the last house at the end of a dirt road and started knocking on doors and said, "Good morning, hey, I've got this white boy over here looking to have a great experience living and working here in Honduras and he pays you for the opportunity . . . are you interested in taking him in for approximately thirty days?"

The people who answered the door would listen to his pitch and then look at me and then say, "No thank you," and close the door. I felt like I was with the Fuller Brush salesman who was struggling mightily to make sales that morning. Turns out, the real reason he brought me to this particular town was he had a lady friend there that he was interested in spending quality time with—killing two birds with one stone. I ended up on a rather large farm/ranch with a very affluent man. The thing I noticed right away once the CODE guy left was, there were no women, girls, or children any-where. It was all guys, and most were in their twenties and thirties.

There were Nicaraguan flags inside the large main house and the barn/processing facility adjacent to it. Lots of rifles and shotguns and ammo canisters around stacked everywhere. The men drank at night and on my second night there, they asked me to see my diary—they wanted to know what I was writing and why was I *really there*? I waited for them to eventually fall asleep, and I put on my backpack and shoes and walked ever so quietly out of the house and down the road. It was about 2:30 am. Once I was well away from the house, I started to run. I ran until first light when I saw an old man on a tractor coming up a road that bisected the one I was on. He stopped, and I asked him how much further to the bus station. He told me about 20 minutes and offered me a ride. I sat on top of the engine cowling with my pack as we putted down the road at about five miles per hour. I was sweaty, wet, cold and frightened. I got to the bus station, purchased a ticket, and the lady said the bus would arrive in about thirty minutes. That was the longest thirty-minute wait of my life. I kept looking back up the road I had come down believing those men from that ranch would be arriving any second in pursuit of me. The bus finally came, and I road several hours back into Tegucigalpa and got a cab to the hotel where I found Dr. and Mrs. Frase. I was filthy and exhausted.

Three days later, our TA Susan took me back out to another home stay on the opposite side of the country in the hills overlooking the valley between Nicaragua and El Salvador. My "home stay" wouldn't be with a bunch of former Somoza para military personnel along the southern border. Instead, I'd be with a thirteen-year-old boy named Erasmo who herded seventy-one goats for his family that lived nearby. He and I lived under a roof top with no walls so that at night time, the goats could gather up beneath our hammocks for safety from predators (getting up to go to the bathroom in the middle of the night took on a whole new meaning). Erasmo was responsible for his family's largest single asset, while his father worked construction in an adjacent town that was too far away for him to return to his home each day. The dad would come back on Saturday night and stay until Sunday afternoon and then leave again. My days were spent grazing goats on the surrounding hillsides, watching out for snakes and preparing meals. We boiled pinto beans in the morning over a fire, and then made what you might call cowboy coffee in an old tin can and then poured it through a piece of a cotton t-shirt into plastic cups. We had eggs from chickens that lived with us, and Erasmo made corn tortillas on a rock next to our fire in the morning after we milked goats. Goats don't like to be milked, and they are hard to catch . . . less you have a handful of salt. As they come to lick it from your hand, you quickly grab them by one horn and lift their front feet off the ground. It's a two-person affair trying to milk goats in Honduras. Sometimes his mom would come down, and she'd bring us a big stack of corn tortillas with a fried egg in the middle of it, so we'd save some of those for later in the day

After the first experience and then coming out to the western side of Honduras, the emotional exhaustion and fear that had been with me went away to some degree. I spent my days with a little boy who had no shoes, one pair of pants and an army shirt he'd gotten second hand from an older brother. He kept me safe, and we became best friends. When I left, I gave him all my clothes, my shoes, my address and a map of the United States showing where I went to school and where my family lived. When I got home, I ordered the book Tom Sawyer in Spanish and mailed it to him.

Two years later, when I was twenty-four years old and back at home for the holidays, my brothers, cousins, and uncles started in on me about being a liberal, wetback-loving ne'er-do-well. My cousin Frank, who was four years my senior and who had too much to drink, made a cruel, thoughtless, and incredibly racist remark regarding a picture I had of Erasmo amongst my personal effects. I punched him in the face and knocked him out. My mom asked me to leave and I didn't come back home for seventeen years. I come from white, working class people—the first and only person in my family to attend college. My brothers and cousins learned on that Christmas day that at no time would they ever disrespect, sully, or denigrate my thirteen-year-old Honduran friend. He was more of a man at thirteen than they would ever be, and I told my cousin Frank that as I stood over him on the front yard that night.

I don't recall wandering onto the campus that fall of 1982 feeling particularly accomplished or like we'd had a great time or even a wonderful experience. It felt more like I had run a gauntlet and still couldn't figure out how I had gotten through it. For the next decade, I spent a lot of time trying to sort out what had happened, what it all meant, and what I was going to do with it. The harsh takeaway for me in those days was quite simply that I had picked my parents a little better than Erasmo had. My world was better than he could ever hope for simply because I was born in the United States, but I had no real answers to the turmoil I felt inside. Thankfully, an answer of sorts would come when Erasmo reached out to me a decade later. He was in New York working at a gas station as a cashier. I flew him to Seattle and encouraged him and Milgian to come and stay with us. They moved out immediately and remained with us until I moved to California. His presence had a calming and healing effect upon me. The gaping hole in my heart disappeared, and I understood from that moment onward what my purpose was . . . why everything had happened as it had

Erasmo and Craig reunited in 1992

In the summer of 1982, I allowed what I saw and experienced there to change me. And the thing that changed me most was a little boy who owned no shoes. I wear a bracelet that I've had for many years. I wear it every day. It doesn't have my children's names on the underside, a scripture, or medical alert. It simply says, "with intention," and it reminds of Erasmo. I live life in mindfulness, purpose, and passion . . . I live with intention. I think I do it out of a sense of honor and respect for Erasmo. Had I not ever met him, I'd very likely be just another beyond middle aged, inauthentic, Anglo Saxon American male parked in my La-Z-Boy watching Fox News mildly wondering what the poor people were doing out in the cold tonight. Thank God for that little boy. He changed everything for me.

Erasmo grew up. He lives with his wife, Milgian, from Tegucigalpa and his three American-born children Alan, Bryan, and Crystabella in Brier, Washington. He took a very small business and has built it into something awesome. He's the most amazing man I know. His kids are American through and through—to them, he's just dad . . . and a little out of touch with what's cool and relevant to their lives. But, I happen to know that he's about as in touch and cool and amazing as a man can get. As the saying goes, Erasmo is the genuine article. Alan graduated recently from New York University. Bryan and Crystabella are still in high school.

And now we have Erasmo's story in his own words:

I grew up in a very small village in the hot southern region of Honduras. Since I was 8 years old I had to go door to door, barefoot, wearing tattered clothing to sell oranges, popcorn, enchiladas, and bread as a way of helping my mom to make ends meet, and I had to accept that as a way of living. I felt different from the other kids, because I was the only one with that "obligation," and I often asked myself "Why? Why is it? Why me?" But I didn't have an answer. As I remember, day after day, nothing changed. Same people, same activities. When I was thirteen, I had found a new occupation: goat herder.

Erasmo with his family

One day my dad came home with some very unusual news: A "gringo" was coming to live with us for a couple of weeks. I wasn't sure what that meant, but the fact that a complete stranger from far, far away was coming to stay with us, in our hut, was a very exhilarating event. I had never heard of it before, let alone imagined it. And there he was at our door, a tall young man with a big backpack on that hot evening of July 1982, and things changed forever.

All the villagers were amused, and I became popular. They asked me a lot of questions, like "What does he do? What does he eat? Is he going to marry your sister?" and so on. Craig spent the majority of his stay with me in the mountains, taking care of the goats, asking questions, taking pictures, and writing things down. For me, all that was so new, different, and very entertaining.

Two weeks went by fast, and I remember the day when Craig had to leave. I felt sad because the possibilities of seeing my friend again were close to none. Sad because after he left, I had to go back to my daily routine, all by myself, again. Yet, things were not the same, and a thirst for adventure started to grow in me.

Two months later we received a letter from Craig with some pictures and a book (*The Adventures of Tom Sawyer* which I still preserve), and after that we didn't hear from him again. Three years later I moved to the city where I got a job, finished my education, met my girlfriend who's now my wife, and life went on.

In 1991 we moved to New York where I decided to find out about my longtime friend, Craig. I was able to get a hold of his dad who then referred me to Seattle where Craig lived. When I called him, needless to say, Craig was speechless.

After many changes in my life, I must admit that going through the experience of meeting that stranger a long time ago impacted me the most. It inspired me. It helped me realize that God's purpose for us is perfect. I found the answer to the questions "Why is it? Why me?" And I am very happy with that. I consider Craig not only a good friend of mine, but my brother whom I love very much. And that's my story.

We moved to Seattle in 1997 where we now live. Craig lives in California, but we keep in close contact and visit often.

Jeff Boyd (1985)

Christi and Jeff Boyd in 2017 at Lake Kivu, Rwanda

MY EXPERIENCES DURING THE Central America Study Tour have helped form who I am today. My memories are not of specific people and places we saw or discussions we had. Rather it is the accumulation of experiences that have left deep impressions and taught me lessons about myself. With shame, I remember getting frustrated with Nicaraguan farmers who spoke Spanish differently than I had learned it. Arrogantly, I internalized "differently" to mean "wrongly." With my 8 months of learning Spanish, I was judging others who have spoken Spanish their whole lives.

After we visited some fruit plantations, we discussed multinational corporations and their exploitation of workers. The specifics of the exploitation in the banana plantations of Central America have since become muddled with those that I've witnessed in more recent years in Central Africa plantations. The concept of exploitation became personal when I realized how I, an unemployed college student with a little cash in his pocket, could also exploit a power imbalance with a man selling woven fabric. The man had beautiful and colorful cloth to sell. It looked nice and I had cash. He needed to sell cloth to care for his family. I did not need it, but I wanted it. I could buy it, or I could walk away. Or I could buy it from any one of the other half a dozen vendors selling similar items in the market. That gave me a power to negotiate an ever lower and lower price, such a price that the vendor would barely earn. In bargaining I could go much lower than what I would actually be willing to pay. So, I saved money to treat myself and meanwhile deprived this man that which could reasonably be considered a fair return on his labor. I exploited my position of privilege to my benefit at the expense of another. Over the years since, I have learned that bartering can play a positive social role in which relationships can be formed. On my better days, I try to do my part so that at the end of the bartering both the vendor and I will feel satisfied, and we can shake hands and smile. On my worse days, I still need to avoid exploiting an advantage that I have. And I need to accept with humility when I, the *mundele/ mzungu/gringo*, occasionally get taken by a vendor.

Doug Segur (student in 1985, TA in 1987)

REFLECTION #1

WHEN I DECIDED TO attend Whitworth College in 1984, one of the key reasons I chose the school was the existence of the Central America Study Tour (CAST). I attended the tour in 1985 as a student and then again in 1987 as the TA. Both experiences I hold as pivotal, life-changing events because they have greatly informed my worldview and more importantly, have impacted and shaped my values and perspectives as a US citizen.

We held a 30-year reunion in the summer after the 1987 trip. As I recalled the trip and its participants in the months approaching the reunion, I kept coming back to a deep, deep sense of gratitude for those at Whitworth who have worked so hard to make the tour possible and to sustain it for over 40 years. In particular, I've been so profoundly grateful to its founder and visionary, Ron Frase. Ron is among four or five people in my life who have had a significant and lasting impact on shaping who I am in the world.

As I've let these thoughts of Ron's presence and influence in CAST percolate within me, the enormity of the impact Ron has had on God's world through the tour has become more and more clear. The mental image it creates in my mind is Ron standing with individual threads radiating out to each and every person who has attended the trip. From each of those people, further multiple threads radiating out to others they have influenced through the values they've formed, the decisions they've made, and the work they've chosen to do. And beyond those, further threads—further impact. When thought of this way I'm left with this reality: Ron, you have changed the world!

This leaves me in awe of God and of the experience. Not only have I been a participant in something so personally profound, but I also have a direct connection to something so fundamentally good and immensely far-reaching in its impact around the globe.

The gratitude I feel flows over to include Ron's wife, and ever-enthusiastic CAST supporter, Marianne. She has made multiple sacrifices at home while Ron has been absent with the needs of the trip and in so doing, has left her own indelible mark on the world. She has always been so very supportive and interested in each individual student who has been on CAST. It also took the work, dedication, and sacrifice of the other professors and spouses (Ed and Leslie Miller, Don and Doris Liebert, Jim and Linda Hunt, Bob Lacerte, and I'm sure others), and to them I'm grateful as well.

Lastly, I'm left with this realization: Whitworth University would be less "Whitworth" if this learning experience did not exist. How appropriate that God chose this place to plant Ron and Marianne to do His work in the world through the Central America Study Tour.

REFLECTION #2

The first time I went to Central America it was the summer of 1985. We left in May and returned in August. I have many memories of this transformative adventure. One of my strongest memories of that trip was a realization that occurred to me in the *campo* (countryside) of Nicaragua. I was staying with a family of seven or eight in one of the few brick houses in the community. My host father was the pastor of this community and a farmer. His house also served as the church and gathering place for the community.

During my three or four weeks staying there, I was able to have multiple conversations with my host family and the various community members. Over the course of time through these conversations and, more-so witnessing how people lived life, a paradox began to emerge. I remember seeing in harsh details the realities reflecting that I had traveled from a very materially rich country to one that was quite destitute. I remember very clearly expecting to find people sad, bitter, and downcast for having to live life in such difficult circumstances. What I discovered shattered my expectations.

What I found was a country poor in material goods but rich, deeply rich, in a spiritual way that was not as evident to me at home. While life was hard, people were for the most part grateful for what they had. I found people living life not with bitterness but with hope, gratitude, and joy. As I interacted with the *campesinos* throughout my stay, more and more I began to see that while we in the U.S. had material richness beyond the Nicaraguans' wildest dreams, there was sort of a spiritual poverty at home. We have material wealth but, in some ways, seemed to be as spiritually destitute as they were materially. I remember wondering if it was the very blessings of our wealth that was keeping us from truly experiencing dependence on God. If we're able to meet our own needs through what we perceive as our own abilities and resources, even when we see them coming from God, perhaps we didn't see or experience our need for God in the same ways. I didn't doubt that faith in God was present at home. That was not the question. What I grappled with was the nature and depth of that faith. Did I truly *depend* on God and see him as my Source, or was my belief in him a convenience; a feel-good kind of faith? Who were the ones that were rich; that were blessed?

In the *campesinos* there seemed to be a richness of life that came from having to depend on God each and every day of one's existence, and in so doing one was daily reminded, and appreciative, of God's presence. It was something I saw exuded in their daily actions, their daily conversations, their way of living life. They were rich in the things that mattered. That's not to say life was easy for them or without complications, or that at home life was devoid of any spiritual depth. It was just this overarching difference that I hadn't expected to find. The difference seemed to be in how they handled, looked at, and approached that life—how they went through their days with a perspective that was centered in deep dependence on, and faith in, God.

Ron Barnes (1990)

FOR ME THE CENTRAL America Study Tour was very significant in my life. I went into it during the second semester of my senior year, and I really didn't have much clarity on where my education (it was called Religion at the time) would take me. Spending significant time in other cultures, learning from the professors and other students and the people we met and lived with in Central America led me to a strong desire to be involved in the larger world, outside the US somehow. I think before I went, my understanding of the Kingdom of God was limited by my cultural experiences as a follower of Jesus in the United States. My understanding expanded so much, it took me a couple years to really begin integrating that in my mind and life. Ultimately, the things I learned during the Central America Study Tour led me on a pathway toward world missions, then to critically examine how the Western Church has pursued the Great Commission. I am currently Global Outreach Pastor at Flatirons Community Church in Colorado, and I am still wrestling with how we should best do our part to fulfill the Great Commission.

DeLona (Davis) Campos-Davis
(student in 1990, TA in 1996)

As a young teen in the 1980s, older members of my church youth group returned from a CAST tour with inspiring stories and a zest for justice, and this led me to apply to Whitworth for college. As a student on the 1990 tour, I gained a lifelong love of Spanish, travel, and cross-cultural adventures. More importantly, I gained an extended family who have sustained me through the decades, the people I still count on to engage my heart and mind.

Serving as a TA on the 1996 tour continues to shape my life. The students taught me about community and embodied grace. This tour faced unique challenges, and they grew stronger together. It was a gift to share the CAST experience with my husband, Martín. We packed up for our six-month adventure hoping to find future job opportunities in Central America. We met many wonderful people and engaged with organizations doing important work. In El Salvador, we found a potential job opening and began planning to relocate.

Delona and Martin Campos-Davis and their Honduran friend Francisco (on the left)

Our final night in San Salvador, over a couple of beers with our host, he said something that reoriented our life plans. "Don't get me wrong," he said, "we'd be very happy to have you two move here and work with us. There is always work to be done. But honestly, the biggest help you could be to El Salvador would be to go home and let people in your country know that how you spend your dollars actually affects us here." This honest statement, spoken after decades of war supported by US tax dollars and in the beginning of the free trade, globalization of manufacturing, stayed with us. It continues to shape our choices. We have never forgotten.

Julienne Gage (1993)

THE LINGUISTICS OF LIFELONG LEARNING

IN A RECENT CONVERSATION with Whitworth University Central America Study Program Professor Kim Hernández I was reminded of the role of linguistics in lifelong learning. As soon as she mentioned how foreign language learning is enhanced by the context in which you do it, I heard the Spanish word *petardo*, or firecracker, shoot off in my head.

On the first night of my homestay in Guatemala at the onset of my 1993 trip, I was rudely awakened by a series of explosions that seemed to be coming from the next room where my host family was sleeping. I hid under the covers thinking about the

war stories I'd only recently learned of during Sociology Professor Ron Frase's historical prep course back on campus a semester earlier.

No screaming or sirens followed, and sleep eventually overcame me until the
next morning when I woke to the smell of freshly brewed coffee and the voices of that
same family happily chattering as they prepared my breakfast. I sat down at the table
looking rattled as I asked my host father in broken Spanish what had happened the
night before: "Were the neighbors okay? Did anybody die?"

He sipped his coffee and stared at me blankly. "Oh, *los petardos*," he finally responded, and then the whole family giggled uncomfortably.

They explained that the neighbor must have had a birthday, and that it's Guatemalan tradition to set off firecrackers under that person's window to ring in the special
occasion. They tried to calm my nerves as best they could in this war-torn corner of
the world. They said they couldn't guarantee I'd never be in danger. They did, however
give me tips for how to watch my surroundings, and they shared lots of stories about
living in a region that had been under fire for nearly four decades. Social and political
inequalities had long fueled civil conflicts there, but during the Cold War, the United
States government exacerbated such disputes by sending military aid to ward off backyard communism

In the months and years that followed, I learned of many situations in which
guns, bombs, Molotov cocktails, and fear-filled public policies had, in fact, destroyed
the lives of people in Central America and beyond.

I associate the word *tiroteo,* or shooting, with that moment our CASP group sat
in a bullet-ridden church in the tiny rural hamlet of *El Mozote*, El Salvador, where in
1980, some 800 civilians were murdered by their own military forces. The massacre
was an effort to wipe out any potential seeds of dissent among poor peasant communities struggling to survive in a tiny, densely populated nation where less than two
percent of the population controlled 80 percent of the land.

BUILDING ON CASP

A few years later, I would return to El Salvador during a yearlong field study as a
graduate student of anthropology, only this time, I would find myself on the metro-
politan end of Sociology Professor Don Liebert's Rural to Urban Continuum.

I was tasked with observing gang members who were both victims and perpetrators of shootings, stabbings, bombings, rapes, and extortions all because they had
grown up witnessing such heinous acts of violence and found themselves struggling
to find a peaceful path to self-preservation. I then hopped over to Cuba to learn how
arts could be instrumental for mental health and critical thinking when lacking job
prospects and geopolitical constraints hampered a young generation's hopes of a pros-
perous future.

Through these experiences, I got fluent in Spanish, better versed in cross-cultural communication, and much more adept at emulating History Professor Jim Hunt, who constantly reminded CASP participants of the ways history enhances our ability to contextualize current affairs and increase empathy toward people whose lives are vastly different from our own.

As I came to the end of my anthropological field studies, I realized my observations could have a wider impact if I could write and publish in two languages, so in 2000, I packed my bags and moved to Spain to study journalism. There, I would specialize in reporting on the country's immigration boom and the xenophobic backlash that followed.

Spain might not have been the beacon of social inclusion—especially if you count the Inquisition. However, my professors had plenty to say about democracy. I was enrolled in a special master's program sponsored by the Autonomous University of Madrid and run directly out of *El País*, Spain's largest newspaper. These journalists had helped to found the publication in 1976, following thirty-six years of right-wing rule by General Francisco Franco. He was known for suppressing Spain's diverse cultural and linguistic conglomeration of kingdoms, and any other identity politics that veered left of his dogmatic form of Catholicism.

I think of those journalism professors every time I watch my fellow American journalists struggle to define the politics of US President Donald Trump, even as he calls our profession "the enemy of the people." If this were Spain, we'd have no problem uttering the term *fascismo* regularly and liberally.

I would go on to report for mainstream news and international aid organizations in Madrid, Miami, and Washington, traveling to thirteen countries to investigate everything from secessionist movements and reproductive health in Kenya to sustainable agriculture and water services back in Central America and Haiti. I would also go back to Cuba several times to reflect on the viability of the egalitarian dream. I even worked as the managing editor of a Miami-based publication called *Cuba Trade Magazine*, which was founded in 2016 on the hope that Hillary Clinton would win the US presidential elections and continue with President Barack Obama's efforts to normalize US-Cuba relations.

On the flip side, I produced a documentary in Argentina exploring the search for children of people—mostly egalitarian idealists—who disappeared between 1976 and 1983 during the country's military dictatorship. Unlike El Salvador, most of these children were not pulled off of battlefields and whisked away to international adoption agencies. Argentina's conflict was far more subtle and cosmopolitan, taking place in a country with relative economic prosperity. These children were born to women who were systematically abducted while pregnant or abducted, raped, and impregnated in clandestine prisons. One of the goals of the so-called Dirty War was to cleanse the population by murdering progressive thinkers and harvesting their babies for adoption and re-education into regime supporting families. Thirty years of forensic investigations and military trials would show this was how most of the estimated five hundred babies born into captivity went missing but tracking adults who may be both victims and evidence of war crimes is a very polemic and heart wrenching process.

I had a nose for the story because we discussed it years earlier in Ron Frase's Latin American History course, and that, combined with CASP, taught me to consider early warning signs of danger and political upheaval, making me a more critical researcher.

THE PEOPLE MAKE THE STORY

Like many CASP students, it was hard to reintegrate on a campus where classmates might not have the same exposure to poverty and international politics. How do you explain the impact of getting dropped off in a remote Honduran village, relying on poor locals for survival? How do you explain the sights, smells, and sounds of a community living on the Guatemala City Dump? The roleplaying we did in Mexico City at the end of our 1993 tour taught me that the best way to relay these often-distressing stories was to mix the data with the emotional stuff. Naming people, places, and the terminology I learned there has given me more confidence in raising public awareness while avoiding self-righteous overtones.

During the first days of Trump's Muslim Ban, I was emboldened to speak up on social media about a time I had the privilege of covering a secessionist movement in Mombasa, Kenya aimed at giving locals—90 percent of them Muslim—a greater stake in their ancestral homeland. I put my life in the hands of a man named Mohamed whom I met at the city's historic Fort Jesus, and he took me on a three-wheeled *tuk tuk* to a slum-based mosque filled with Mombasa natives and Somali refugees, and then to a rural dirt-floored church. At both stops, I found non-violent Muslims and Evangelical Christians organizing around this illegal cause. He taught me that this ancient center of global trade is the birthplace of the Swahili language and *salama*, Mombasa's word for peace, is derived from the Arabic term *salam* or peace prevails, which sounds like *shalom* or *šālōm* in Hebrew.

During a translator shortage in Haiti, I was able to rely on a Spanish speaking Haitian doctor with a medical degree from Cuba to translate for workers at a cholera clinic where everyone spoke French and Creole. Our conversations moved well beyond the United Nations' involvement in introducing cholera to an already vulnerable nation by not educating their peacekeepers on where to set up latrines. We talked instead about what to do now, what to do over the long haul, contrasting Haiti's almost non-existent public health services with those he studied under in Cuba. This young doctor was so indebted to the Cuban Revolution that I nicknamed him *Che Comandante*.

I wasn't raised in Haiti or Cuba, so I will not judge his revolutionary romanticism, but he did remind me of how I lost the edge on some of that same sentiment I developed in the first post-war years of Central America.

Every time I light a gas stove, I think about the time I told an Argentinean tourist in Havana how hard it was to cook in an apartment with only one "what do you call the burner again?"

"Ah! La hornilla," she replied with a thick Argentinean accent.

I hoped to troubleshoot by taking this information back to the Cuban tenants in the old mansion we shared by explaining that my garage apartment only had one "orn-knee-sha."

This is how I would learn that Cubans let off steam through a variety of communication styles—some verbal, some not. They silently wrinkled their noses and raised their eyebrows.

"Oh! La hornilla (or-ni-ya)!" One of them declared. "She learned the word from an Argentinean!"

It was times like these that Cubans would burst into hysterical laughter, looking over their shoulders as they chided, "Yeah, join the club!"

The collective experience of lacking access to basic goods—largely because of the US embargo, but also due to slow moving bureaucracy—could make people hilariously sarcastic. Sometimes that type of expression was welcome. Sometimes it was cause for reprisal. It was hard to know.

And today, nobody can help me appreciate the absurdity of life's uncertainties better than La Gata, an elderly, undocumented tango singer I followed for an independent film in Miami in 2004.

Central America taught me that neighbors are part of your extended family, and older people, are to be treasured, no matter how crotchety. As a result, losing touch with La Gata after the documentary premiered in 2006 just wasn't an option.

Now in her 90s and living in low-income housing in Buffalo, New York, La Gata will give me an earful if I don't call for regular check ins, and even when I do check in, I sometimes still get an earful.

In the winter of 2016 a series of unfortunate events that included a project cancellation brought on by a budget crisis, a grueling schedule as a freelance reporter during the tumultuous 2016 elections, and a fall in my apartment building had me feeling vulnerable and disillusioned. During my studies in higher education, no one could have guessed that the digital revolution would destabilize the budgets for all kinds of humanities and communications roles. And now I couldn't even make ends meet by waiting tables because I had a broken arm.

I wondered to what extent I chose such an exciting yet unstable life and to what extent it chose me, and I just had to go with it. Surely that's a lesson I picked up early in Central America where the choice to live or work in a dangerous environment or in a precarious economy is hardly a choice at all.

And surely that's a lesson La Gata also taught me. She had escaped life as an orphan in a convent by learning to sing tangos on the streets of Buenos Aires in the

1940s. Exciting, yes, sustainable sometimes, but not always, so I figured we could commiserate.

"Thank God you've called," she said as she picked up the phone. These friends installed a landline for me, but it doesn't have any long distance."

I happened to know those friends because Latinos have taught me to coordinate social services in the absence of sufficient public assistance. That includes poetic ways of saying when enough is enough. None of us were going to pay for long distance on a landline, so I explained to dearest, most beloved *Gata* —for the millionth time—that she had a government-issued cell phone on which she could call us and then we would immediately call her back so that she wouldn't use up the free airtime.

"Look *Flaca* (Slim)," she protested, "That's just too complicated. That's just not how I want it to go!"

Yes, I know by now it's not appropriate to talk back to old people in any culture, but *Gata* does have that *je ne sais quoi*.

"Well *Gata*," I replied dryly, "I'm laying here flat on my couch with my broken arm in a sling. I've got a terrible head cold and I haven't seen my freelance checks. It's not exactly the way I want it to go either."

I cringed as an uncomfortable silence penetrated the phone line. It was broken by yet another awkward linguistic life moment.

"*No jodas marquesa*," she bellowed with a deep throaty laugh. Let's just say that's Buenos Aires street slang for "shut the front door your Royal Highness."

"I got a row of missing teeth and I'm hard of hearing," she shouted, and then, ever the cabaret queen, she chuckled again as she recited the wise cracking lines of old down-on-your-luck tangos.

One of her favorites? "Cuesta Abajo" or "Downhill" by Carlos Gardel, the first musician to write lyrics for tango music.

> Now, downhill in my defeat
> the illusions of the past
> I can no longer manage.
> I dream of the past that I miss,
> the old days for which I cry,
>   that will never come back.

The bad news is, life everywhere is increasingly uncertain. The good news is, we can manage the stress by learning to speak more openly with those around about our hopes, needs, and fears. For me, it all began with the linguistics lesson my Guatemalan host family offered when they saved me from the fear of *petardos*.

Authors' Note: Julienne Gage is living in Miami. She continues to work as a journalist as she looks for ways to segue into project management roles for long-term disaster recovery and community development

Alycia Krieger Jones (1993)

WHEN I THINK BACK on the Central America Study Tour, so many images come to mind, like a patchwork quilt with its multitude of intricate squares: playing sticks in the *parque central* of Quetzaltenango, bathing in the river during my homestay in Honduras, squeezing nine people into a hammock like a can of sardines, crying in the parking lot of a supermarket in Nicaragua because we have so much and they have so little, watching Ron wander along a deserted beach in his drawers . . . All of these images, and so many others, shape my trip to Central America.

How can we quantify what this trip gave us? It was a shock. It was our savior. It was everything we could ever hope for or fear. It fed us and starved us at the same time. It forced us to ask uncomfortable questions and to question where we came from. It pushed us to ponder the state of the world and the direction of our country. It humbled us.

I must say that, while I live in France and not Central America, and my job is not at all linked to Central America, the effects of that trip are an integral part of my life. The friendships I developed, both with students and professors, the way I approach the world, the way I live today—these are all influenced by a trip I took more than twenty years ago.

During my homestay in Honduras, I lived in the remote village of Texiguat. At that time, there was no electricity and very occasional running water. I had fourteen brothers and sisters in my family, not to mention the multitude of nieces and nephews. I had a hard time figuring out who everyone was. I had to ask one of my "sisters" to make me a family tree just so I could sort out all the names.

For the first few days, the family treated me like a visiting dignitary rather than a member of the family. I took my meals alone at the table, and I was not allowed to help with anything despite my many offers. It would have been a very unfulfilling month if I'd accepted that situation and not made an effort to change it. It took several days and a fair amount of stubbornness to begin weaseling my way into the family unit. First of all, I refused to eat alone. After that, they tried to make me eat with the men (who were always served first), but that was not very appealing either. So, I spent a lot of time hovering in the kitchen. Every time something needed to be done, I was waiting in the wings to jump in and do it. Before long, I was serving the men (who, to my great shock at first, bellowed "tortillas!" when they wanted fresh tortillas brought to the table, without a please, thank you or nod of acknowledgement).

Alycia Krieger Jones with daughter Julia and her husband Olivier

Before long, my family became a real family. I attended bingo sessions in the *parque central* after dinner each evening, where the whole village turned out for the game. There is not much to do when there is no electricity! I learned how to make tortillas, to wash my clothes both in the pila and in the river, and how to haul water up from the river in buckets (though I was rarely allowed to do this heavy work—the older kids of the family were recruited for that). I also got used to using a latrine, which is not so bad until you get a vicious case of amoebas and you have it coming out of both ends. Sorry to be so explicit, but another thing we all got used to during the trip was talking about our bodily functions!

Leaving my family at the end of that month was bittersweet. I was so excited to see everyone from Whitworth again, but so sad to leave my family.

But that departure was not the last time I would see my family. I was lucky enough to see them again several times in the years that followed my stay there. I experienced the (for me) disappointing arrival of electricity to the village, which brought an abrupt end to bingo night. Everyone was glued to telenovelas in the evening and quickly lost interest in bingo. Despite the big television that arrived in my family's house, my "mother" continued cooking over a wood fire—and coughing. When I asked my brothers and sisters why they didn't buy her an electric stove, they said she flatly refused. Change is hard.

And now for the surreal part of the story. Today, several members of my family are friends of mine on Facebook. How strange is that? How things have changed over the past few decades! From no electricity to sharing posts on social networks. What's next?

If I have to summarize what this trip represents to me, I think friendship is one of the first words that comes to mind. Laurie, godmother of my daughter, Julia; Renee and Tracey, lifelong friends; Krista, a dear friend whose life was sadly cut way too short; Ron, who touched my life in more ways than I can count; Jim, who came to visit us in France just a few months ago and with whom I share such a close bond; Don, one of the only ones who will ever truly understand my Honduran experience; la *familia* Mejia in Texiguat; so many others as well.

I am so grateful to have participated in this trip. I cannot imagine what my life would be like if I hadn't been on the Central America Study Tour.

Dan Plies (student in 1996, TA in 2005, consultant in 2008)

CASP leadership at Punta Mona: Wayne Beymer, Esther Louie, Michael LeRoy, Dan Plies and Robin Plies

RON FRASE RECOUNTS A message that he received from Dan Plies:

On November 30, 1998, I received an email from Dan Plies who first went to Latin America on Whitworth's 1996 trip where he visited the destruction of *El Mozote* and later served on the staff of several subsequent trips (as a Teaching Assistant and as a Consultant). He had just returned from the annual Fall protest against the US sponsored School of the Americas (SOA) which trained 60,000 Latin American soldiers in counterinsurgency. The purpose of this annual protest was to urge the US government to close the school whose graduates had been the perpetrators of the most heinous crimes. These crimes included the massacre of *El Mozote* where ten of the twelve officers cited for the crime were graduates of the School of the Americas. Of the twenty-seven officers cited for the Jesuit massacre, nineteen had graduated from the SOA.

For two days, protesters gathered at the entrance of the SOA. By law, this military base prohibits the public from protesting. To cross a line painted on the ground is to invite being arrested. In past years, protesters who crossed the line were arrested. Last year twenty-five people returned for a second year of civil disobedience and were each fined $3,000 and six months in prison.

Dan resolved to cross the line with 2,400 and to carry a photograph of Rufina Amaya in one hand and a cross in the other. As he crossed the line, his mind was filled with memories of Central American victims like Rufina Amaya and others he had known. This was a cleansing experience for him. A bus stopped, and the head colonel of the SOA jumped from it to inform them that the Army chose not to arrest anyone and that they would be given a letter banning them from the property for twenty-four hours.

Dan concluded his email with the words, "Acting in civil disobedience is such a small act of solidarity, such a small risk of my personal time and privileges, in comparison to the call that I have to be a witness to a higher (call and a higher) law of peace, love and justice. The strength of that higher call is an amazing force that empowers me to act and live out my convictions."

Jacob McCoy (2002)

Jacob McCoy with friends along the beach in Honduras

THE FOLLOWING "AMERICAN DREAM" was written by Jacob during his home stay in rural Honduras on March 5, 2002:

AMERICAN DREAM

Written in the rural backcountry of Honduras, at night by lamplight

Lately, I've been feeling a desire to be somewhere else. Not sure why I feel discontent; I keep telling myself this is the experience of a lifetime, the month I will look back on in the years to come when I am buried in the barrios of American suburbia with a smiling plastic wife, 2.3 kids, two gas-guzzling SUVs, a 12,000-sq. ft. home with four TV's, overstuffed furniture, cream-stuccoed walls, vaulted ceilings, a pool out back with manicured lawn and a hot tub, a NordicTrack collecting dust in my four-car garage next to my [limited edition] Mastercraft ski boat and my vintage Harley-Davidson which I can no longer work on like I used to because of my large gut preventing me from kneeling, and since my hair implant operation I've been forbidden from touching metal objects. Then, when my wife and I are no longer speaking and my children only slur monosyllabic responses to my questions as they sit for hours in their virtual reality entertainment system, and after I haven't seen my parents in over six years since they moved to Florida, because I just haven't found the time off from the office, and the only communication we have is the generic Christmas letter we send them and in return receive a picture of my parents in a computerized beach scene, my dad's head perched atop the huge crustacean body of a crab and my mom's face pasted in the center of a giant starfish under balloon letters painted in the sky saying, "Surf's Up in the Keys with the McCoys." This picture we will stick on our fridge-freezer unit, inside of which, heaps of leftover food rot in disposable Tupperware containers. This picture will hang for months next to revolving sports schedules and a fading church bulletin announcing a congregational meeting to discuss whether we want a traditional tree or a flocked one in the sanctuary this Christmas. Then, as I open the fridge to drink eggnog straight from the carton at 3 a.m. because I have insomnia brought on by the anti-depressants I am taking in combination with the prescription for social anxiety that also promotes cuticle growth, stimulates the sex drive, and turns your eyes an opaque green every 12th of the month, then will I stare out through the full wall of windows into the inky depths of the night, listening to the motor in the fridge and the falling rain on the patio with matching lawn furniture, and recall the still night

on which I sat listening to the rain fall on a thin tin roof,
writing by the light of my headlamp spilled on the page
long after my host family went to sleep,
their even breathing and sleepy murmurs wafting over
the nylon divider separating our rooms.
I will recall the days of endless rain and nights of clear skies,
waking and sleeping with the sun,
eating beans and tortillas and sometimes more,
working beside my father, picking coffee or cutting firewood,
learning to wield a machete or turn a tortilla with the same hands,
hands of flesh and sinew and bone,
hands with which to love and to build.
I will recall how I sat in mud, ate in mud, walked in mud, dreamed in mud,
lying awake at night,
stiff-legged from cramming my oversized frame into an undersized bed with paper-thin sheets,
living with nothing more than you could fit into a school day-pack,

when I was the town gringo,
a walking entertainment show for every kid under 15, and everything I did,
even brushing my teeth, was fascinating and exciting,
when I saw children cry from fear of the dark and men fall silent for fear of
tomorrow,
where the day's work depended on the weather,
where I showered once a week and forgot how to spell *"deodarant"*,
where I learned the knife edge of hunger and the precipice of poverty,
how to finger it, to walk the edge and know its power.
Then, standing there on my linoleum floor in cotton socks and sweatpants I
will wipe away my eggnog mustache, turn from the night and say, "For one
month, there I was alive."

Fifteen years later Jacob was asked how the Central America experience affected his
life and career after Whitworth. He responded:

> The trip was wonderful and challenging. It was very tough to confront the
> reality of some of the darker chapters of American foreign policy, as well as
> seeing crushing poverty up close. It took some adjustment after returning
> to the States. For a while I considered changing majors (I was as an English
> major) to International Studies or Political Studies. After college I did a vol-
> unteer year in Spokane and was a Krista Colleague through the Krista Foun-
> dation for Global Citizenship, a nonprofit started by Jim and Linda Hunt.
> I did the Peace Corps in Ecuador and was often reminded of the Central
> America trip and frequently found myself comparing my experiences. The
> trip continues to inform my life. I probably think about the trip every month
> or so, either because I am in touch with friends from the trip, or because I
> see something in the news about Central America. I am now an attorney and
> am currently representing a client seeking asylum from a town in Guatemala
> not three hours by bus from where I studied Spanish over a decade ago. I
> know of at least two other classmates from the trip who are working in im-
> migration law.

He was also asked what he wanted people in the United States to know about Central
America. His answer was:

> I think the greatest thing that United States citizens can keep in mind is that
> our politics and our policies, even if they only seem to be about national
> issues, reverberate far beyond our borders and have deeply felt consequences
> for citizens in Central America and around the globe.
> And on a lighter note, "If you have not yet tried *pupusas*, get thee to your
> nearest *pupuseria*."

Lora Burge (2005)

Chelsea Peterson, Lora Burge and Laura (Thaut) Vinson

IT IS HARD FOR me to pinpoint a singular experience or event of CASP 2005 that was most transformative. I remain deeply grateful to the experience as a whole for the ways that it shaped me and who I am today. There is a set of experiences that I have been ruminating on recently because of its intersection with some of my current work and ministry.

In San Salvador, we attended a mass at the Divine Providence chapel where Monseñor Oscar Romero was assassinated while saying Mass. I remember the artwork on the walls documenting the martyrdom of the Salvadoran people. We saw graphic pictures of Romero's death, of the nuns rushing to his aid, of a community surrounding this beloved leader in the tragic moment of his death. We met with Dean Brackley and walked the grounds of the UCA where the six Jesuit priests were martyred. We visited the cathedral downtown San Salvador to visit the final resting place of Monseñor Romero.

I remember the chapel being eerily quiet. I remember having a felt sense of being on holy ground. That a prophet and priest of the people had walked, preached, and broken bread in this holy place. And because of the brave words of truth and justice—in defense of the Salvadoran people—he was killed. I remember studying his work and words: Stop the repression! Stop the violence!

I recently stood in the streets of Honduras declaring similar things: Stop the repression! Stop the violence! Stop the impunity! Because of my work as a chaplain and training volunteers to be human rights accompaniers in Colombia, I was invited to be a part of an emergency accompaniment delegation leading up to the January 27, 2018 presidential inauguration. We were invited by a Jesuit priest known as Padre Melo. Profound militarization, deep corruption at all levels of government, rampant impunity and increasing repression of the people and human rights violations—it's a story long familiar to the region. Padre Melo, who has been a passionate and outspoken advocate for the people and for justice, has received death threats. Many of his colleagues—human rights defenders, lawyers, journalists, activists—have also been intimidated and threatened. Colleagues of mine on the delegation likened what we witnessed in Honduras to El Salvador in the 1980s. The El Salvador that killed Monseñor Romero and martyred thousands of other Salvadorans before it was done.

When the call for accompaniment to Honduras went out earlier this year I couldn't not go. Father Rutillo Grande, Monseñor Romero, Father Stan Rother, the US churchwomen, the Jesuit priests at the UCA and many more. Too many prophets have died in the region. And Honduras is now watching their brothers and sisters be bullied, beaten, and martyred.

I still reflect on the work and legacy of Monseñor Romero. I'm inspired and encouraged by the brave work of Padre Melo in a country in political crisis. I imagine I will always be connected to Central America because of the many ways it shaped and formed me in 2005. May the martyrs and the prophets continue to inspire our accompaniment, advocacy, and on-going solidarity work for peace and justice in the region.

Danielle Wegman (student in 2005, TA in 2011)

MOST SIGNIFICANT TO MY CASP experience was my homestay in the eleven-family village of *El Marmol*, Honduras, at the end of an offshoot of a long, mountainous dirt road. I shared a one-bedroom home with a family of four, without electricity or running water for one month. The village girls and boys brought me to the stream in the mornings to collect water, and in the evenings, I joined the men and boys for soccer games and cards by candlelight. I learned to co-exist with a tarantula who had made its home above the pila in the backyard.

When my host NGO dropped me off in *El Marmol*, they suggested I make an effort to meet Doña Vilma during my stay, a widow who lived at the bottom of the hill with her five small children. She lived in a small one-room shack with all of them and cooked outside over a fire. I played with her children, and when I was about to leave, she gave me an egg. It was my first experience of hospitality from someone who had essentially nothing in the way of material possessions. I accepted, as one of our pre-departure conversations with Esther Louie was about acknowledging the dignity of others not only by giving but in receiving. I will never forget Doña Vilma's generosity and purity of heart. She gifted me something almost every time I went to visit and play with her children.

I returned to *El Marmol* in 2011 while on a brief vacation from the Teaching Assistant role for CASP that spring. Most everyone in the village was still there, except for Doña Vilma and her family. Before leaving the area, I was able to find her in the nearest town, living with her mother, traveling two hours by bus to San Pedro Sula each week to work as a housekeeper and send her kids to school. Her kids are teenagers now with Facebook accounts, so I have enjoyed keeping up with them from a distance!

I credit my participation in CASP as what prepared me most in my life for intercultural communication and relationships. It taught me more resilience and a greater capacity to engage on many levels. It taught me to see the complexities of poverty, wealth, and relationships in the context of social, political, and historical dynamics. The education and exposure CASP provided transformed me from someone who simply wanted to help others, to someone who understood the value of being present, learning from, and participating with people who were different from me. I am forever grateful for my experience and participation with the CASP program.

Annie Aeschbacher (2011)

Annie and fellow CASPian Erica Yoder with children at La Pedrera in Xela, Guatemala

I WALKED UP FROM the metro station into the LA sun. My eyes squinted against the glare as I looked around and, to my surprise, realized that I was in front of a bustling market scene. Spread out all around the sidewalk were vendors selling clothes, shoes, CDs, fruits and vegetables, *pupusas*, hot dogs, and anything else you could imagine. People were browsing and bartering in Spanish with the driving beat of a *regetón* song blasting into the air. I smiled and took it all in, lifting my gaze across the street out to a park and then, to my even greater surprise, a big inflatable chicken perched on top of a roof.

What? That can't be . . . I thought, shaking my head at the prospect of seeing a *Pollo Campero* (the Guatemalan equivalent of Kentucky Fried Chicken) right here in Los Angeles. Still, my mind was too excited at the idea not to take a closer look. As I walked closer to the chicken, past an elderly woman selling freshly squeezed orange juice, a goofy grin spread across my face. I realized that the chicken was wearing a sombrero, and that it was, indeed, a *Pollo Campero* sitting across the street.

I can't believe it; I thought. This is too good to be true! Just minutes later my friend Abi found me, that goofy grin still plastered across my face. She laughed at my delighted awe at what I had already seen.

"Well, are you ready?" Abi was going to give me a tour of the MacArthur Park neighborhood, a place that she has now called home for five years. "Absolutely!" I replied. "Let's go." Abi walked me up through the sidewalks lined with vendors, past colorful murals and storefronts advertising call plans to El Salvador, Guatemala, Honduras, and Mexico, and restaurants with Central American specialties like *paches* and *pupusas*. Spanish music played out of the stores that we passed, and with every sign and advertisement that I saw, I was reminded of places I had gotten to live and travel during our four months together on CASP.

I slipped between reverie, memory and reality, especially when we turned a corner and saw a big Home Depot and Food 4 Less right in front of us. Oh yeah, we're in Los Angeles, I reminded myself with a disbelieving shake of the head. But it was the closest to Central America I had ever come in the United States, and I loved it. It was an exhilarating, confusing, surprising mix of reality. And it was home.

You see, when we left Central America I never actually left. Sure, we physically passed through customs, and I finished out my senior year at Whitworth, but I knew that somehow my life would always be tied to Central America and to its people who I had come to love and admire so much. The people I met in Central America and the things we experienced there challenged and inspired me, especially when it came to the intersection of injustice and faith.

A young Honduran woman who at the age of twenty was already a mother and a widow, with a sixth grade education and few job prospects. She was one month younger than me, almost to the day, and yet still had so much faith and gratitude for her life. I was struck by the heart-wrenching reality that I could easily have been in her shoes had I been born in a different part of the world and struggled to imagine whether I would have so much hope and faith. I was humbled to realize that I didn't think I would and challenged by her tenacity and bravery.

A group of farmers in Nicaragua whose bodies and lives had been broken by a poisonous pesticide called *Nemagon*, illegal in the United States because of its devastating effects. People we met had chemical burns all over their bodies; some had become blind, or lost limbs or clumps of hair. Other effects had passed onto their children; young ones born with physical deformities and mental handicaps. Some children never were born at all, due to infertility caused by the poison. Others were ravaged by cancer. The land was destroyed. They all had come to seek justice for what had happened to them, their families, their livelihoods and their community. And still they spoke of the grace of God amidst their suffering and pain.

A woman we met who was the *abuelita* of *La Chureca*, the gigantic garbage dump in Nicaragua. She had been forced to live in the dump for a number of years because she was no longer able to pay for a house. Her son was so ashamed that he no longer acknowledged her existence; she was isolated from her entire family, trying to make her way off of what the dump could provide. Still, she greeted us with one of the biggest, warmest smiles that I have ever seen. She radiated love, hospitality and compassion.

My six-year-old Guatemalan host sister, who cried that she wanted to be "pretty" like her three-year-old half-sister. Both girls were beautiful, with bright almond-shaped eyes, sweet smiles and thick, dark hair. The only difference between them was the shade of their skin. The older girl had a Mayan father, while the younger girl's father was mixed or ladino, with more Spanish / European ancestry. She had inherited a lighter skin tone, while her older sister was *morena*. My heart broke to see how racism already grasped and twisted my *hermanita's* perception of beauty and self-worth . . . the sins of prejudice and the lies of superiority / inferiority run deep. The thirty-six-year civil war and the deaths of over 200,000 Mayan Guatemalans is a testimony to that. And yet even after my country's direct involvement in this war, I experienced such a depth of grace, hospitality and love. It was humbling beyond words.

Visiting La UCA, a university campus in San Salvador, which is also the site of the brutal murder of six Jesuit priests, their cook, and her daughter. It was a murder that happened in the middle of the night, by soldiers who had been trained in techniques of torture at the School of the Americas—right here on US soil. These men, like many other martyrs during the civil wars, were killed because of their staunch advocacy for justice; especially for the poor and those who were most vulnerable in society. The women were disposed of so that there would be no witnesses. Seeing the gut-wrenching photographs, and then walking into the rooms and through the corridor where the murders happened, is something that is seared into my memory. I was glued to the spot, silent tears of anguish rolling down my cheeks. The group had to move on, but afterwards I returned alone. I needed to pay respects; I needed to lament the pain and injustice; I needed to cry; no, I needed to sob; I needed to pray. And as I stood there in front of eight rose bushes, one planted for each person who lost their life that day, the heavens let loose one of the most torrential rain storms I have ever experienced. The rainwater mixed with my tears, soaking me and the ground. Dewy drops landed on rose petals; I stared at the flowers and the thorns, acknowledging the tension of beauty and pain's coexistence. And then I just let the water soak over me and soak the ground . . . and I have no other words to describe it, except for a sort of baptism. An overwhelming feeling, from deep in my soul, that God was making all things new. A cleansing rain. A rain—a reign—of justice and of peace and of restoration that can only come from God. And my tears of sorrow turned to tears of joy, clinging onto the very real hope that we have of ultimate restoration . . . that day when all things will be made right and new. Looking at the eight names carved on the headstone, I knew that the world is still very broken. There is still so much pain; so much injustice. And it breaks God's heart. But pain and death does not have the final word . . . God does. That hope and faith are what Central America gifted me with; a hope and faith that are not just idealistic or theoretical, but very real, flesh-and-blood faith that fights against poverty, pain and injustice; holds onto hope, beauty and joy in the midst of suffering with courage, tenacity and perseverance; turns power and privilege on its head and reveals glimpses of God-with-us in the most beautiful and unexpected ways.

So, that very real faith, that very real struggle against injustice, that very real hospitality, that very real hope, joy and love . . . those are gifts that I received and knew that I needed to continue to give back in return. I returned to the US with a burning desire to continue to connect with the Latino community, invest in them, and bless them as they had blessed me.

After graduating from Whitworth the following year, I returned to Central America, living and working for a year as a Young Adult Volunteer (YAV) through the PCUSA. I lived with a beautiful family who remain dear to me to this day. My host mother, Juana Herlinda, is one of my lifelong heroes: working full-time as a single mother since her son was three years old, she has been an advocate for environmental stewardship, women's education, especially for low-income Mayan women, and access to health care—especially for impoverished mothers and children. She is a firm advocate of social justice, believing that it is at the heart of every Christian's calling to care for the least of these. She is one of the most joyful, loving women, and one of the strongest and most humble disciples of Christ that I have ever met.

While I was in Guatemala, I worked at the health center that served our town and the surrounding communities (10,000 patients), and a daycare for the children of working mothers. I learned much about myself through that work, and continually learned lessons about patience and humility. When I had time, I would go help out with the InnerChange team in Xela, a thirty-minute bus ride away from where I lived. The team had remained good friends since I first met them on a Jan Term trip during my sophomore year at Whitworth, and it was a blessing to have my YAV placement site so close to where they lived and worked. Their work was primarily with boys who shine shoes in the Parque Central, as well as making visitations to the women's prison in Xela. I would often come to Friday bible studies and hang outs with the boys and the team, sharing life, God's love (and *pan y café*) with them.

It was during a Friday hangout that a friend on the InnerChange team asked me what I was thinking of next in my future. I told her that I wanted to go to grad school and was still very interested in working with low-income / at-risk Spanish speaking kids and families in some capacity. She looked up at me and said, "You should really check out the Intercultural Studies program at Fuller Seminary. They even have a Children at Risk emphasis! I did that program at Fuller and it equipped me really well for my work. "Plus," she said with a sly grin and raised eyebrows, "There is an InnerChange team in LA that is driving distance from Fuller. You could help out with the team while you're in school." I admit, it did peak my interest . . . but seminary?? I laughed and said I would think about it, tucking it conveniently away in the back of my head. Out of sight, out of mind, I thought. But God had other plans.

Over the course of the next month or so, a series of events made it clear that God was nudging me towards Los Angeles in the near-future. I still didn't know if that call was for seminary or InnerChange or both, but it was a clear invitation to the City of Angels. And it scared and confused the heck out of me. You see, I have never really identified myself as a "city girl." I tend to thrive in nature and open places where my soul has a little more space to breathe. So, the thought of moving to Los Angeles, one of the super cities of the United States, was more than just a little bit intimidating. But just like any call, that nudge did not go away. So, I paid attention.

I finished my year in Guatemala and returned home to Washington, knowing that the time was right for me to be at home. My mom had just undergone a major surgery, and I was happy to provide extra help around the house while figuring out the next step. I ended up finding a job teaching Spanish at a few elementary schools in an extracurricular program and looked into grad school options. The more that I learned about Fuller, the more it seemed to fit with my passions and interests in an incredible way. The InnerChange team in Los Angeles also held many striking parallels to ways that God had been working in my life—working primarily with Spanish speakers and Central American immigrants, many of them children (and some families who were K'iche' speakers—the same language spoken in the town where I lived in Guatemala!). The doors to Fuller flew open, and the next fall I found myself driving down to Los Angeles to start the next adventure . . . very aware, and very grateful to God, of how connected all of this was with my first forays down to Central America so many years ago.

The two years at Fuller Seminary were incredibly rich and transformative. I was blessed to learn from professors and classmates from around the world, and to live so close to a city with so many different people. One of the biggest surprises to me was the way that God grew a great love in my heart for Los Angeles. I came to love it in a way I have loved few places in my life; I came to long to "seek the welfare of the city" to which God had taken me (Jer. 29:7), and to seek the welfare of the people there who were my neighbors. Throughout my studies I continued to volunteer with the InnerChange team in LA in MacArthur Park. And, surprise of all surprises, on my first visit I found myself in that mini-Central America, with *mercados* and *Pollo Campero* and all. In the craziest way, I truly was home.

Upon graduation, I sensed God extending an invitation to answer this call of "home" with the InnerChange team in Los Angeles. With InnerChange LA, I had found a group of people who love God, love their neighbors and who love the city. A group of people who are working with many hard-working, low-income, Central American Latino immigrant families on the margins. A group of people who are partnering with God's work in this little corner of the world, partnering with the Holy

Spirit to bring hope and healing and the flourishing that God desires. And in the midst of all that work, we are transformed by the immense gifts of God, given to us through those neighbors who God loves so deeply. Those neighbors who we also get to love. And so, I embarked on the journey of raising support and building up a base of ministry partners, so that I could soon join in this work full-time and truly make MacArthur Park home.

Just the other day as I was praying, I saw myself in Honduras again. I was lying on a bed after having been horribly sick. The room's lights were dimmed, and my host aunt was sitting right next to me, stroking my head and rubbing my stomach. It was exactly the comfort that I needed; her love reminded me of what my own mom (who was a couple thousand miles away) would do. I was entirely helpless yet receiving an abundance of love and care and grace so freely from this woman. There was nothing I could do or give her in return. And as I was back in this scene, God showed me clearly the abundance of love and grace and care that I would receive from my new neighbors in LA, just like I did in Central America. How they would become vessels of God's love and grace and care to me in moments when I have absolutely nothing to give. I saw parties in crowded apartment complexes, with an abundance of food and laughter. I saw hugs and tears and looks that spoke volumes. I saw hugs and hands helping me up when I fall. And I knew, in that moment and even now, that this new step will be a blessing far beyond what I can dream or imagine.

Kelsey Grant (2014)

As PART OF OUR CASP academic coursework, we were asked to compose photo essays using Appreciative Inquiry guidelines to reflect on several important themes. Following is the first essay I wrote near the end of the first month in Guatemala.

Lago Chicabal, a sacred lake in Guatemala

"SUFFERING"

In those days they climbed the mountain to reach the sacred place. Except they didn't bring their *agua pura* in Nalgene bottles; the women shouldered babies, the men machetes. They walked through and up an down in dust with the rhythm of ceremony. They were walking to reach the place where *Nawales* send a man searching and the water receives prayers. I trekked to the same destination, but without so much grace.

I complained and there were rocks in my Chacos and the view was cool, but we were going to climb down 600 more stairs to get there anyways. Then I wondered how I may have walked differently were I an indigenous Guatemalan woman, carrying physical and emotional cargo, but with quiet perseverance. Feet steadied with familiar steps.

It's like when I had amoebas. My heart and mind weren't quiet. I could not rest in the moments between puking my brains out, nor could I look forward to a time when I would maybe not be dying. My mind was on the next bout of sickness. My feet were pointed toward the next hill around the corner. Which is the funny thing about an ambiguous destination. I can't seem to focus on the present nor the end goal, but instead gravitate toward the what-will-go-wrong. Problems become the certainty, suffering the stronghold. When you are climbing and your lungs are begging mercy, or when you are laying on the bathroom floor thinking about just sleeping there for lack of energy, the near future and the present are both crappy options. I am in a foreign place experiencing foreign things, and sometimes suffering—homesickness, frustration, self-pity—disguises itself as a comfort because at least it feels certain.

I saw her by the lagoon, that woman I could have been, wearing her huipil and leading two small children by the hand. She seemed to walk with so much familiarity and therefore purpose; in that moment I envied her because she had reached her destination. Now, however, I realize my mistake. Too often struggle is my end point for lack of a firmer stronghold. I travel and travel with the intent of getting somewhere, but I am never *there*. I am always climbing the next hill, imagining the lagoon on the other side, and so forget that I have made it. I am here, and that is enough for now. Suffering is not the journey in and of itself, and it is not the destination. That is what they knew, and I didn't, when we climbed the mountain to reach the sacred place.

Hannah McCollum (2016)

Hannah McCollum and host mom and sister

ONE YEAR AGO, I was getting ready for the adventure of my life as a student; my every thought was preoccupied with my upcoming semester abroad in Central America. I was scared and excited and filled with high expectations—in other words, I was experiencing a completely normal mix of emotions. Professors Lindy and Kim, and students from previous years did a good job of hyping up the CASP experience: I, along with thirteen *compañeros*, were going to make flying leaps forward in our Spanish abilities, we would build friendships that would last forever, and we would be converted to a life of service in the mission field or development work. Above all, we'd become crazy about *gallo pinto*.

I'm home now, my tan is gone, and my life has returned to normal. My Spanish is better but nowhere close to fluency. I don't anticipate I'll ever work for a non-profit to help save the world, and I don't know if I'll ever go back to Central America. All that remains visible from the trip are a few trinkets from Guatemala displayed on the mantel, watercolors of Granada and Volcán Mombacho hung slightly crooked, and a frayed bracelet with my host family's initials tied around my wrist. It's back to the same life in Spokane, the same routine of class and homework. When everything appears to be the same, I wonder what's changed.

A peek at Facebook shows what's different. I spent three months in Nicaragua interning at a school, and besides the political cartoons posted by my host mom, I am privy to the teachers' birthdays and cute pictures of their kids. A few of my friends from the school still randomly message me, demanding I mail some snow back to them. Besides my casual Facebook friendships with Nicaraguans, I am blessed with a dozen new friends at Whitworth. I live with two *compañeras* from CASP and running into any of the others on the Hello Walk feels like a mini-family reunion. Somehow, without my fully realizing it at the time, I made connections that are very real and special.

Making these connections wasn't easy at first. My motive for studying abroad in the first place was to force myself to get over my fear of speaking Spanish to strangers, and to some extent that worked, but crafting friendships from scratch is difficult for me even in my native language. I was afraid, not only to mispronounce words, but to engage my host-parents and the people at my internship in personal conversations. For a month, I let my trepidation get the better of me. It held me back from practicing Spanish, but more importantly, it made me feel alone and isolated.

I blamed everyone but myself for my frustration and sense of awkwardness at home and at my internship. My host mom was too standoffish, my host-dad was always at work, how could I get to know them? The principal put me in the wrong place at the school, where I had nothing to do. I looked forward to the evenings when I helped my host mom and her sister roll and pat Salvadoran *pupusas* and wait on customers. I felt useful. Silences didn't feel as uncomfortable because our hands, coated in vegetable oil, were occupied. Although I quickly became the favorite playmate of my little host brothers and a clingy cousin, I longed for adult interactions.

One night, my host dad gave me a tough love pep talk: "You need to start conversations with people, ask them questions! When you have nothing to do at work, find someone and ask about their day or their family." He placed the responsibility for my happiness squarely where it belonged: on me.

I did my best to take his advice, making it my goal to have a personal conversation with one person every day. Once I said "hola," the rest got easier. First Martín befriended me, he practiced his English and I replied in Spanish; then Aminta, who loved to watch me try new foods and react to them, and brag about her two daughters; and only a few weeks before I left I befriended Johana, the school nurse, and Rosa, a high school math teacher, who were both the same age as me, nineteen. The simple choice to eat my lunch outside instead of sequestered in the air-conditioned office acquainted me with more friends: a third grader claimed me as her best friend only a day after we'd met. She liked to ask me what Americans typically eat, and then reject my answer because she had an aunt in Los Angeles who said we eat hamburgers every day.

On the last day of my internship, I was surprised by the number of hugs I gave and received. The teachers brought treats to morning devotionals and I assumed it was a holiday, not realizing it was a going away party for me until the principal presented me with a card everyone had signed. Honestly, I didn't expect to be so affected by parting ways with people I had only just gotten to know. I lasted the entire day without crying until, as I was leaving the school grounds, I walked past Martín and two overall-clad groundskeepers whose names I could never keep straight. It was their chorus of "*Hannah, no te vayas*" that made me realize I had friends who would miss me and who I would miss in return.

Looking back, I wish I had pursued those conversations with more energy right from the beginning. I imagine how much better I could have known Johana and Martín and mustache-guy if our friendships had started at the beginning of those three months instead of the end. I wish I had asked my host mom more questions instead of waiting on her. I'm trying to look at it as more than a missed opportunity, but as a lesson learned in the value of opening up to the people around me and asking for their stories. It was selfish of me to possess the language abilities to understand someone's story and to shy away from asking while I benefited from their hospitality in a strange country. The only thing I could offer in return was simple friendship, and I undervalued that gift.

Now I'm home, back in Washington *(el estado, no la ciudad)* where it's cold and rainy instead of hot and humid, trying to figure out where to place my experiences last semester in relation to the rest of me. The little blue house I share with Karli and Emily, fellow CASPianas, is often filled with the heavy scent of *plátanos* frying, and Karli prefers to make tortillas from scratch on taco night. Sometimes, we'll gather in the kitchen and laugh as we revisit our memories of Guatemala and Nicaragua—Emily's obsession with the thick, Guatemalan tortillas, the time Karli broke her foot stepping out of a cab, and my intense struggle to find a decent cup of Earl Grey tea. Sometimes, one of us will pause while washing a dish and realize out loud, "Guys, we actually did that!" On the outside, it's true, not much has changed. I still want to be a freelance editor and stay in the northwest United States for the rest of my life, just as I did before my trip. From where I am now it's not immediately obvious how Spanish or my short time in Central America will influence my career or life. I know my experiences in Guatemala and Nicaragua will stay with me, even as memories fade, because it was an important time for growth. And growth is often invisible, it doesn't have to be expressed through a major change in my goals, but it makes me realize my values and in what ways I still need to grow. I am excited to see the surprising ways Nicaragua will pop up in my future, and the relationships I'll form because of it.

Micah Allred (student in 2016, TA in 2018)

Micah Allred with his host mom and host brother

DURING OUR THREE WEEKS in Quetzaltenango, Guatemala, I made up my mind that I would try to attend a Catholic church once I got to Nicaragua. Since high school, I had had a growing interest in Catholicism. Raised in a non-denominational Christian home, I absorbed early on the belief that Catholics are not Christians. When my family began worshiping in a Presbyterian church when I was in high school, I was "reacquainted" with Catholicism and gained a respect and curiosity for it. The first mass I attended was in the national cathedral of Honduras, during a two-week long trip with my pastor during Jan Term of my freshman year at Whitworth. By the time I arrived in Guatemala on CASP, I was more knowledgeable about Catholicism, but it was still new enough to me that I was eager to learn more about it and to experience the liturgical and theological insights that it might have to offer. Moreover, I knew that I would experience enough upheaval in Nicaragua as I attempted to fit into a completely different culture. I figured I would appreciate the stability and relative normalcy of weekly mass, as opposed to the often emotionally draining charismatic, Protestant services that I knew I would find in abundance. Attending mass would be simpler, also, since there would likely be one or two churches to choose from, as opposed to the plethora of Protestant mission church plants and break-offs.

I was happy to find out ahead of time that my Nicaraguan host mom—and my internship supervisor—was Catholic. I was disappointed during the first week of my internship, however, when she attempted to avoid my requests to attend mass, "forgetting" that I had asked her multiple times and making us late to the service when she finally relented. Yet, deep beneath her overbearing personality, beyond the anxiety of being responsible for the safety of a North American sent to work with her, Sara really did care for me. (When I carelessly remarked to a friend of hers that she was my *madre nicaragüense*, she latched on to the term, proudly repeating it to all who would hear.) So, after the initial spat about attending mass, Sara made a point of either going with me or sending her adopted son—her grandson, John,—to go with me.

One Sunday mass, during the part of the service where the congregation stands to pass the peace, I returned to my seat and was warily eying my hostmom as she continued to make the rounds. It seemed like she knew the entire congregation, which was impressive to me, not because the parish was large, but because it seemed like the only time Sara went to mass was when I did. Likely, Sara knew the people at mass from her work outside the church; she was an activist just as much as she was Catholic. My wariness became astonishment when Sara not only greeted everyone in the pews but proceeded to the platform. Working her way from right to left, she greeted the acolytes, with the air of a queen greeting her most ardent supporters. The priest, meanwhile, was preparing to create the body and blood of God himself, seemingly unaware that Sara was approaching him. I watched with horror—and strangely, embarrassment—as Sara stepped close behind the priest and slipped her hand under his, depositing something that I couldn't quite make out on the white table cloth of the altar. As soon as I realized what Sara had placed on the table, I guessed why she had done it. By placing her multiple rings—her *anillos*—between the bread and wine, Sara was ensuring that her jewelry would share in the sacramental blessing, receiving perhaps enough blessing to last until the next time that she came to mass.

When I asked Sara later that day about what she had done, her explanation—that she placed the rings on the altar so that they would blessed by the priest, and that I, too, could get something blessed if I left it on the altar—captured well my experience with her over the three months that I lived with her. I thought what Sara did was wrong—her theology of blessing was entirely off base. But I could tell that Sara was proud—no one else had had the nerve to put their rings on the altar. Finally, I realized that Sara had something that I, a well-off North American, didn't—a certain insight into the process of blessing. She affirmed her own dignity and showed her love for me by choosing to share her knowledge with me.

Jessica Langdon (2018)

Jessica Langdon and members of her Nicaraguan host family

I FIND IT DIFFICULT to sum up how all I have experienced on CASP has changed my values, goals, and passions. I do not think it is possible for me to know how exactly my experience will shape who I will become. However, I do recognize that I have a different way of viewing myself as a result of CASP. When I was living in León, Nicaragua, I would often come across situations and interactions that would highlight this privilege in contrast to the people I was living with and working alongside. Recognizing this privilege would make me feel upset, disconcerted and sad. The injustice of living on a different "playing field" economically than others out of luck seemed irreconcilable.

Post-CASP, there have been many times I have returned back to a guilt-ridden reaction to my own privilege. When I look at the current Nicaraguan news on my Facebook and see injured victims and unrest, I look at my own privilege with disgust. Why do I deserve to enjoy the comforts I am surrounded by? Why do my worries seem so superficial when compared to deep hurts and injustice in the world? I recoil from the thought of forgetting how my standard of living is vastly different from most people living in the world. As a result, I sometimes put myself in a space of grief so as to not forget my privilege. I tend towards using guilt as a tool to keep me "grounded" in life's large problems.

However, I am beginning to recognize that while my reaction is valid and warranted, my self-enforced guilt could be more harmful than helpful. Sure, this guilt can help keep me in a critical mindset that reminds me of inequality and pain—and this grief is important to create the passion it takes to propel toward shalom and fight for justice. But living in mental grief is not a great way to make my privilege a source to help serve others. In order to contribute and act, I cannot be paralyzed by guilt. I am convinced that this kind of guilt is not productive and resembles a poisonous sort of shame more than anything.

As I was reminded many times during my CASP experience, we are commanded and commissioned by God to use the gifts He has given us in the world. He wants us to live alongside others as ministers of His love and share our story. I do not want to grow stagnant in shame after CASP. I hope to be able to successfully move forward in my processing in order to allow myself to share my CASP experience with others. I hope to utilize what I have experienced on CASP as I serve God in whatever career I end up choosing. God does not desire that I sit in shame—he did not create and have me be born to parents in the United States so that I could sit in shame about my privileged situation. God desires that we move, act and seek His kingdom on earth.

The question that follows: "How can I best transition from Jessica pre-CASP, to the Jessica post-CASP?" I think this will come with time and patience. As I become exposed to ways I can get connected to Latin America and share my story, I will feel more connected to the newly transformed Jessica.

In all, CASP has grown my passions in immigration, feminism, foreign affairs, politics, and history. I am able to draw upon real-life experiences in order to explain these passions. I have gained cultural competency and know how to be more culturally sensitive when talking about other cultures. However, I ought to utilize my awareness and passions in a productive manner. This way will not always be clear and obvious, but I hope I will never stop pursuing it.

I am incredibly appreciative to partake in an experience that allows me to question my identity so deeply. To have an experience that molds your passions and motivates you to action is something to be grateful for. I believe that God chose for me to partake in this experience during my time at Whitworth—and I am excited to continue to grow and learn from it in my future.

Erik Blank (2018)

Erik Blank and coworkers at a women's march in León, Nicaragua

I CAN SAY WITHOUT a doubt that this experience has changed my life. While my Spanish speaking abilities greatly improved during CASP, I was most impacted by the way the program forced me to confront real problems and injustices in the world that became apparent through experiences and personal relationships in Central America. I learned about culture, history, and sociopolitical dynamics through my relationships with my host families, internship supervisors, and friends that I made in both Guatemala and Nicaragua. Learning in this way is nothing like learning from a textbook or a lecture. It allowed me to associate historical events and issues with people whose reality has been and continues to be affected by those events.

While in Guatemala, our group had a number of opportunities to confront these difficult truths, and it was here where my worldview truly began to be challenged and grow. I remember one particularly challenging day was when we visited a deportation center for Guatemalan minors. This government center works with minors who have been just deported back to Guatemala after being picked up in Mexico attempting to cross into the US. Upon arrival we came face to face with kids whose eyes showed devastation as their dreams of a brighter future had just been ripped away. The rest of our time there was spent playing games and hanging out with these kids, hoping to let them feel like kids even if it was just for a moment. After this experience, I heard many stories from my host families and friends in Guatemala and Nicaragua who have family members who have attempted to immigrate or who are currently living in the US. It is these stories that have shaped the way I think when discussing issues like immigration in the US, and I have CASP to thank for that.

In both Guatemala and Nicaragua, I stayed with incredible host families who treated me like their son. These families taught me more about their culture than I could have imagined. They showed me how to make their food, what they like to do for fun, and shared their beliefs with me, for which I am very grateful. Both of my host families also taught me about what it looks like to care for someone who is different than you. They took me in and accepted me as their own despite our differences, something that a lot of people in our culture (including myself) have a very hard time doing. I found this very impactful as we were learning about many things the US has done throughout history (most of them pretty bad) in these countries. My host families were aware of the harm the US has done, but still loved and accepted me despite the rough history. As I said before, they also shared a lot of stories with me. The importance of story is something that the CASP program heavily focuses on, especially the privilege we have to be both givers and receivers of stories. It was through stories with my host families that brought us to become family.

Learning about many of these hard truths and injustices in the world made me feel very convicted and anxious to start doing something about it. In my internships in Nicaragua, I began to think about my vocation, and discern what it is I can start doing to fight injustice in the world. I began working in a community clinic where I was giving health education classes, and while I enjoyed working with patients, I came to realize that I could not see myself working in a clinical setting for any extended period of time. This was a worthwhile investment in my first month in Nicaragua; however, I decided to pursue another internship for the rest of my time in Nicaragua. I began working with a women's advocacy organization that revealed a passion I didn't realize I had. I worked with the anti-violence sector of the organization where I helped with workshops and efforts to educate women and children about their rights and worth as humans. While working at this internship I was confronted with many current injustices happening to women all over the world today, like domestic violence and sexual abuse. This internship allowed me to discover a passion in me of advocacy and fighting for human rights that made me consider more of a future in social work or law. CASP also created a new budding interest to become a Spanish professor and educate students about the importance of learning another language as it allows you to learn about more people and become a more compassionate person. While I'm not certain which direction my future will ultimately take, I can definitely say that my CASP internship opened my eyes to new possibilities and gave me exposure to things that I could not have seen and done in the US. Thank God for CASP!

Anna Waltar (2018)

Anna Waltar and her Nicaraguan host sister

As a theology student, one of the major questions I found myself asking over and over again throughout our experience was, "What does good, faithful cross-cultural ministry look like?" I started wrestling with this question almost as soon as we got to Guatemala in January. Guatemala has a very prominent indigenous population, and many indigenous people still actively practice their traditional religion. So, the month we spent there in January was a rich time of getting to learn about and witness so many aspects of Mayan spirituality—whether that meant watching a spiritual guide burn an offering of thanksgiving or coming across whole families hiking up to the peak of a volcano early in the morning to worship at a sacred site.

Alongside this ongoing influence of Mayan spirituality, Guatemala is also a country with deep ties to the Christian faith, a legacy which dates back to the arrival of Catholic missionaries alongside the Spanish *conquistadores* centuries ago. These missionaries, while praised by some for bringing salvation to native people groups who had never before heard the gospel, are condemned by many for their frequent acts of violence and oppression against those who refused to accept their message. All too often, these missionaries took on the conquest mentality of the soldiers they accompanied—those who were not like them and refused to bend to their rule were enemies who could be robbed, enslaved, or slaughtered as they saw fit. And so, these missionaries denied the humanity of the Mayan "pagans" they encountered, giving them the choice between conversion and the sword.

Other missionaries took a different approach. Rather than presenting the gospel of Christianity or death, they sought to adapt the Christian faith to fit in seamlessly with the Mayan religion they encountered. During our month in Guatemala, we got to see many examples of this phenomenon known as syncretism, which is basically the attempt to somehow integrate one religion with another—in this case, merging Christianity with elements of indigenous culture and spirituality. We visited cathedrals, for example, that were originally built in typical European style, but later repainted with the bright colors and images that are so much a part of the vibrant Mayan culture. Similarly, inside the churches we frequently found statues of Jesus and the disciples that had been dressed in traditional woven textiles. At times, there would even be space at the front of the church for people to observe their traditional Mayan rituals and offerings right there inside the cathedral. For me, it was beautiful to see ways that missionaries and Christian leaders from within the Mayan community had sought creative ways to make the gospel message more accessible and relevant to the lives of indigenous Guatemalans. At the same time, there were certain cases where I had to wonder whether the truth of the gospel was even being proclaimed at all, or if the message had been watered down so much that it had eventually been left behind altogether.

So, these experiences kept me wrestling with my original question of what it looks like to share the gospel well within the context of another culture and spirituality. Being there in Guatemala, I could feel a pretty heavy influence of what I would say are two dangerous extremes when it comes to answering that question.

The first extreme is that conquest mentality I mentioned earlier, where the assumption is that any culture or spirituality other than traditional Western Christianity is inherently wrong and dangerous and needs to be wiped out. During CASP, it was such a hard experience for many of us in the group to have to learn so many painful truths about how the Christianity we grew up in has been abused so much throughout history as a way to justify wiping out indigenous communities and their cultures.

Then there is the other extreme of pluralism, which basically says that all religions are the same and that the Christian message has nothing distinctive to offer to the world. And as I mentioned before, this is where I got a bit cautious about syncretism. I felt so privileged our whole month in Guatemala to have the honor of learning from the beauty, the generosity, and the humility that are all so central to Mayan spirituality, but as a Christian, I can't lay aside my conviction that the gospel message holds truth that all people of all cultures need to hear, and I worry that at some point, syncretism moves from adapting that message to fit a cultural context to abandoning the unique importance and saving power of Christ.

The more that I witnessed what, in my view, were unhealthy and dangerous forms of cross-cultural ministry, the more I found myself growing angry and disillusioned with the idea of Christian missions as a whole. A major turnaround point for me came one weekend when we went to visit Lake Atitlán and saw a powerful example of what I would call incarnational ministry—a concept I'd talked a lot about in theology classes at Whitworth but was hit by in a whole new way through this experience.

That weekend, we took a little boat across the lake to visit a small rural village called Santiago. This community was mostly indigenous, and as we walked through the markets we got to see women working on their weaving and men wearing their traditional pants with colorful birds sewn all over them. When we reached the steps outside the cathedral, we all sat down and Micah (our TA) told us about the man who had served as priest in that town during the Guatemalan civil war some thirty years ago. His name was Father Stanley Rother and he was a Catholic priest from Oklahoma.

Stanley Rother memorial in Santiago de Atitlán, Guatemala

When this priest came to Santiago, he didn't reject the culture of the people like the Spanish *conquistadores* had done—instead he saw the beauty in it and looked for ways to empower his community and to stand in solidarity with them in the midst of all the oppression they were facing in the midst of the civil war. Even as he sought to respect and learn from their culture, however, he didn't shy away from teaching them the truth about Christ and inviting them into the kingdom of God.

One of his main projects in the community was working with the women to help them organize businesses to sell their weaving. Along with the clothing and blankets that they would normally make, he also encouraged them to start weaving stoles—the cloths that priests wear around their necks as a symbol that they've been chosen and anointed to do God's work. Father Rother would always remind his congregation that every single one of them was a priest and was called to use their gifts to do God's work in the world, a remarkable message to a village of poor, indigenous peasants accustomed to being shoved to the margins of their society.

As he continued living among these people and teaching them about the good news of God's love for them, Father Rother also began to see that his ministry had to push him to raise his voice against the dictatorship that at this point was disappearing people left and right and massacring whole villages of innocent indigenous families. With time, he became such an advocate for indigenous rights that the government started to see him as a threat and put him on their list of opponents to kill. When the church found out about the danger he was in, they flew him back to the US. Only a few weeks later, however, Father Rother decided to return to Guatemala, against the wishes of the church and his family. He knew full well that he would be killed by the government, but he also knew he couldn't leave his congregation behind for the sake of his own safety when they were experiencing such great suffering. Only a few months after his return, some soldiers came in the middle of the night and shot Father Rother in the chapel. During our visit to Santiago, our CASP group actually got to go into that chapel, which has now been converted into a memorial for the priest. Bullet holes and blood stains on the floor still mark the place where this man gave his life for the sake of his beloved people.

As odd as it sounds, the story of Father Rother gave me so much hope for the church. It helped me to know with confidence that the kind of ministry God calls his people into doesn't look to conquer and lord it over people. Nor does it minimize the powerful message of the gospel just to make it easier for people to accept. The kind of ministry God calls us to requires us to stand in solidarity with people. To eat what they eat. To live with them and accept their hospitality. To delight in the beauty and richness of their cultures even when they differ from ours. And even, if and when the time comes, to be ready to make real sacrifices as we seek justice and wholeness for others—not because we're strong enough on our own to make those kinds of sacrifices, but because we trust that God will be faithful in giving us the strength. I recognize that we're not all called to be martyrs, but I do know that we're all called to live in this kind of bold solidarity with people, even when that means making true and painful sacrifices.

Before we left Santiago, each member of our group had the chance to buy a stole from the women in the market who continue to weave and sell them to this day—a tradition handed down from one CASP group to the next. And if you've ever been to a Whitworth graduation or ever choose to go, you'll see each graduating CASP alum wearing their stole with their graduation robes and cords. For us, these stoles serve as a sign that all the gifts and passions we each have, the education we've gained at Whitworth, the experiences we've had through CASP—none of these are simply for our own benefit. The stoles are reminders for us, just like they are for the congregation in Santiago, that we've been chosen and anointed to give ourselves over to God and to the work he wants to do in and through us for the sake of the world. And that's what ministry is, I've learned, whether it's here in Spokane or in Guatemala or anywhere else—it's giving ourselves over to God to be used and trusting that he'll be faithful in revealing himself to the world through us.

This poem (translated from the original Spanish) is a reflection on my experience of visiting the chapel of Santiago Atitlán and learning the story of Father Stanley Rother. The first half of the poem imagines what this priest might have experienced on the night of his death and the second half captures my thoughts from the day we visited as I stared at a framed photo of Rother that now hangs in the room where he was killed.

You trembled, brother.
I have to believe that.
When the door creaked in the darkness,
Just as you knew it would.
When they entered into your room,
Perhaps shouting,
Perhaps with the silence of impunity.
In that moment,

Your blood, brother—so alive just a beat ago –
Now turned to ice in your veins,
Pleading with each pulse,
"Not yet! My God—not like this."
We fix eyes.
You, from paradise.
Me, here in your Gethsemane,
Desperate,
Searching for answers.
Against my will, my tears betray me.
I can no longer hide my fear –
The immensity of the call
Bears down heavy on my heart.
This soul, how it yearns to obey,
But this body?
Cannot.
But yours, it did.
Tell me how.
I must know how.
You stare back at me with the confidence of glory,
A son, even now, of the victory fulfilled,
The kingdom soon to be revealed.
Don't fear, my sister.
You whisper.
This God—our God—he is faithful.
It is he who calls us, yes,
But he, too, who trades our frailty
    For strength.

Henry Estrada, Teacher at Casa Xelajú in Quetzaltenango, Guatemala

JESUS CHRIST SAYS, "My peace I leave you." Many of you have come to share with the poor of Central America, to be peacemakers, and to interact with other young people and let them know you are different and that you want a better, more just world; a more humane world; a world with more God. In light of Christ's words (a Christ that is the way, the truth, and the life), I ask you this question: What kind of peace? What kind of peacemaking do you come to share with us, compared to the peace offered by the world? Please indulge me a few more lines to paint the portrait of this "peace" that you have come to share and seek in Central America.

Is it a personal peace that somehow makes everyone see things my way?

Is it the kind of peace based on having everything possible—possessions, money, power, living like first-world consumers?

Is it the kind of peace that turns people into machines and dehumanizes them, so that they reach the end of their lives obsolete and good for nothing in the world?

No! Christ's peace is the one that each one of you carries inside you and is the most valuable part of you. Human beings are life, spirit, and love, and with those things the peace of God can always be built.

As I reflect on my experiences with many Whitworth students in my Spanish classes at Casa Xelajú in Quetzaltenango (Xela), many images come to mind. Your unique paradigms have shown me that you want to be different, that you are enthusiastic and joyful about sharing with different cultures (especially with the Mayan people), that you sincerely desire to share life with new families and friends here, and most of all, that you are willing to invest of yourself in social projects to benefit our community. Your adventurous trips to smaller communities in Guatemala (author's note: "the Plunge") have allowed you to really get to know the sociopolitical and economic realities of our people. Personally, I have enjoyed teaching sessions with you about Liberation Theology, which have been cordial times to share, analyze and reflect on the poverty, suffering, and injustice of the countries in this region.

I truly believe that this program has allowed you to grow in your academics and professional aspirations, but more importantly, it has allowed you to become humanists. The impact you have made all these years on your teachers, host families, and community members in Guatemala and many other places in Central America, has been what I would dare to call necessary and indispensable for our world. The impact not only benefits all of you university students and those you meet during the program, but most of all, it transforms the human family.

I only wish this kind of program could happen all over the world to show how we really can be in solidarity with one another and not selfish toward the preferred of God's Kindgom—the needy.

I am so happy to have the opportunity to get to know so many students with different philosophies who are committed to building a better world and sharing the peace of Jesus Christ. I hope we will have Whitworth groups in Central America for many, many more years to come. The world needs you and the peace you bring. Continue in your mission of solidarity through justice and love for all. *¡Con un abrazo fraterno para todos!*

Freddy and Leonor Méndez (2011–present)
Nicaragua In-Country Consultants

BACKGROUND HISTORY

I (FREDDY) MET WHITWORTH University Professor Lindy Scott back in 2009 at a Latin American Theological Fellowship conference in Costa Rica. At that time, I was the National Director of Nicaragua's university student ministry affiliated with the International Fellowship of Evangelical Students (IFES). At that time, he shared with me Whitworth's plan to establish an academic center in Heredia, Costa Rica. A year later, when Whitworth's Costa Rica Center (CRC) was getting started, I met the two Teaching Assistants of the CRC, Emily Dufault and Kristina Kielbon, who had been students on CASP in 2008. After many conversations, we arranged for the first group of CRC students to visit Nicaragua for a week in November 2010. That trip was such an academic, cultural and relational success that we hosted CRC students for a week every semester for the next four years.

In 2011 we received our first CASP group for a three-week period. My wife Leonor and I coordinated their lodging and travel within the country as well as arranged many academic and cultural learning experiences. We were able to introduce them to Nicaraguans deeply involved in the religious, political, and social activities of our country. The CASP leaders and we all agreed that the experience had been overwhelmingly positive.

During the 2013/2014 academic year, Whitworth implemented the new internship format for CASP. After a summer or fall at the Costa Rica Center and January in Guatemala, the students would come to Nicaragua where they would be placed with host families and internship sites for three months. We had the privilege of finding and vetting the families and work sites. We were able to use Freddy's network within the Christian subculture to find placement opportunities with Christian NGOs where the CASP students could serve God by loving Nicaraguans through their academic majors.

Freddy and Leonor Méndez, their children Saraí and Josué

LESSONS AND IMPACT UPON THE MÉNDEZ FAMILY

CASP has had a positive impact upon our family. We have been able to serve CASP as a team using our individual skills and talents during the preparation, coordination and implementation of the CASP programs in 2014, 2016, and 2018. I (Freddy) dedicated myself more to the areas of relationships with families and institutions and with educational activities, and I (Leonor) have worked more in administrative and bookkeeping tasks.

CASP has enabled us to establish and strengthen relationships with Christian sisters and brothers from North America. This has expanded our vision of the world and what God wants us to do. Given that our cultures are different in many aspects, Nicaraguans and North Americans have somewhat differing ways of knowing God and following in his steps. We trust that the CASP students and our Nicaraguan Christian students have learned from each other in our complementary ways of obeying God.

Through our service to CASP we have been able to supplement our family income and have been able to pay for some essential needs, such as the education of our children Saraí and Josué. We have also grown professionally. I (Leonor) have become much more confident in my skills as an Administrator and Accountant. I (Freddy) have developed my student ministry abilities, especially with those from a culture different from my own. We have received over fifty CASP students since 2011 and they have become dear sisters and brothers in the Lord. We have also developed deep and enduring friendships with the CASP Teaching Assistants (Travis Walker, Danielle Wegman Sagen Eatwell, Dana LeRoy, and Micah Allred) and Professors (Kim Hernández, Terry McGonigal, and Lindy Scott).

IMPACT UPON THE HOST FAMILIES

CASP has enabled more than twenty host families to develop and affirm healthy, intercultural relationships with North American university students. In most cases, these families have become the students´ mentors and teachers in areas of Spanish, faith, politics, culture, economics and ecology. The students have been received as if they were true members of the families.

Of course, the families have received modest remuneration for hosting the students. With these funds, the families have been able to make improvements to their homes or cover other expenses.

By having an international student in their homes, each Nicaraguan family has been able to expand their understanding of God's Kingdom in our world. They have learned more about what God is doing through their student, and indirectly, through the student's family and home church. Each family has learned about how these university students follow Jesus in the United States.

IMPACT UPON THE CHRISTIAN MINISTRIES

We have had the privilege of placing the CASP students in over fifteen faith-based service organizations as well as in a few secular institutions. These agencies have included medical clinics, schools, and community development organizations. They have opened their doors and their hearts to receive our students and enable them to carry out their internships.

In most cases, these internships have been win-win situations for the agencies and for the students. The agencies receive three months of hard work performed by enthusiastic interns . . . for free. The students receive three months of supervised, intercultural work experience. What a great deal for all!

The agencies have also strengthened their professional stature as they have grown in their own intercultural abilities. Having supervised a student from another culture, the agencies and their staff have also broadened their horizons and improved their supervisory skills. In the best cases, the agencies and the interns have learned from the strengths of the other's culture.

Esther Louie (2002–2005)

Former Assistant Dean of Student Life, Faculty Leader, and Intercultural Specialist

THIS WAS A LETTER that Esther wrote to the parents of the 2002 cohort in April 2002:
Dear Moms and Dads,

I have just returned from Managua, Nicaragua. It's been almost twenty-four hours since I left the Central American study tour group, and I miss the group. I've been writing this letter since I joined the group on March 20. My husband, Wayne, and I flew down to San José, Costa Rica to join the group and continued on with them through Costa Rica and Nicaragua.

The first evening we were all together, I was so amazed and impressed that I wanted to thank you, to thank you for raising such incredible young people. One of the ways I thought that I could do this was to write about your son or daughter and tell you about my experience.

Where do I begin? I know that what I've written here will show my inadequate writing skills, and you will forgive me because I want to tell you how absolutely wonderful your son or daughter is. I write this also to give you an idea of what's been happening, and what you might see and hear on the return of your son or daughter—here goes.

When your son or daughter returns, you might notice that the first thing in the morning is a conversation about your poop —firm, soft, or the dreaded diarrhea. If you declare that you had a firm bowel movement, they will gleefully cheer. Don't be alarmed at their choice of topic. It's perfectly natural—all of them have had diarrhea on this trip, and some for multiple times. There are amazing stories about diarrhea and bathroom behavior. Some of you may have heard these stories already, and you can bet that if anyone in the family has diarrhea, your student will be the expert on how to take care of yourself. You must ask them about the "diaper" awards.

You might also notice that at the table, they'll be eating with their fingers, totally disdaining the use of utensils, or scooping their food up with a piece of tortilla. Don't be alarmed—they learned this skill in Honduras where in most of their home stays, the families did not have or use utensils. They've developed a connectedness with their food and an appreciation of what food means to their bodies.

They may launch into a lecture about the coffee that you are drinking because they've seen from the ground up how coffee affects the livelihood of so many people. Many of them during their home stays in Honduras picked, sorted, dried, carried, and helped get the coffee to market. They know about the economics of coffee and how the world treats Central America and one of its largest exports. They know what the *campesinos* get for growing, picking, and supplying the coffee and it seems so unfair.

They may have a new attitude about eggs as many saw their very hungry "brothers and sisters" not eat the home-grown eggs because the price of one egg could sustain the family for a few days.

They may appear moody—or more quiet—or want to spend time by themselves. There's nothing wrong, this may be their new-found sense of tranquility and the changing pace within. It's a process they've learned—to reflect, to sit quietly writing in their journals, to pray and to meditate even when all around them is a hustle and bustle.

You will notice their deepened sense and connection with God and Jesus. To their core, many of them relied and surrendered to Him in the most uplifting way. We all learned during the toughest times that He is faithful, that He is the greatest companion. Many have learned to have a deeper conversation with Him during these months. It has been what has sustained them.

They may have a new attitude about the US. They've heard from an amazing array of speakers on many different subjects. New perspectives on the role of the US and the impact we've had on their politics, economy, government, and ultimately on the people of Central America. Some of this information was hard to listen to. Don't misinterpret that your student has become less patriotic but do listen to what they have heard.

Your student may not want to stay home after having been gone for five months. They may make a beeline back to Whitworth to see their friends. Do not be disappointed. But understand that the fellowship with their travel partners and the bond is incredibly strong. They started out the trip without knowing hardly anyone in the group—maybe a few acquaintances. And now, they are so deeply connected, my guess is that they will feel a bit lost without "da group."

(Esther then describes with flair both heartwarming and heart wrenching anecdotes about the participants. The complete list of stories is found in the chapter about the 2002 trip in the first section of the book.)

The stories go on and on. If you don't play pinochle—you may want to learn and be ready to play. All the students have learned on this trip to play and many a night when they could have gone out, they made the choice to stay and play some killer games. The tournaments were hot and fierce. This is not just about playing cards; it is about life and fellowship.

They worried about how to be able to tell you what has gone on with them these months. They know they will have a hard time putting all of their experiences and their transformation into words. I would say that they might not be able to fully understand the enormity of personal growth during this time. They will be processing this experience for the rest of their lives.

Their perspective about people, ways of doing things, ways of thinking, problem solving, arguing, may subtly change or shift. Their reference point to the world, awareness of politics, social, spiritual, environmental and interpersonal may have increased or expanded. Their world and their insistence of what is right or wrong, good or bad, conservative or liberal, light or dark, funny or serious has increased by many dimensions and facets.

They may not insist that in life that it is—all or nothing, either/or, but now can see more clearly the both/and, and that differences and similarities have many shades of gray. In short, they are becoming more of the intelligent, sensitive and caring people you wanted them to grow up to be. Your handprint is clearly on them; and the work continues.

They will or may have a hard time explaining this to you in the moment they get off the plane, or at the next morning breakfast, or even in those first few days they are home. They expected to be changed by this trip, but they had no idea how. And some know the changes, but not sure what this may all mean.

Their focus has sharpened. This doesn't mean they know exactly what they will be doing, and in fact they may question hard which direction to go. They may be confused or perturbed by all they've learned. Some may feel they've been affirmed in their life goals and will work hard to reach these goals.

I've asked them to listen to understand, to listen to hear the messages, to listen with all their heart, to listen with compassion, and to listen to get all of the message before they discount, defend, dominate and deny. I've asked them to reflect on this experience as it is full of the riches of life and to continue to plan, hope, and dream for world peace and understanding. They are doing hard life work and you can be proud of the passion and faith with which they approach this work.

In my opinion, the success of this trip lies with a lot of different factors. You and a cast of thousands have helped with their success. Two of the most important people on this trip are Amber and Jero. My guess is that you've heard of them already. They are the glue to this group; they are the constants that have cared, nurtured, challenged, supported, and helped transform this group. Having been former students of this tour in 1999, they have returned as the teaching assistants. They have kept us all on course even when we couldn't remember what the mission of the trip is, or why we decided to come along. Their devotion to the vision and mission of this tour is inspiring. Their fluency in Spanish and their cultural understanding is incredible and professional—from working with border guards, politicians, officials to taxi drivers, they have guided us safely and graciously and moved the group all over Central America.

Amber and Jero's medical expertise has helped your student to get through diarrhea, bug bites, sunburns, diarrhea, dehydration, infections, head lice, diarrhea, stomach aches, many unnamed itches and scratches, and diarrhea, to name just a few. They have modeled true leadership for this group. I have watched them continue giving and serving the students even when they were tired or hungry. They slept less to get up in time for those early morning bus rides; they ate less when for some reason there was less food. They itched and scratched along with us, but they ministered to all before themselves. They worried more about the condition of the group and paid close attention to those that needed it. They would jump into action to take care of all other's needs before their own. They managed more details than they should have, but because they were often the only ones around, they stepped up and took care of any issue. I trust them with my life.

Jero has helped pull your student back to safety when they have wandered away from the group whether physically or spiritually. He has provided a sense of safety with his rock steady ways, and clear thinking—no problem is too large for Jero. I have watched Amber handle five students standing around her and all asking different questions at the same time. She takes care of each one in the most grace-filled way. They are fun to watch, as they are such great friends to each other. They know each other well and are so grooved that they allow for each other's strengths and gaps. They know when to lead and when to follow—there is hardly a misstep as they take care of the feeding, housing, transporting, and motivating of twenty-five students and the faculty. When they may clash, we have fun watching them as they stand nose to nose and work it out. Better than most marriages, they walk around from that clash with no grudges and no hard feelings. They are amazing young people. I am privileged to have worked with them, and I am humbled by their devotion to God, their sense of social justice, and the passion to live their lives of commitment. They have been friend, confidant, nurse, teacher, and parent to your student.

I can write and write about my impressions and observations and experiences for the short few weeks that I was with the group. I hope that I have given you an idea of how this has gone, and perhaps what you can expect when your student returns. Most of all, again, I want to thank you for the young person you have raised. This has been a letter written with love for your sons and daughters. I have learned so much from them.

I look forward to meeting you.

Esther

Dr. James B. Hunt (1981–2009)
Faculty Leader and History Professor Emeritus

I BECAME ENGAGED IN Central America through both academic interests and friendship. Through friendship.I met Drs. Ron Frase and Don Liebert in 1973 when we all arrived together to Whitworth College for our professional work as faculty. I became intellectually aware of Latin America through my graduate course work in Latin American Colonial history at the University of Washington. These two factors began my journey towards my involvement and engagement in the Latin American Study/Service Program. I had heard of Ron Frase's work since an undergraduate at the University of Washington and my involvement with University Presbyterian Church's World Deputation program in that my peers in 1963 had gone to Brazil to be with Ron and Marianne in their summer assignment. One of those, Dick Boyer, became a professor of Latin America History at Simon Fraser University in Canada and others came back with engaging stories of what they learned while in Brazil. Our families met at the start of school faculty retreat held at Priest Lake and have remained colleagues and friends ever since meeting monthly for prayer and sharing in various combinations of faculty and administrators. Our wives participated in both book groups and collaborative writing projects including a children's cook book and gardening book. The friendship has undergirded our work as colleagues together on the Central America Program, the vision of which was guided by Dr. Ron Frase without whose commitment and dedication, the program would not have existed, nor the impact on both students, other faculty, administrators and curriculum and alumni of Whitworth.

My first involvement in the Central America Tour (as it was called in the early years) began in 1981. I had taught Latin American History and was brought on by Ron Frase, who began the program in 1975, to provide additional faculty support for the program. For me, Latin American history had been an academic study and discipline. Throughout undergraduate and graduate school I had not traveled to Latin America even though I studied both the language just to pass a graduate school reading test and in-depth work in Colonial Latin American History. My first travel and engagement with Latin America was landing in San Pedro Sula to meet up with students who had been, for a month, in their Honduran service assignments and then help lead them to Copán where they learned about the ancient Mayan Civilization, then to Guatemala, where we learned about the civil war, US foreign policy, and met with a Catholic Priest whose work with the indigenous populations put his name on a hit list for death squads; a retreat at Lake Atitlán, then travel by bus to Oaxaca to learn about Mexico's Ancient civilization at Monte Alban, and then completing the trip at Cuernavaca to learn about the realities of barrio life and from the work of Ray Plankey and his staff about economic and social injustice. This first trip with students was an eye-opening experience for me. I learned so much from Don Reasoner, our TA, and definitely felt so under-prepared in the Spanish language, knowledge of current Latin American problems, that I deferred for almost a decade my re-engagement in the Central America program. While at the College, I continued to be involved in Latin American issues, however, including the Latin America theme dorms and an extensive program called *The Stranger Next Door* which brought in Latin speakers such as Camilo Cortez from Chile and representatives from the US State Department. As we were raising our children in the 1980s, it also became difficult to leave my family behind especially during our difficult Spokane winters and with our kids in their critical teenage years.

The impact of the Central America Tour, later known as the Centra; America Study and Service Program (CASP), was definitely significant for the students, but also for the College as well. Whitworth secured grants from the Fund for the Improvement of Post-Secondary Education to assist professors in both language training as well as travel experiences in the host cultures. To prepare for both my involvement in CASP as well as to augment my regular teaching of Latin American history, I and my wife spent a summer in Seville, Spain and a summer in Mexico City, Mexico to learn Spanish. I moved from a bare reading level to some degree of functionality in Spanish. I also brought cultural materials including photos, experiences and even documents back from Spain and Mexico which enriched my course work. In the late 1990s these materials were incorporated into my PowerPoint slides I would use in my Latin America classes. Thus, I kept up in the field of contemporary Latin America problems and thus overcame the deficiencies I felt in 1981.

I also found that I began to integrate this work with my own professional interests in American history through two intellectual threads that began to weave into my scholarly and research interests. The first was work in faith development. I began to note the impact travel experience had on the lives of students who had gone to Latin America. The transformation of ideas, values and perspectives was evident in their journals and perspectives once they returned to campus. This resulted in a scholarly article on the faith development of Frederick Douglass that emerged from a National Endowment of the Humanities Summer Seminar on Autobiography led by Dr. James Olney at the University of North Carolina I began to note how the travel experience shaped Douglass's autobiographies and faith journey. Certainly, the Central America experiences of students informed these insights. Second, while most of my training in history had a social science bent, the Summer Seminar also broadened my perspectives into a more holistic consideration of development which is a hallmark of the interdisciplinary, reflective and experiential approach used in the CASP program. These insights persisted in my published scholarship on Jane Addams, John Quincy

Adams and, eventually, John Muir. The CASP program had no small impact on my scholarly interests, questions and published results; rather, it was a driving force that gave me insights that shaped my research and scholarship.

Beginning in 1990, I resumed my engagement with the CASP program by providing preparation courses in Latin American History, participating in the Preparation course specific to the five-month program and helping with the planning of the itinerary, budget, leadership, student selection and the curriculum. Both of my daughters participated in the program with Susan Hunt (Stevens) in 1990 and Krista Hunt (Ausland) in 1993. Thus, the Program had a deep, personal and family impact on my life. By now, the design of the program involved considerable pre-trip preparation with language, preparation course work, and content classes in history, sociology, and religion classes required of the students. There was also added significant debrief both during and immediately after the program's completion. These later components were shaped so that students had a way to process their profound experiences. For many students this was the first time in their lives, they had direct lived experiences with poverty, injustice, and questions of foreign policy. At the same time, students gaining a deep appreciation for the families they lived with and the bonds they made with one another during this five-month intensive program of learning. I was involved in the CASP program from 1990 to the close of my retirement in 2008–09.

A number of students influenced by CASP returned to live and/or marry in Central America including Kay Eekhoff, Leslie Vogel, Jefferson Shriver, and Tracey King. Many students sought to return to visit their host families including Laurie Werner, Alicia Jones, and Julie Gage, for example. Some students married and lived their newly shaped values in the United States including DeLona Campos-Davis and Karen Murphy, just to name two. Other students found new direction in their careers as a result of the impacts. Marc Archuleta worked in the Los Angeles police departments with Hispanic communities; Paul Brassard sought business opportunities by going to the Thunderbird School of International Business; Julienne Gage has been active as a freelance writer and worked at the Inter-American Development Bank; Mick Cunningham, Sharon (Glasco) Bailey, Michael Barram, and Sagen Eatwell sought out and found careers in international education. Their direct involvement at an experiential level resulted in their committing their lives to people and issues they engaged with on this five-month program.

In the case of my two daughters, Susan's acceptance to Dartmouth Business School for an MBA was facilitated by her essay on the Central America Program even though she was a graduate of Wesleyan University. In the case of Krista, who got her teaching certificate from Whitworth, she and her husband, Aaron Ausland, sought a three-year volunteer assignment with the Mennonite Central Committee in Bolivia as a preparation for their intended careers in international development. Aaron went to Guatemala when Krista chose to go on Whitworth's program. Krista was killed in a bus accident in Bolivia in May 1998, just three months into the assignment, but Aaron returned; worked for three years in micro-loans and financing, and was admitted to Harvard's Kennedy School in International Development. He is currently working for World Vision in an African entrepreneurship program. As grieving parents, after I returned from the CASP program in the spring and that fall, my wife and I co-founded The Krista Foundation for Global Citizenship. The model for the processing of the service experience was the Whitworth CASP program, because we wanted our Krista Colleagues who engage in service, to develop a lifelong ethic of service. To date, the Foundation has supported over 280 Krista Colleagues in areas Krista sought to serve: inner city, developing nations, and the environment. A good number of these Krista Colleagues are Whitworth alums. The inspiration for the formation of the Foundation came directly from my experience with CASP in 1999.

So, what has been the impact of CASP on the College, now University? First, CASP students shared their experiences with fellow students, many of whom were recruited for the next class of CASP. Their stories widened out to the student body. The students also held College-wide Forums which were well attended and appreciated by their fellow students. Second, CASP helped to internationalize Whitworth's curriculum. Courses like Western Civilization in the History department became a World Civilization class. American History eventually became America in the Atlantic Community. The "other" culture requirement became a requirement in cross-cultural learning and global studies. Study abroad programs began to proliferate on campus to include programs in France, British Isles, Mexico, Thailand, China, Africa, and South Africa. Consideration for international education became a focus for the selection of Academic Deans including Darrell Guder and Michael LeRoy. The campus embarked on an ambitious program to build a learning campus center in Costa Rica. In addition, CASP students have come back to Whitworth for ten year and multiple year reunions. They often retain a positive appreciation for the power of their learning experience.

Whitworth has prided itself on being an open and committed Christian university that takes its faith seriously while at the same time engaging in the real problems that confront humanity. The CASP program has undergirded and supported that justifiable identity. As the nation appears to be turning inward, will Whitworth follow the culture? Hopefully, the CASP program will continue vibrant, alive and effective in the future. There is no doubt the CASP program had a profound impact on this professor, his family and, in turn, the entire Whitworth community. I have only to thank my colleagues, Ron Frase and Don Liebert, for making this opportunity available to me and to Whitworth and, especially to the students who went through the program.

Terry McGonigal (2002–2018)

Faculty Leader, Theology Professor and Chaplain

WHILE I TRAVELLED WITH CASP students throughout Central America, my primary focus on each journey was the experience of CASP students in Nicaragua. I had travelled to Nicaragua several times in the 1980s and 1990s. I was in Nicaragua the month before the election between Daniel Ortega and Violeta Chamorro, which Violeta surprisingly (for some) won. I experienced first-hand, through discussions with US Embassy personnel and meeting with candidates across the political spectrum, the vast economic and political resources of our nation as it exerted its will to influence the outcome. Of course, the US had been doing this for decades in every Central American country. The 1970s and 1980s saw the tragic consequences of that intervention in the prolonged wars in so many countries, as well as embedding violence into the very fabric of each affected nation.

But somehow Nicaragua seemed to be different. They had stood against US intervention and been victorious. But slowly over time the regime of Daniel Ortega slipped into familiar patterns of favoritism, corruption, and failure to fulfill promises to enhance the life of the people in Nicaragua. Tragically, those failures have now come full circle in the violence which has broken out in that country in the spring and summer of 2018, with the tragic deaths of hundreds of protestors at the hands of Daniel's national police and military. We sat with CASP 2018 alums who were forced to leave Nicaragua early because of the violence, their minds and hearts torn asunder by their rapid extraction from Nicaragua and return to Spokane. My mind drifted to countless conversations I had been a part of over several decades with CASP alums. These most recent CASP alums were responding in the same ways I had seen so many times before. Deep sorrow and sadness as they mourned the loss of the precious relationships they had with their homestay families, expressing worry about their host families' wellbeing. I had heard these questions repeated over and over again about the root of violence, the seeming absence of God in the midst of the bloodshed, wondering about how this cycle of relentless violence can ever be broken. If any country in Central America could have forged a different, more peaceful way, it seemed that it would have been Nicaragua. The questions the 2018 CASP alums raised reverberate with echoes familiar to all of us who have made this journey, going all the way to the beginning in the 1970s when Ron Frase first envisioned this risky life-transforming educational experience. Perhaps those questions, and each of our attempts to answer those questions with our lives since we experienced CASP, whether three months ago or three decades ago, is the greatest living testimony we can offer to the power of CASP and the mysterious work of God in the midst of all the mayhem which daily invades the villages and cities and mountains and *campo* of Central America.

And yet the story of Nicaragua in particular, and for every Central American country as well, is laced with stories of countless courageous followers of Jesus who have risked everything, including their lives, in the cause of peaceful intervention on behalf of justice. Those people, many of whom have been martyred, rehearse for us once again the story of Jesus. As Jesus entered into Jerusalem on Palm Sunday with the crowds shouting praises in their mistaken belief that this was the moment when he would initiate the violent overthrow of Roman oppression and re-establish the glorious Kingdom of Israel, Jesus wept. "If you, even you, had only known what would bring peace—but now it is hidden from your eyes." (Luke 19:42) His followers' blindness was caused by their complete misunderstanding of God's work. They thought violent vengeance was God's way. But Jesus' way was, and still is, the way of peace (*paz, shalom*)! And the faithful remnant of Jesus' followers who for decades have pursued his peace in his way throughout Central America know in their hearts, minds, souls and bodies the struggle to live in the Jesus' way of peace.

Throughout all the decades of CASP these faithful Jesus' followers have invited us into their communities and their homes. They have shared their lives, their food, their stories, their grief, their hopes with those of us from Whitworth who have been fortunate enough to receive their gracious hospitality. By knowing them, each of us has been molded and shaped in the Jesus' way. The best commendation of our Central American experiences is for every CASP alum to continue to live in the Jesus' way— each day in our own communities as we pursue the way of peace for all people in all places at all times.

Kim Hernández (2008–present)

Spanish Professor and Coordinating Faculty Leader

Kim Hernández helps Xela friend, Isabel, with a cooking class

WHITWORTH'S CENTRAL AMERICA STUDY & Service Program has a rich history and legacy over more than forty years. Hundreds of students have had their lives transformed by their studies, their travels, and their learning experiences in CASP. Likewise, many people, communities, and local organizations in Central America have been enriched by their interactions with Whitworth students and faculty. I am grateful and proud to think that Whitworth has been present in Central America for more than four decades. The students have been able to live, learn, and serve in a way that is unique to any other kind of study abroad program. They have left a lasting impact and gained an enduring change in perspective.

The past ten years of memories, challenges, ministry, learning, and relationship building have been some of the most enriching moments of my life and career. I have had the privilege to accompany, teach, guide, and learn from five cohorts of CASPians and several other CASP faculty colleagues. Being part of my students' academic and personal development and education through the CASP experience has strengthened my vocation as an educator, informed my faith as a servant of Christ, and expanded my understanding as a global citizen.

My own family has been transformed by the CASP experience, too. My husband, José, a native of Venezuela, co-led the 2008 and 2011 Januaries in Guatemala with me. He became enamored with the culture and people of Guatemala, discovering a part of Latin America that he didn't really know much about before CASP. The opportunity for him to interact with and speak into the lives of mothers and children who live on the margins of society in Xela brought back the memories of his similar childhood in the barrios of Caracas. There have been many sweet moments when he was able to instill hope in a discouraged young person or a desperate mother. God's presence was clear on these occasions and the frailty of humanity was uplifted by these interactions. Our sons, Ilan and Isaiah (now 20 years old) also accompanied us in 2008 and 2011. They attended language school and participated in all the activities and service projects alongside the Whitworth students, all the while keeping up with their schoolwork in the evenings. During these trips, our boys gained about forty Whitworth brothers and sisters and had the chance to experience things that most ten to twelve-year-olds never understand at their young age. As biracial, bicultural young men growing up in Spokane, Washington, their experiences in Guatemala helped shape their own intercultural identities, their acceptance of their father's native language, and their understanding of "the other." They became strong, insightful, empathetic, and inquisitive people who also began to embrace their own sense of difference back home. I will be forever grateful for the impact CASP has had on my family.

Kim and José, their sons Ilan and Isaiah, and TAs Emily and Ryan in Guatemala (2008)

CASP's impact on my vocation as a teacher of Spanish language and culture has given me significant new insights about experiential learning and language acquisition through immersion. I have been amazed by the progress the students make with their Spanish in just three to four weeks in Guatemala as they begin their journey through Central America. As a mentor and companion on the adventure, each CASP cohort has taught me something new and helped me make memories that will last a lifetime. I consider each student an exemplary pupil and a beloved friend. Each time I returned to the US after my leg of the program was finished, it was difficult to re-enter my own culture and life, which always feels strangely foreign to me for a while. I always have a hard time leaving the CASP students, wishing I could continue to be a witness to their transformative experiences and sharing the joys and sorrows of the journey with them. The experience of living in community with them for a month makes a profound impact on me every time, and I go through the spring semester feeling like I'm missing a piece of me until they all return to campus in May.

To the students, I want to say *gracias por todo*. I admire your tenacity, courage, humility, and openness to participate in CASP. I pray that you will each continue to unpack your experience in Central America, to be grateful for all that was shared with you, and to live your lives as witnesses of injustice and reconcilers for the voiceless. As I have been known to say (many times!), we are entrusted with people's stories, and it is up to us to figure out how we will honor that privilege and fulfill that responsibility. I am blessed to be the carrier of stories, too. Among the most treasured, the stories I honor and cherish belong to Isabel, Julia, Telma, Henry, and many others.

To the parents of the CASP students, I want to say *thank you* for the amazing sons and daughters you raised. Each of them has such incredible gifts to share with the world, and I count it a huge blessing to be one of the recipients of their contagious joy, genuine love, and compassion for others. It is a humbling experience as a professor to learn and grow so much as a result of my time with these students.

To my sovereign. loving God, I want to proclaim your *justicia* (justice and righteous!) for this broken world. I am thankful that God chose me, along with every other faculty, staff, and student that has gone on a Whitworth Central America program, to be sent as his ambassador into the homes, communities, workplaces, and hearts of the people of Central America. It is a region that needs and deserves our understanding, cooperation, reconciliation, and friendship. May God make us all peacemakers and participants in his good work in this part of the world!

I have loved the CASP adventure! Here's to many more years of living, learning, and serving alongside Whitworth students in Central America!

Lindy Scott (2011–present)

Spanish & Latin American Studies Professor and Faculty Leader

MY FIRST CONTACT WITH Whitworth's Central America Study Program goes way back to 1982, before I began teaching at Whitworth. At that time, I was the Academic Dean of the Comunidad Teológica de México, a consortium of Protestant seminaries in Mexico City. A group of North American students from Whitworth that had been in Central America for several months came through our Center. They were being lodged at a seminary's facilities while they did an extended debriefing of their Central American experiences. Although they seemed tired, they were also enthusiastic about they had learned through their travels. I was encouraged that they wanted to go deeper in their knowledge, both informational as well as experiential of the land and people that I had also grown to love.

My direct contact with CASP started in the Fall of 2007 when I began teaching at Whitworth. Several students from the 2008 cohort took some of my classes in Spanish and Latin American Studies. They were eager to know about the history and culture of the region they would be encountering. Upon their return, many took my Core 350 course on US/Latin American relations. I was impressed by the changes that I had seen in them. They were more mature, more disciplined, more realistic. They still wanted to change the world, but they had realized that they had to know the world better before they could make it better.

In 2011 I became an active CASP faculty member. My assignment was to visit each of the CASPians in their rural home stays in Honduras. Together with the TAs Danielle Wegman and Travis Walker, I walked the dusty roads of Honduras to check in with each one of the participants. I became more and more convinced that although these rural experiences were difficult, they were very important. Many students had experienced bouts of sickness and loneliness, but they had all been able to develop strong relationships with their Honduran families. They had learned that the "rugged individualism" so highly prized in the United States is not all that healthy. They were beginning to grow into a more mature "mutual interdependence."

The 2014 CASP group was quite unique. Each student spent the summer or the fall semester at our Costa Rica Center with intensive studies in Spanish, Creation Care Ecology and Latin American Studies as well as host family home stays and a one day a week internship in areas of their majors. In January they met up in Guatemala for their intensive advanced Spanish acquisition and additional cultural experiences. I joined up with the group for an academic retreat over spring break in Granada, Nicaragua. They were wrestling with tough issues, but they were well equipped to deal with the personal and intercultural challenges they faced. The overwhelming consensus was that the in-depth internship experience was well worth the investment of their energies. Their feedback led us to continue the internship component in the successive programs.

I accompanied the 2016 CASP group during their January sojourn in Guatemala. Their intensive Spanish language acquisition at the Xelajú Language Institute was combined with excellent host family stays and a variety of cultural and service experiences. Two new events were the presentation by two Catholic nuns and an exploration of the "miracle" city of Almolonga. The fourteen students were able to hone their linguistic and cultural skills during their "plunges." After a brief debriefing time in Antigua, I accompanied the students to Managua, Nicaragua, where they were placed in their internship sites and with their host families. I also had to privilege to be with the CASPians in the academic retreat in Granada and for the final debriefing back in Spokane. Again, and again, I have been amazed that our Whitworth students are more than able to move beyond their comfort zones. Although some of the internships were better "fits" than others, students were able to meet the challenges. This has led me to emphasize that CASP can be "tough" and leads to greater maturity.

During the 2018 CASP program I spent February, March and April in Nicaragua, accompanying the students who were dispersed throughout the country in their internship sites. The program advanced well as the students made great strides in their Spanish, intercultural, and work skills. Most of the students were having deep and powerful experiences in their internships. Then in mid-April, Nicaragua's president, Daniel Ortega, made some unpopular decisions regarding retirees' pension and Social Security programs. Peaceful protests erupted throughout the country, but these were met with violence from the country's police and military forces. Citizens were being killed by the dozens. We CASPians were brought face to face with the distressing dilemma: What should followers of Jesus do when faced with an elected president who has become increasingly authoritarian and dictatorial? Personally, I was impressed with many Nicaraguan Christians who chose to express their peaceful protest. It seemed to me that it was Nicaragua's "Martin Luther King moment" when followers of the Prince of Peace went to the streets in their commitment to justice. The CASP program was curtailed a week early. During the debriefing and the months that followed, we have continued to struggle with these difficult decisions.

Accompanying our students on these recent CASP trips as well as researching about the earlier tours, I have become more and more convinced of the fallenness of humanity. Although we have been created in God's image, sin permeates all areas of the human race. This is clearly seen in the world of politics. Many Central American politicians have abused their power and used it for their own enrichment. All too often, interference by the United States government and corporations has caused great damage to many people in the region, especially the poorest Central Americans. Although it is legitimate for the US government to seek the well-being of our own citizens, this does not justify treating people in other countries as inferiors. Especially during the Cold War, both the Soviet Union and the United States used their ideologies to fuel civil war around the world, but especially in Central America. God will hold authorities responsible for their hypocritical actions of using false promises of democracy and economic well-being to cover their own economic and political motives (see Luke 22:25).

We followers of Jesus form the Church, the Body of Christ. As such, we show both signs of God's grace and power in our lives, but also the lingering and damaging aspects of our sin. I have been both encouraged and disappointed by the Body of Christ in Central America and in the United States. At times, Christians have been complicit in these acts of injustice. At other times, followers of Jesus have given of themselves in loving sacrifice for neighbors. Archbishop Romero was an example of a life poured out for others that continues to inspire me.

For this book project, I have had the privilege of interviewing many CASP alumni and professors. I have been impressed by the role of truth in their lives. As disciples of Jesus (the Truth), we are urged to know, to speak, and to obey the truth. One conversation about following the truth stands out in my mind. During the 1980s, the United States government was funding the Contras in an attempt to overthrow Nicaragua's Sandinista government, even though the US Congress had prohibited sending funds or arms to the Contras. The Central America Study Tour participants, upon seeing the disastrous impact of such "aid" on the people of Nicaragua, came back to campus and witnessed to the truth they had observed. Such truths were not welcomed by everyone at Whitworth. The controversy reached such a crescendo that college president Robert Mounce asked Ron Frase to resign. After much prayer and conversations with other leaders on campus, Ron refused to resign due to his commitment to the truth. Ron told the president that if he wanted him to leave, he would have to fire him. The president backed down and Ron continued as chaplain, professor and director of the Central America Study Tour. Obeying the truth is costly.

I am most grateful for CASP because it has pushed me over and over again to seek a deeper walk with God. This has moved me to incorporate issues of God's justice into my classes and to encourage my students to become persistent agents of change in our broken world.

Appendix

Exchange of Letters in the Whitworthian regarding Nicaragua and the Contras

A HEALTHY, HEATED DEBATE took place in the *Whitworthian* that was sparked by the CAST 1984 group. A bit of historical background is necessary. Ronald Reagan was running for re-election in 1984. He was supporting the Contras (mostly men who had served as soldiers in Somoza's army) with arms and money so that they could overthrow the Sandinista government which Reagan had labeled as communist. Although Congress had originally agreed to fund the Contras, later Congress voted to prohibit that support. Nevertheless, that did not stop the Reagan administration from funding the Contras. Lieutenant Colonel Oliver North, who was on staff of the National Security Council, went around Congress by making trade deals with the Iranian government and then had Iran send arms and money to the Contras. This illegal maneuver became a political scandal known as "Irangate."

In the March 9, 1984 issue of the school newspaper, there were two articles that portrayed the Reagan administration's support of the Contras in Nicaragua as being quite good. The CAST students had learned just the opposite, that is, the killing of hundreds of innocent civilians by those same Contras. They wrote a group letter to the *Whitworthian* editor to express their understanding of the truth. That letter was published on April 20. Todd Robertson responded with a letter to the editor in which he wanted to clear up the misinformation that the CAST letter had expressed. This received a counter-response on May 4 by student Mark McDonald. An article by CAST student Kurt Dale also appeared in that May 4th issue. He gave a general description of what the CAST students had experienced and again mentioned their serious disapproval of Reagan's support for the Contras.

Many issues raised during this exchange of letters are important for every generation, including our own. How do we know which sources to trust when we seek the truth, especially when those sources give conflicting stories? If the Lord Jesus Christ should permeate every area of life, including politics, how do we avoid allowing governments and politicians to use and abuse the faith of sincere believers? Does religiosity, such as frequent attendance at church services, equal faithfulness to God, in light of Jesus´ rebuke of many Pharisees and Sadducees?

We present these letters in their entirety so that you may see the full debate.

STUDY GROUP EXPERIENCES CENTRAL AMERICA (APRIL 20, 1984)

To the Editor:

We received the March 9, 1984 issue of the *Whitworthian* while in Managua, Nicaragua and were greatly disturbed by some of the comments we read. We refer particularly to John Worster's article titled "Somebody Forgot to Tell the Russians" and Tommy Ellis' article, "Democrats Pick Reagan." We hope that the sentiments expressed in these two articles are not felt throughout the Whitworth campus.

What we have been learning about and living in, here in Central America, does not reflect the so-called "Christian" action of our nation. In fact, it is just the opposite.

We consider it hypocritical to have printed on our money "In God We Trust" when it is used to kill the Nicaraguan *campesinos*, children and internationals building a nation by the people, for the people, and of the people.

We find it ironic that the Nicaraguan government, which is allegedly "anti-religious," also has "*En Dios Confiamos*" (In God We Trust) on its money.

Nicaragua is a poverty-stricken nation, building itself from the roots up. Everyone now has basic staples to eat, free medical care and medicine (which we have made use of), education and housing (incidentally, a university education here costs about $5 a semester).

We visited a cooperative in Jerusalén, in the Nueva Guinea district of the Southeast of Nicaragua (which is attacked nightly by US-supported contras). After this year's harvest, they will be able to pay off all debts, including a tractor. This cooperative also has a child day care center, providing three meals a day, a clean facility and care for children while their parents work in the fields of the cooperative.

Incidentally, money for this day care center comes from the government and international funds. This is a small example of how Nicaragua is providing for the needs of its citizens, something that has never occurred here before.

From Jan. 1, 1984 to Mar. 7, 1984 Nicaragua has been attacked twenty-two times by US-supported counter-revolutionaries. All the principal ports of Nicaragua are mined with US mines which have damaged Japanese, Dutch, Panamanian, Soviet and Nicaraguan merchant and fishing ships.

Thousands of families are refugees because of the contra activity in the North and South, fleeing their farms, homes and livelihood in order to survive.

These are the "Christian" actions of the God-fearing nation of the United States! This not only happens in Nicaragua but also in Guatemala, Honduras and El Salvador. We deplore the actions of our nation done in the name of Christianity and democracy.

We are appalled at the way our taxes are spent for our "defense" in this offensive war, which is killing our Nicaraguan brothers and sisters. Did you know that:

- 1,700 U.S. troops are still in Honduras following the termination of Big Pine II maneuvers.

- 2,000 U.S. troops from the 82nd Airborne Division (those that invaded Grenada) are arriving for the Granadero I maneuvers, in which they will participate with 2,300 Honduran troops, 3,000 Salvadoran troops and possibly Guatemalan troops,

- The Defense Department says it sent forty US parachutists to Tegucigalpa (Honduras) from the Southern Command in Panama. Honduras claims the number to be 600 Green Berets.

- Between mid-February and mid-March, there were 119 violations of Nicaraguan air space for spy and exploration missions.[1]

This does not include the millions of dollars for covert military aid to the contras, nor the aid to the Salvadoran military. This, my friends, is the "Christian" help our United States of America is giving. We implore you to think twice, three times, even four before you support the policies of President Reagan.

If you ask what you can do, work on the Democratic campaign so that Reagan won't be re-elected; write to your representatives demanding that they vote "no" on the $21 in covert aid to the contras and aid to the Salvadoran government and/or register to vote.

We thank you for your time in reading this. We implore you to do something to stop the non-Christian, violent, murderous actions of our government. You can make a difference, so do! It is as much your responsibility as ours.

God bless you.

The Whitworth College Central America Study Group

CENTRAL AMERICA LETTER REVISITED (APRIL 27, 1984)

Dear Sir,

I am writing in concern for the people who read the Central America Study Tour letter in the April 20th edition of the *Whitworthian*. I feel some of the implications stated in the letter were misleading. First, I'd like to address the issue of the Christian Nicaragua. I don't doubt there are as many or more Christians per capita in Nicaragua in comparison to the U.S.A. I am questioning the Nicaraguan government whose leadership includes many Marxists and a Catholic priest who has violated the Canon Law. Here are the reasons for my doubts:

1. At the end of the letter it was stated that this information was provided by the Committee of US Citizens living in Nicaragua

"In Nicaragua today it is strictly prohibited to preach the gospel today," reports a Nicaraguan Trans World Missions leader. "One can be arrested for distributing Bibles, and hundreds of civilians have been specially trained to make citizen's arrests of individuals who share the Word of God publicly."

Raul Diaz, a Christian medical student from the capital city of Managua, recently stated, "While Nicaraguan propaganda claims that it is for religious freedom, clearly it is on their own terms. Although they also claim that churches are wide open, in reality the churches that are open and operating freely are ones known as the Popular Church, which is their own creation. These churches generally preach Liberation Theology and upon entering them the worshipper comes face to face with the posters of Marx, Lenin, Che Guevara and Sandino . . . among other champions of socialism. Biblical doctrine is taught alongside Sandanista (sic) ideology and more often than not confuses the person who is not well-versed in either doctrine."

The Trans World Missions leader revealed that the Sandinista government has now required all churches to register their buildings, leaders, sermons, and congregations. In order to receive approval as a recognized legal body, the church must be approved by the Ecumenical Council set up by the government. (*Open Doors,* March/April 1984, pp. 22-23).

Because the government officials in Nicaragua wanted the world to believe nothing had changed since the Marxist regime had taken over, they allowed a Christian crusade to take place in the city. But, they gave them the smallest arena in town to hold it in! Then, when they felt that the crowds would be small—many were planning on watching it in their homes over TV—they changed the meeting at the last moment (just hours before it was to begin) to the largest soccer stadium in the city!

They felt that a small gathering in a stadium holding 25,000 would ridicule the Christians and show the world that people were no longer interested in Christian beliefs.

However, they were wrong! Even though there was no way to publicly announce the last-minute change in location, 18,000 people showed up the first night!

Pope John Paul II and most bishops have condemned the Popular Church because it tries to separate the people from the church and their bishops in order to rally the people with the Sandinistas. The list goes on, but I hope you get the picture. This alarming information is important because after the overthrow of the Marxist regime in Grenada, more information on how the Marxists squelch out the Christian churches became available.

". . . if serious measures are not taken, we can find ourselves with the Polish situation, said one report stamped '*Top Secret*' by the Ministry of Interior. Another report told of the government consulting Cuba on how to control the churches." In a list of recommendations, the interior ministry report urged establishment of a "register of association" to monitor church activities, membership, and the financing. "Greneda (sic) Marxists planned religious suppression" *Christian Enquirer* April '84).

I think it is also important that we realize our priorities when we vote for a president, senator, or any other politician. When we vote, do we vote morally as a Christian, or is it always an economic factor? President Reagan's morality seems to be questioned and he is deemed Anti-Christian, when in reality he is the only candidate of the top three who has publicly made a commitment to the Christian church and attended church regularly.

"Seek ye first the kingdom of God, and then all things shall come unto you." Does that fit into your politics?

Another concern is the character assassination of El Salvidoran (sic) presidential candidate Roberto D'Aubuisson. US Ambassador has repeatedly made accusations and brought (or bought) a witness to prove that D'Aubuisson was a leader of the death squads. Mr. White now faces a multimillion dollar suit because of his accusations. Also, no substantial evidence can prove this supposed relationship. The witness, who won't reveal his identity, or speak publically (sic), was paid roughly $80,000 for this service.

Perhaps some people do wrong in the name of Christ. Are we perfect? Do you ever think people will be perfect? The intent of this letter is to keep your mind open in the hopes for some human integrity. I might imply that some politicians are worse than others, but that really isn't my intent.

I write this in hoping that you'll judge a candidate on the individual level, not party line. I also hope you vote on the issues that are on the top of your list of priorities. God bless you all and thank you for reading this.

If you have any questions concerning this letter, please feel free to confront me. Sincerely,

Todd E. Davidson
P.S. "Do not think that I have come to bring peace on earth, I have come not to bring peace, but a sword." RSV Matthew 10:34

DAVIDSON LETTER CRITICIZED; SANDINISTAS DEFENDED (MAY 4, 1984, P. 5)

To the editor,

I was very disturbed after reading Todd Davidson's critique of the letter sent by the Central America study group. He states that his purpose was to clear up some "misleading" implications in the letter, which had referred to the social improvements since the revolution in 1979 and the extensive support the United States has given to groups against the Nicaraguan government.

I do not worship the Sandinista party; I try to make justice my primary criterion when evaluating issues. I recognize that all of us have only the information presented to us (books, media, people, etc.) on which to form our opinions.

After substantial research on the Nicaraguan issue, and after recognizing that the Sandinistas have made some serious mistakes, I am of the opinion that their overall program is worthy of American support. If the Sandinista party was to be shown as against basic human rights, I would be the first one to stand up against them.

Having stated that, I sharply criticize Todd's letter which he supported by questionable sources, both of which I had never heard. They are contradicted by more reputable sources, some of which I will provide in this letter.

My overall purpose in writing this is to stand up for what I believe to be right and to urge readers to consider and check sources when forming their opinion on issues. After checking Todd's sources, I was anything but impressed and have asked him to supply to the *Whitworthian* any other sources he might have.

I am afraid it is Todd's letter which is very "misleading" and in need of some clearing up. Consider the sources. In his letter he quotes an anonymous Trans World Missions leader who claims, "In Nicaragua, it is strictly prohibited to preach the gospel," and a medical student who claims people can be arrested for distributing the Bible.

This is a remarkable claim in light of the reports of four of our professors who have been to Nicaragua: Don Liebert, Ron Frase, Townsend Shelby and JoAnn Atwell-Scrivner. These people are always available for anyone who has questions on this issue.

Todd's sources also contradict Nicaraguan pastor Norman Bent who spoke here last semester, the report of the task force of the Presbyterian Church (USA) and the report of several Spokane pastors who visited Nicaragua in January.

An article in Christianity Today (April 8, 1983) titled "Why the Gospel Grows in Socialist Nicaragua" states: "Evangelicals here preach the historic gospel and freely evangelize. Since the Sandinistas took power in 1979, distribution of Bibles has increased fivefold, distribution of New Testaments ninefold . . . even a skeptic such as the U.S. ambassador to Nicaragua does not believe the Christian faith is in jeopardy as long as the Sandinistas hold the government."

The Joint Pastoral Letter of the Nicaraguan Bishops titled "Christian Commitment to a New Nicaragua" in the section on evangelism makes no reference whatsoever to any type of persecution, nor does the report adopted by the Presbyterian Church (USA).

A letter to the American Baptist Churches from The Baptist Convention of Nicaragua (May 4, 1983) also does not make one reference to religious persecution—it speaks only of the suffering of civilians attacked by the US backed Contras and pleads with the American Baptist Churches "to have the U.S. government stop backing and promoting the groups that are trying to overthrow our government."

In the past there has been some persecution of the Miskito Indians, but this has long since been resolved (Norman Bent is a Miskito pastor and made this clear).

There were also some restrictions on evangelical churches in 1982, but most evangelical churches in Nicaragua had supported the dictator Somoza.

The same Christianity Today article reports that in the spring of 1982, opposition church leaders had been preaching that the harsh spring floods were God's judgement on the Sandinistas, which was not only untrue but potentially disruptive in a society trying to get its feet solidly on the ground. Since then, the Sandinistas have publicly admitted their error in persecuting the people. The evidence is clear that the religious situation of today is quite free.

Regarding President Reagan's Christian commitment, Todd's claim about his church attendance is incorrect. The President has stated that he is unable to attend public worship because of the security risks involved and the inconvenience to the congregation.

Lastly, I find it difficult to comprehend how anyone could defend Robert D'Aubuisson concerning his involvement in the death squads. He is not, as Todd implied, accused only by ex-ambassador Robert White.

An article in *Newsweek* (February 22, 1984) reports that D'Aubuisson has been accused by several human rights groups, and an article in the reputable periodical *Foreign Affairs* (1982) states: "Major Roberto D'Aubuisson [is] a man long identified with rightest death squads and [is] even thought to be linked to the March, 1980 murder of Archbishop Oscar Arnulfo Romero."

While he has not been proven guilty, the accusations are certainly coming from more than just one man "buying off" one witness.

I, too, will make my sources available to anyone who is interested. The situation in Central America is complex and it requires some effort on our part in making responsible judgements. It is not as simple as keeping the Soviets out of the region.

I stand behind the position adopted by the 195th General Assembly of the Presbyterian Church (USA) to "immediately cease all efforts, direct or indirect, to destabilize the government of Nicaragua or to intervene in its internal affairs."

Mark McDonald

Student[2]

'FRANKLY, I GET SICK WHEN I SEE WHAT I'VE BEEN SEEING . . ."
(MAY 4, 1984, P. 4)

Hello Friends,

Well, the Central America study tour gang has just returned to Managua, Nicaragua after three weeks out in the boonies of this beautiful country, and I figured it was about time that we tell you a little about our trip.

2. Author's note—It is obvious that Cold War rhetoric deeply colored this exchange of opinions. In addition to serious flaws in Mr. Robertson's logic, many of his sources were of dubious merit. Several of his affirmations were known to be false at the time (ex. Reagan attended church less than any other U.S. president) and other claims have been shown by history as being fallacious (ex. Both the *United Nations Commission on the Truth for El Salvador* and the *Inter-American Commission on Human Rights* concluded that D'Aubuisson gave the order to execute Archbishop Oscar Romero.)

So far, our trip has included a six week stay in Costa Rica, studying the language, attending seminars, and living with Costa Rican families.

Then it was off to Panama for another week of seminars and sightseeing, and now we're coming to the close of our six weeks in Nicaragua.

Basically, we've been learning and experiencing life in Central America. For the overwhelming majority "life" means poverty, disease, war and incredible suffering.

We're all under the firm conviction that the economic and social structures of these countries are terribly unfair and are a far cry from the just system I think God demands.

The rich own the land and rake in huge profits, while the poor generally don't make enough to live like human beings.

Frankly, I get sick when I see what I've been seeing down here, especially here in Nicaragua, where our government is sending millions of dollars to put down what I would consider a popular revolution.

Overthrowing a popular revolution involves slaughtering thousands of human beings, and that's exactly what we're hearing about down here.

People die horrible deaths every day here in Nicaragua, and it's becoming more and more clear that the fault is on the side of our government. That means indirectly we're all responsible.

We're hopeful, however, because we see the people of Nicaragua investing their lives into making life better for *everyone* in the country. I'm also hopeful because I believe God is somewhere, here in the midst of this suffering, identifying with these people.

Someday, somehow justice is going to roll down here into Nicaragua and eventually throughout all of Central America.

In this short note, I cannot begin to express all the feelings that are welling up in me—or in the rest of the group. So, I'll close by saying thanks a billion for the letters of encouragement and all your prayers.

A 50 Años . . . Sandino Vive!